Text Classics

PETER ROSE was born in 1955 and raised in Wangaratta, in northern Victoria. His father was a legendary player for, and later coach of, the Collingwood Football Club. His older brother also played for Collingwood, and opened the batting for the Victorian state cricket team.

After graduating from Monash University, Rose became a bookseller and eventually began working in publishing. His first book of poetry, *The House of Vitriol*, appeared in 1990.

Throughout the 1990s Rose was a publisher at Oxford University Press in Melbourne. During this time he produced two more volumes of poetry: *The Catullan Rag* (1993) and *Donatello in Wangaratta* (1998).

In 2001, two years after his brother's death, he published *Rose Boys*. Critically acclaimed and the winner of the 2003 National Biography Award, the memoir became a bestseller.

Rattus Rattus: New and Selected Poems and *A Case of Knives*, Rose's first novel, were published in 2005. *Roddy Parr*, another novel, followed in 2010. His fifth collection of poetry, *Crimson Crop*, won a 2012 Queensland Literary Award.

Peter Rose has edited two poetry anthologies and his literary journalism has appeared in many publications. Since 2001 he has been the editor of *Australian Book Review*.

BRIAN MATTHEWS has been a weekly columnist for the *Weekend Australian Magazine*. *Louisa*, a life of Louisa Lawson, won the 1987 ALS Gold Medal; *A Fine and Private Place*, a memoir, won the inaugural Queensland Premier's Literary Award for non-fiction; and *Manning Clark: A Life* won the 2010 National Biography Award.

ALSO BY PETER ROSE

Fiction
A Case of Knives
Roddy Parr

Poetry
The House of Vitriol
The Catullan Rag
Donatello in Wangaratta
Rattus Rattus: New and Selected Poems
Crimson Crop

Rose Boys
Peter Rose

Text Publishing Melbourne Australia

textclassics.com.au
textpublishing.com.au

The Text Publishing Company
Swann House
22 William Street
Melbourne Victoria 3000
Australia

First published by Allen & Unwin 2001
This edition published by The Text Publishing Company 2013

Cover design by WH Chong
Page design by Text
Typeset by Midland Typesetters

Printed in Australia by Griffin Press, an Accredited ISO AS/NZS 14001:2004
Environmental Management System printer

Primary print ISBN: 9781922147202
Ebook ISBN: 9781922148278
Author: Rose, Peter, 1955–
Title: Rose boys / by Peter Rose; introduced by Brian Matthews.
Series: Text classics.
Dewey Number: 796.358092

CONTENTS

Extreme Days
by Brian Matthews

ROSE *Boys* begins on 22 August 2000 in 'an upstairs study in Adelaide', not far from St Peter's Cathedral, where for the moment the bells are 'blessedly still'. Further down the road from St Peter's, and in sound of the bells when they are in full voice, is the Adelaide Oval, perhaps the most beautiful of Australia's cricket grounds, and the venue for a Sheffield Shield match between South Australia and Victoria in January 1973. Forced to follow on after being 205 runs behind on the first innings, Victoria was rescued by an opening partnership of 217 between Paul Sheahan and Robert Rose, who batted for five hours to make a 'dogged' 94.

Reading through family records in the silence of that upstairs study, Peter Rose relives scenes from his boyhood with his brother, Robert, and their parents, Elsie and Bob (one of Collingwood's greatest footballers); but it seems there is no escaping a truth that is as insistent as the cathedral bells when the hour turns. Too quickly, brutally, a random choice opens his brother's scrapbook 'at a front-page story drawn from the Melbourne *Herald* of 15 February 1974'—'ROSE PARALYSED IN CAR ROLL', runs the headline. The *Australian* that same day is unequivocal: 'CRICKET, FOOTBALL STAR IS PARALYSED'.

No matter what diversions the scrapbook turns up—a riotous wake after the Magpies' legendary 1970 Grand Final defeat; the moods of coach Jock McHale; Bob and Elsie's courtship and marriage; flashing scenes of young Robert, the brilliant batsman and mercurial footballer—the merciless narrative to which Peter Rose has tentatively, fearfully committed himself will out. About to turn away from the scrapbook's intolerable reminders, the pasted-in clipping about the 'transformation' wrought by 'a driving accident—just another of our crashes—and a second or two in time', Rose is brought back into the unremitting penumbra of memory, the unreachable silence of the dead and, above all, the unanswered questions the dead leave in their wake.

And so the first chapter, 'Scrapbooks', a skirmishing with the past—now intense and tight-lipped, now genial and indulgent—becomes a magnificent prelude to confronting again the pain that awaited the Rose boys and all their family when Robert's Volkswagen spun off the road near Bacchus Marsh on St Valentine's Day in 1974.

What exactly is the message of Robert Rose?
One year after his death, twenty-six years after

just another of our crashes, knowing the effect it had on his family and friends, and thousands of others who hardly knew him, I want to go back there, I want to examine my brother's life and reanimate him...Here, in my Adelaide eyrie, with my documents and my pent cathedral bells, I want to examine his achievement, what he symbolised, what he gave and what he withheld, what he divulged and what he never said, as a son, as a brother, as a husband, as a mate, above all as a tragic victim of that 'second or two in time'.

And so I hold on to the outsize scrapbook for a while longer. It is time to listen to my brother whose message, laconic but self-evident to many in his life, I somehow never fully heeded...

Again I turn to the handsome lad, the vaunted youth, the rage recruit, and will him to speak to me.

Like all fine, evocative prose, Rose's splendid re-creation of the place and mood in which he set out on his memoir journey has echoes of, and is intensified by, other voices seeking the same truths: his fellow poet Kenneth Slessor, for example, who, willing the dead to speak to him, hears only 'five bells coldly ringing out...the bumpkin calculus of Time'.

Rose Boys is the story of Robert Rose's transformation from a quintessentially Australian sporting life of brilliance, promise and sheer physical energy to the confined and cribbed world of the quadriplegic. More broadly, it is the wrenching account of a family living for a quarter of a century in the sometimes tightening, sometimes loosening, never absent grip of catastrophe.

The book begins unannounced, in a brief prologue that moves with the pace and fractured logic of a dream: 'Electric afternoon. Hiding from humanity, I drift through burnt spears and withered grass. My walk is soothing but fraught with snakes and goannas. They rustle in the flammable scrub, reminding me that anything can happen to a solitary. In the distance a minor cemetery catches the sun…A woman appears, frantic and dishevelled…'

The prologue ends inconclusively, when a small boy with 'uncanny vision' 'takes pity' on the wavering intruder and speaks to him. This dream—inchoate, compelling—resurfaces at the end of the book in the form of Peter Rose's splendid poem 'I Recognise My Brother in a Dream'. From the remorseless heat of the trials that Robert and the family had endured there issued at long last, shaped and graspable, the product of 'seven years and thirty drafts', a hard-won serenity, the pitilessly even-handed but reconciling equilibrium of art.

In contrast to the disorienting dream and the richly allusive poem, the main narrative between the two is spare and tense: 'Robert was lying on his back, looking rather beautiful. His head was shaved. They had already drilled holes in his skull and inserted calipers attached to eight-pound weights. Robert's head was pulled back, immovable. There was a tube in his mouth. Mum kissed him. His first words to her were, "I'm in trouble."'

Artless on the surface—telling it how it was, you might

say—this tremendously moving moment is unerringly timed from word to word, sentence to sentence, to deliver the hammer blows of disaster without breaking up under their force. Like Nick Adams in Hemingway's story 'Big Two-Hearted River', who keeps panic at bay with a succession of small, deliberated tasks, Peter Rose, scarcely knowing what to feel or think, controls surges of panic and grief within tight, unadorned prose. It was just about the only way he could write it.

Rose Boys is relentless: when you think it can't get worse for Peter and his parents and their circle, it does. When you think Robert can suffer no more, that torture upon torture must kill him, he endures, suffering before the gaze of his loyal, loving, helpless family. The telling of this story is so right that it is easy to overlook the nature of the task Rose set himself. No feelings are spared here—not the reader's, not his own—least of all his own.

The book's trajectory is a descent that ravages and cauterises the Roses, strong though they are, and threatens all bulwarks, structures and props. Disintegration flickers through the story with increasing certainty, and that sense of pervasive illness which afflicts tragic households becomes a sub-theme in Rose's memoir. 'The extreme days had begun,' he writes in his journal, 'days of futility, days of grief', days of 'volatile, ungovernable' emotions. 'No one was in good shape' and at times, he says, conceding how graphically the image of Robert's broken body commanded their thoughts and imaginations, 'it felt as if we were all crippled.'

They had been gathered into what Susan Sontag called 'the night-side of life…a more onerous citizenship…in the kingdom of the sick'. They would return at last from this drawn-out crepuscular gloom incalculably altered, damaged, but glimpsing a hard renewal.

For himself, Rose looks down for the last time on his brother with 'a pang of something that would never fully dissipate—incompletion, incomprehension, rich regret...' There seems to be no resolution available to him. Even his last-minute attempt to see the Collingwood team honour Robert is foiled by rain and confusion.

Yet this story of fractured lives, unassuageable grief and nowhere-to-turn desperation becomes, in Rose's hands, a triumph. Though seeming, in retrospect, unrelieved— I read it at a sitting when it was first published, in 2001, and its images and episodes ghosted round me for days— the story of Robert Rose's tragedy is both ennobled and lightened by a context that calamity cannot diminish. Friends, children and extended family populate and colour the 'shifting text': Bob's parents, Bert and Millie, with 'one cow but no fence'; Uncle Rusty, 'a wheat-farming bachelor with a roll-your-own cough'; and the Rose family's Nyah West home, in Elizabeth Street, 'named after one of the little princesses but commonly known as Blowfly Flat'.

And there is Peter Rose himself, ironic, witty, 'Thicko' to his equally witty and ironic brother. His account effortlessly ranges across past and present, and is variously enriched by glimpses of Melbourne's football culture, his emerging sexuality, his discovery of the depth of his fraternal love, his growth as a poet and his affection for Robert's daughter, Salli.

Through it all there is the selfless devotion of Elsie, devastated but indomitable, resilient; and Bob, a wonderful human being, unassuming, dogged, loving. And there is Robert Rose, whose inspiring courage, lost promise, shattered body and tortured soul this great book unflinchingly documents, celebrates and gently lays to rest.

Rose Boys

for
Robert Rose 1952–1999
and
Brian Martin 1945–2000

Living is more dangerous than anything.
Randall Jarrell

There is no such thing as forgetting. The secret
inscriptions are waiting to be revealed when the
obscuring daylight shall have withdrawn.
Thomas de Quincey

Everything is what it is, and not another thing.
Bishop Butler

ACKNOWLEDGEMENTS

This composite portrait of Robert was only possible because of the generosity and goodwill of the people who knew him best: our parents of course, to whom I am grateful for everything, Salli Caruana, Terry Butler and Jenny Mackay. Other people gave me helpful information: Steve Bernard, Joe Fairhurst, Kate Breadmore, Paul Sheahan, Peter Harris, Dr David Burke and Jeff Kennett.

I am especially indebted to Robert Bird, who spoke to me freely about the accident in which he too was injured, and to the late Brian Martin, who saw me shortly before his death.

I doubt whether this book would have been finished without the encouragement of friends and advisers, especially Sonja Chalmers, Craig Sherborne, Kerryn Goldsworthy, Louise Sweetland and Morag Fraser. Christopher Menz has been the subtlest and most supportive of critics.

The late John Iremonger commissioned the original

edition for Allen & Unwin (2001). I am also grateful to his colleagues Rebecca Kaiser and Julia Stiles, who was a thorough and sympathetic editor.

Soon after Robert's death his family created the Robert Rose Foundation, a bona fide charity which helps people with spinal cord injuries. Readers wanting to make donations or seeking more information about the Foundation should consult the website: www.robert rosefoundation.com.

The quotation from Janet Malcolm is drawn from *The Silent Woman: Sylvia Plath and Ted Hughes* (Papermac, 1994). Two quotations are drawn from Robert McCrum's *My Year Off: Rediscovering Life after a Stroke* (Picador, 1998). Peter Porter's poem 'Basta Sangue', from which I quote, appears in his *Collected Poems* (OUP, 1999).

Electric afternoon. Hiding from humanity, I drift through burnt spears and withered grass. My walk is soothing but fraught with snakes and gonannas. They rustle in the flammable scrub, reminding me that anything can happen to a solitary. In the distance a minor cemetery catches the sun. I know it contains hidden ancestors. I study the stones but am defeated by hieroglyphics. Sheep ring the fence, and beyond them the Ovens—or is it the Murray River? My two rivers. A woman appears, frantic and dishevelled. I know her. She is one of the eminences in the library where I work. This acquistive god might have been conceived inside one of the reference books she guards like gold. Breathless, she tells me that a power failure has blacked out the entire region. She urges me to return to the library and describes the chaos I will find. The moribund computer is in a state of crimson riot. All the records are lost. No one can borrow or return. Midgets of literature stagger through gloomy compactuses. The chief librarian is a write-off.

I hasten to the library down clamorous streets. It feels like a film, but then, less real than film. More fluid. The old hotel near my parents' shop has been plausibly renamed the Jewel. Anxious women scuttle into attics clutching decorative hatboxes. Empty prams flash across the street. Oozing insects crawl into surfaces that creep like flesh. I long for the radical ceremony of scavenging birds. I am frightened and then strangely unfrightened.

Turning into the main street I waver briefly. The library, standing between the blood bank and the football oval where all the men in my family have played, and played, is ablaze, everything in it presumably lost.

Primitive flames shoot from the roof. I think of plunging my right arm into the fire. I will rescue the clueless and the knowing alike. But then firemen appear with their suggestive hoses, and the burlesque of evacuation begins. I move on, no longer misgiving.

At the end of the street stands a two-storey block of flats. Are there really flats in our town, let alone two-storey buildings? I hadn't noticed before. Three boys are leaning from a window decked in purple ribbons. I move towards them, studying my excited trio, not the blaze. The boy in the middle is jeering at something in the distance. He is slender and vivid and blond as an angel. His two companions stare at him open-mouthed. I almost recognise this boy, but he is younger than me, which feels wrong. He is clearly the oracle because of his uncanny vision. Creeping up to the foot of the flats, I listen to his sunny description of the pandemonium in the library—the pillage, the recriminations, the reign of blisters. He laughs at the firemen and their theatrical efforts to douse the blaze. He mocks the townsfolk who cluster behind barriers, gripping their cameras.

And then, looking over the window ledge, he takes pity on me and addresses me directly.

1
SCRAPBOOKS

August 22, 2000. In an upstairs study in Adelaide, the bells of the neighbouring cathedral blessedly still, strong coffee at the ready, I open my brother's old scrapbook. It is just one of several I have brought with me. Curious documents: these bibles of scrap, collages of self-delight. I have never kept one myself. That would be a thin volume anyway. Perhaps my diaries, stacked in a trunk, fill that need. I will draw on them, too, as I contemplate my brother.

I open his scrapbook at random. It parts at a front-page story drawn from the Melbourne *Herald* of 15 February 1974. The old gothic masthead is sallow with age but full of information. The newspaper, costing six cents, seven by air, comprises thirty-eight pages—quite puny, I think. There are no lifestyle or gourmet or computer sections to bolster it. After a long career in publishing, editing thumping dictionaries and reference books, I find thirty-eight pages innocent, pamphlet-like.

But there is nothing derisory about the circulation, proudly advertised to the right—'495,133 daily sales'. Quaintly, beneath the masthead, there is a telephone number, with six digits. I want to ring it. I want to speak to someone there. Perhaps I would get through to a night editor, lighting another cigarette, waiting for a disaster. The front page, neatly clipped and stuck in the scrapbook, is eclectic and prompts reflections about 1974. Patty Hearst had just been kidnapped. Brandt and Brezhnev, Heath and Franco, Trudeau and Tito—all those fascists and bourgeois reactionaries we vilified at school—were in power. Richard Nixon hung on grimly after Watergate. Billy Snedden, incredibly, was Australia's alternative prime minister.

The front page is dominated by a photograph of a white Volkswagen. It is a confronting image, for the car has been badly damaged, its front crushed. I don't recognise the pale weatherboard house in the background. I wonder how the Volkswagen got there, who moved it. The car's roof, like the numberplate, is missing. A caption tells me it was removed when they freed the driver. Both doors are open. I wonder if the radio is still playing, the horn wailing unstoppably. The lights are missing and the bumper bar lies buckled on the ground. It all reminds me of one of those expensive crumpled sculptures you see outside office towers.

The bonnet is stained with oil or paint from a passing truck. Bits of metal poke out dangerously. A man in short sleeves, posed by the anonymous photographer, stands by

10

the passenger door. He peers into the car in a kind of stupor. Judging by his Brylcreemed hair, muscular arms and stern mien, he lives in the country. I wonder what he saw in the wreckage. I want to ask him what was left. Cigarette butts? The Ballarat racing guide? Myriad sporting pages? Crushed cans of soft drink, beer? A thin suede tie for formal occasions? A baby's dummy, spat out during some weekend outing? Pizza containers? Pizza, even?

My eyes, blank as the short-sleeved witness's, avoid the long accompanying report on the front page. I am not ready for that yet. But I note the weighting of the main headline and the awkward construction: 'ROSE PARALYSED IN CAR ROLL'. It sounds almost contradictory, like a pratfall. There are three other smaller headings—'Trapped for 90 minutes', 'At races', 'Sedation'—plus three photographs of the victim. In one, weedily moustached, he grins at the camera. In another, longer-haired, he cuts a cricket ball to the boundary. In the bottom one, taken during his schooldays, he kicks a football with an intensity that reminds me of a much earlier photograph. His young wife is there too, near my father, who looks away.

Next to this clipping is a front-page story from the *Australian* of the same day. This headline is blunt: 'CRICKET, FOOTBALL STAR IS PARALYSED'. Subheadings tell me that Dad was hastening to join him and that sympathisers had already sent money. There are two photographs of Robert. In one he defends his wicket with a characteristically straight bat. The top one, much larger, is arresting. A handsome young man with fair hair and a five o'clock shadow stares at the camera. Lips parted,

11

eyes wide open, he seems shocked to find himself in this company. So profound is his surprise I almost expect his prominent Adam's apple to gulp.

But something is wrong—or should I say, more wrong? This is not the right face. It's not the paralysed cricket and football star we know. He is not, in short, my brother. In their haste the sub-editors chose an image from the wrong photo file.

Nevertheless, I knew our startled interloper, Dennis O'Callaghan. He played football for Collingwood while Dad was coach. A quiet young man, he never expected to end up on a front page, headlined and paralysed.

It was the first mistake.

Not that Dennis O'Callaghan wasn't accident-prone. I vividly remember one mishap at our house. This was after the 1970 grand final, in which Dennis played. I had often wondered how my parents' new spindly olive-green Scandinavian Fler lounge suite would stand up to the weight of all those footballers. It seemed too fine, too chic. I fancied that we would find out that night, given the chaotic atmosphere.

My parents had arranged the party before the grand final. Everyone, even the knockers, expected it to be a celebration. Collingwood, coached by my father, had a superb team that year. After two narrow losses in recent grand finals, a premiership seemed inevitable. Carlton, under Ron Barassi, was no less talented, but Collingwood had beaten them three times that season, including the second semi-final.

Things went according to plan during the first half of the grand final. By half-time Collingwood led by almost eight goals. Peter McKenna already had five. But he had also collided with his bullish team-mate Des Tuddenham a few minutes before half-time. McKenna was seriously concussed and shouldn't have played on. Tuddenham wasn't untouched, either. Ron Barassi didn't know this, of course, but he did have an idea. It was called handball, handball, handball.

Many furphies surround that most famous of grand finals. One has it that Collingwood started opening the champagne during half-time. Dad denies this. He was too worried about the injuries to his stars. Play resumed. The second half was calamitous and horrible to watch. Carlton surged forward and overwhelmed Dennis O'Callaghan and the other defenders. Barassi's rejuvenated handballers snatched victory in the last few minutes. Collingwood, unbelievably, had lost.

After the game my mother and I fought our way through the despondent/triumphant mob to get to the rooms. Our progress was slow, for it was a record crowd—121,696 people. My brother wasn't with us. A huge crowd had assembled outside the rooms. Later, George Harris, Carlton's provocative president, damned the club by saying that its supporters heckled the players as they emerged. I very much doubt this. Everyone was too busy crying. I myself was devastated by the result. Apparently I became so upset during the final quarter, as Carlton overhauled Collingwood, that my maths teacher, who was sitting with us, became worried about me. He rang up later that night to find out how I was. I'm surprised that we heard the telephone above the din.

The atmosphere at the party was shaky at first. Most of the guests were in bad shape. A kind of collective shock had stunned people. No one remembers when the party got under way. Dad thinks we called at the club en route to our house in Lemana Crescent, but he can't be sure. Peter McKenna doesn't even recall playing in the second half, let alone the aftermath. When Martin Flanagan interviewed 'Twiggy' Dunne for his book 1970, Twiggy remembered playing billiards at my parents' house. We didn't own a billiard table.

Our small house was soon overflowing. I had never seen so many people seriously out of control. All of fifteen, I knew it was going to be a great party. The noise was impressive as people began to relax. They had dressed up. Several of the women were wearing lace-up hotpants with long leather boots. The players removed their official ties and blazers. A business acquaintance of my father chainsmoked in a corner, using our television as an ashtray. His wife, considerably younger and taller than he, wore a tight-fitting leopard-skin dress. She reminded me of Ava Gardner, of whom I had seen photographs in my movie magazines. She had long dark hair and a majestic throat. It takes a lot to turn footballers' heads, especially when they have just lost a grand final in bitter circumstances, but the leopard skin seemed to work.

Well after midnight, my mother went into the kitchen and began mopping the floor, which was under several inches of champagne. 'Christ, Elsie, you're fussy!' someone said. Meanwhile, a sophisticate in a little black dress sat on our gramophone and played Mum's EP of Sinatra's

'My Way' over and over again, as if it were the only record we owned. My brother, smoking and drinking on the balcony with his mates, must have been desperate to play Led Zeppelin, Jimi Hendrix or the incomparable Cream.

The party lasted all night. It was still going in the morning when Dad left to appear on *World of Sport*, a mandatory Sunday morning commitment for coaches. Dad hadn't slept at all. Nowadays, a tennis player, defeated so mortifyingly, would avoid such an interview, happily incurring a ten thousand dollar fine, but Dad felt he had to 'front up'.

Just as the interview began, Lou Richards and Jack Dyer, two of the programme's hosts, came up with an unsubtle mock-rendition of Collingwood's theme song. They were off-camera but quite audible. 'Good Old Collingwood for Never,' they sang merrily. The interview went ahead, but when it was over Dad went looking for Lou, who had been his captain when Collingwood won the 1953 premiership. Dad, a former boxer, intended to confront his old team-mate. He went right through the television studio but couldn't find Lou, who had disappeared.

That afternoon, when it was all over, we cleaned up. While Dad, Robert and I surveyed the heap of empty bottles and Scandinavian kindling, Mum polished the kitchen floor and tried to disguise the burn marks on the television. Domestic order swiftly regained, Mum knew she had to get Dad away from the media, and from himself. They packed a few things and drove around Victoria for several days, stopping at a different motel each night. One evening they found themselves in Gippsland and had dinner in a small timber

15

town. The waitress recognised Dad but couldn't think of his name. Perplexed, she kept asking him who he was. He didn't enlighten her. Meanwhile Robert and I stayed at home with the dog. Years later, during an interview, Robert recalled that the house was like a morgue for days.

We thought it couldn't get any worse than that. We thought it was one of those tragedies they write about so freely in the sporting pages. We wondered if Dad would recover from such a perverse loss.

But had he courted defeat? I remembered something he had said after the 1966 grand final, which Collingwood had lost by one point. Dad gave a press conference that night. During it he wondered aloud, in his self-deprecating way, if he was jinxed. He later regretted this speculation, for it stuck. By 1970, after three grand final defeats in bizarre circumstances, people were beginning to believe him.

Three decades later, studying Dennis O'Callaghan's amazed and likeable face in Robert's scrapbook, I can still picture him and a fellow backman crammed on the chic Fler sofa with their girlfriends. And I can still remember the sound it made when it collapsed, sending the four of them toppling onto the floor. People laughed at them and joked about the Rose jinx. The end, as Frank Sinatra repeatedly sang, was near. Everyone agreed it was ironic. Dennis and his mate, the dispirited defenders, were the quietest people at the party.

And I wonder what Dennis O'Callaghan's mother thought that morning, four years later, when, alerted by some bewildered relative, she went out and bought the *Australian* and saw her son's photograph beneath the brutal headline.

My father's newspaper cuttings are even more voluminous. He began keeping them soon after leaving Nyah West in the Mallee to play football for Collingwood. That was in 1946, when he was seventeen. Collingwood's coach in those days was Jock McHale, then in his seventies. He had been coach since the 1920s and had won eight premierships, four of them in succession. Dad was awed by the legendary old man in black knee-length shorts. He was just as impressed by McHale's great ally John Wren, whom Frank Hardy wrote about in *Power Without Glory*, a novel of which Collingwood people still disapprove. As Dad's career progressed he got to know Mr Wren, as he always called him. He was grateful for his patronage. When Dad played well, as he often did, Wren's chauffeur-driven car would pull up outside my parents' sports store on Johnston Street and Wren would give him ten guineas—a handsome sum in those days.

Jock McHale was just as imposing. My father still talks about the chilly reception the players got from him whenever Collingwood lost a game. As they trudged off the field, past the rueful spectators, McHale was waiting for them at the end of the race. He eyeballed each player, saying nothing, daring him to look away. Dad still gets a frisson thinking about that piercing gaze. He says it was a major incentive not to lose the following week.

At other times McHale, though naturally or tactically taciturn, was more encouraging. My father recalls an early turning point in his career when McHale said to him, 'You'll be all right, Rose'. To coach a football side you must know something about the vagaries of human nature and masculine pride. McHale doubtless sensed that my father was a needful and respectful youth. But McHale's advice wasn't always palatable. One day McHale asked Dad what he had for breakfast before a match. Disapproving of Dad's preferred steak and eggs, he recommended tripe. Dad tried it once, disastrously. McHale also asked him if he kept a scrapbook. Dad told him that his mother kept a small one, up in Nyah West. McHale urged him to start one of his own, because he wouldn't regret it. Dad took his advice.

I had never seen the earlier scrapbook until recently. Slim but compiled with great care, it covers Dad's brief boxing career, which ended soon after he went to Melbourne. On the inside cover is a large photograph of Dad taken when he was about fifteen. He had learned to box in Harry Shaw's gymnasium in Nyah West. He is bare-chested, smiling and ornately Brylcreemed. To accentuate his muscular physique, he keeps his hands behind his waist. Inside, several clippings anoint him 'Best Boy of the Week'. Floral allusions begin to appear. 'A new Rose was discovered on Saturday night, having come fresh from the "garden" of Harry Shaw. This Rose was in full bloom…It was a fistic Rose that Bendigo people saw, and they liked it.'

I like that 'fistic Rose'. I must use it in a poem.

Not so long ago, during an interview, Dad said of his own scrapbook, 'If there was a fire, that's the thing I'd grab'.

The smallest scrapbook in my family is the one I treasure most. My mother gave it to me years ago, as though glad to be rid of it. She has never asked to look at it since. Her

18

mother—known as Daisy—kept it in the 1940s when my mother was a singer. Daisy was a loving but haphazard archivist. Everything went higgledy-piggledy into the tiny Embassy memo book. Chronology was not her forte.

My mother has always been reticent about her childhood. (That can stand as the first understatement in this book, in which I prepare to violate old privacies.) She has never mentioned her father to me. The little I know about my grandfather I gleaned from others. To someone like me, a devotee of Henry James's 'temple of analysis', unashamed of frankness, this reserve seems hard, too exacting for the curious and secretive alike. I do know that my mother grew up in the Goulburn Valley. (Douglas Nicholls—later 'Pastor Doug' and governor of South Australia—drove horse-drawn lorries for my grandfather and remained a devoted friend of Daisy and my mother. His autobiography tells me that he buried my grandfather.) My grandparents' marriage ended when my mother was a child. Nan took her four children to Melbourne and settled in Brunswick. I don't know how these domestic upheavals affected my mother. Lifelong silence is a kind of testimony. There was also the latent tension between her and Nan which troubled me as a child, my mother's seeming frustration with something Nan had or hadn't done—some old wound that haunted every conversation for her.

My mother rarely indulges in family anecdotes. One Christmas she surprised us by relating a story about her upbringing. My parents were talking about their childhood Christmases. Dad recalled being given a toy tank during the war. For Mum it was a boxed doll, given to her as a little girl. But she wasn't allowed to remove it from the container. Nan said she would spoil it. A few days later, the doll vanished. 'Knowing Nan, she probably gave it away,' I blurted out, remembering her largesse. 'Probably,' Mum agreed with an air of resignation.

At the age of sixteen Mum joined the Ordnance Revue Company, based at Puckapunyal. Her two brothers were away with the Sixth Division. For three years she toured the camps with a concert party that entertained the troops. These were mixed troupes comprising vaudevillians, coloraturas, popular singers, instrumentalists and 'the ballet'. Elsie was a croonette. Her repertoire included standards such as 'Melancholy Baby', 'Embraceable You' and 'Pennies from Heaven'. Admirers still talk about her clear diction, her identification with the lyrics, the discernment of her phrasing, and a certain pathos. After the war, soldiers remembered her performances. Their printed tributes appear in the scrapbook. 'Digger (Kew)' wrote to *Listener In*: 'Orchids to Elsie Rowlands…Having seen Elsie at quite a few camp shows, I, and thousands of other troops, think she is wonderful.' 'An Admirer (Heidelberg Military Hospital)' is complimentary: 'I wish this talented dark-eyed beauty all the success in the world'.

After the war Elsie began performing on Melbourne radio. There are winning photographs of her singing ardently into classic microphones belonging to 3AW and 3KZ. In one, the long-necked, wavy-haired young singer is accompanied by a bald violinist. In the adjoining box, 'Pat "Bambi" Tuckwell (well-known model)' leans over a wedding cake—not her own on this occasion. 'Bambi', now

Lady Harewood, is sporting the power shoulders of the 1940s. Both are beautiful women, born in 1926, like Joan Sutherland and the Queen.

Elsie's following grew during the next five years. 'Orchids galore,' writes one fan, adding, 'Judy Garland must look to her laurels.' Mum's voice reached as far as the occupied empire, as 'Back from Lotus Land' attests: 'In Japan I heard a recording of the first heat of the "P & A Parade" of 1946, in which croonette Elsie Rowlands appeared. On Sunday last I saw her in person at the Savoy Theatre, and was most impressed. Lotus blossoms and orchids to her.'

By then Elsie was appearing with vocalists such as Edwin Duff and Frank Wilson, and with 'Nicky', the doyen of Melbourne radio and Graham Kennedy's mentor. She was appearing on 3XY when the actor Ronald Colman's brother, Eric, made a guest appearance as an announcer. The imported American had golden tonsils and a drinking problem. One day this became so acute that Jack Davey, florid with rage, marched into the booth and completed the broadcast. Colman was never seen again.

Oddly, there are no references in Nan's miscellany to Mum's appearances at Mario's, the legendary Melbourne restaurant owned by the Viganos, Mietta O'Donnell's grandparents. Mum was singing there in the late 1940s when a member of the touring Italian Opera Company heard her. A tenor advised her to stop crooning and concentrate on opera.

In 1950, the year my parents married, the scrapbook ends. A last, floating clipping records the nuptials: 'College

Chapel, Parkville, was the setting of a charming wedding on the occasion of the marriage of Elsie Rowlands, the young Melbourne vocalist with Mr Robert Rose, the Collingwood League rover. A feature of the reception was a magnificent wedding cake made by the bride's aunt.'

Another feature was the blizzard of confetti. One piece of conjugal shrapnel landed in the bride's eye, troubling her for the rest of the day.

After the wedding Mum retired from the stage, though she would put it more modestly than that. My father, who loved her voice and knew how fulfilling it was to be acclaimed by an audience, wanted her to go on singing, but a family member, whom Mum adored, told her that she couldn't possibly go on singing now that she was married. She was twenty-four. For myself, revering music as I do, it seems like a bad joke, the sort of fatuous advice that subverts a life. I feel complicit in that social conspiracy. After all, I was the son of her sacrifice.

Lotus blossoms and orchids to her.

There was more family lore on my parents' ruby anniversary. I wrote about it in my poem 'The Living Archive'. We dined in a restaurant with some family friends. Dad regaled us with familiar tales about my childhood. There was talk of narrowly missed snakes in the Warby Ranges, near Wangaratta, and my fecklessness as a footballer at school. When someone asked Mum about her adolescence she surprised me by saying that she couldn't remember her life before she was married:

the twenty-odd years romanticised by a
fantastical son: waitress, stenographer,
the stoic girl outbraving rheumatic fever
(not once complaining, an uncle said),
one of Mario's dark-haired croonettes,
advised to concentrate on opera by a
visiting Italian tenor, but already
contracted to a bantamweight from the bush.
I have files on you, and fingerprints,
and photographs, yet the shards of memory
disintegrate under our feet—
leave me sentimental and otiose,
Antonia's archivist in the Offenbach,
the last romantic to convert to disk.

Poets lie, of course, for the sake of euphony
and alliteration. My father was a lightweight, then a
welterweight, never a bantamweight.

Mum didn't fall completely silent after her retirement.
She always sang while dressing us or doing housework.
Inspired, perhaps envious of her gift, we all became
inveterate singers. Nietzsche was right: life without music
is an error. I used to wonder what the neighbours thought
of the Rose family concert party, everyone whistling or
humming or singing, everything from jazz to rock to
opera. Dad's high notes were unforgettable. Unfortunately,
Robert was tone-deaf, but not without pretensions. One
night, alone in the house, he borrowed my tape-recorder
and recorded a Beatles song. Foolishly, he didn't erase the
torturous evidence. I teased him about it for years.

Another solo stands out, more melodiously. This happened a few years ago, one Christmas Day, the morning after our conversation about fugitive gifts. I withdrew to the deck to read a book, escaping the Christmas cheer for a moment. Mum was in the kitchen preparing lunch, unaware that I was seated a few feet away. An old fifties song came on the radio. Mum sang it right through, in that sweet pristine soprano of hers. (Her speaking voice is similarly dulcet. A colleague of mine once described it as interestingly feminine.) Sitting there listening, I knew how fortunate I was to have grown up with that gorgeous sound in my ears, a mother's unaffected musicality, consummate but unrealised, innocent but not naïve. Unlike her sons, she had never forced her voice. It was unscarred by time or vibrato. In her sixties, she sounded forty years younger. Putting my book away, I marvelled at this uncanny sound—a lasting therapy.

It's different now. The songs are few. Mum told me recently that she can't listen to music any more. The events of 1999 spoilt it for her.

My father's and brother's scrapbooks are identical, which seems fitting. They are also huge—more than a metre high. Originally, there was only one. I was there when Daisy presented Dad with the undivided original. Conscious of the groaning tea-chest containing Dad's clippings, she had decided to buy him a grand scrapbook. This was in 1964, soon after Dad, in his first year as Collingwood coach, lost his first grand final, by a margin of four points. The unveiling took place in Clifton Hill, where Nan ran a boarding house,

24

often billeting young footballers down from the country. I always looked forward to Nan's stupendous chips, the bric-a-brac she collected for me during her visits to the local opportunity shops, and the glimpses of anonymous life in the boarding house, with its succession of hefty, amiable boarders—always men, two to a room.

The scrapbook, duly unwrapped, proved colossal and unwieldy. Only Dad could lift it. Even he agreed it was too big for his reputation. Then someone had a bright idea. Why not cut it in half and give one of them to Robert? He would need a scrapbook soon. Not yet a teenager, he had begun to taste success as a schoolboy cricketer and a great future was predicted. Nan kept the tome and had it rebound into two, more practicable scrapbooks.

Robert's stands beside my desk as I write this. It is striking, if a little worn. Soon I will return it to his daughter. First, though, I will study it, noting the omissions as well as the feats and statistics. The type on the cover is confusing: R.A. Rose, 1946–1962. They are my father's initials and the dates of his playing career. Nan, after all that binding, must have economised on gold lettering. It should be initialled R.P. Rose, for Robert Peter Rose.

Robert's scrapbook opens with schoolboy clippings. One headline reads, 'BOBBY ROSE JNR TAKES 8 FOR 10', while a bolder one greets 'ANOTHER ROSE: Little Nyah West, near Swan Hill, has given Collingwood five Roses and a sixth made his appearance with them recently. He was nine-year-old Rob.'

Five Roses and a sixth. Dad had four younger brothers: Bill, Kevin, Colin and Ralph. They all played for

Collingwood, none quite as successfully as Dad. They were known as the Rose brothers.

Then we find that early photograph of Robert. He is about two, so it must be 1954, the year before my birth. Robert was born on 6 February 1952, the day George VI died. He was born in Melbourne near St Patrick's Cathedral. All Mum could hear after the labour were cathedral bells. Still groggy, she thought it was ethereal music and that she had died.

The two-year-old is playing football with his father in the yard behind the sports store on Johnston Street. Robert is wearing dark corduroy overalls and what may be a baby tie. I like his little boots. The toes are grooved, as if he has kicked a football before. His hair is wonderfully blond, as it would remain until 1974. Dad, very attentive, props on his haunches as the little boy kicks the football. It flies off to the right, catching the sun, perfectly focussed. The expression on Robert's face is remarkable for its portent of what he would become. He grimaces, so great is his intensity. His kicking technique is flawless. His right arm shoots back out of range and his left one crosses his body and touches his outstretched leg. His toddler's instep is doubtless taut. Young Robert is kicking for his father, and he knows how to do it. All his later determination and obsession are printed on his face.

For a time it seemed as though Robert's scrapbook would prove inadequate, despite its bulk. We teased Dad that Robert would eventually encroach on his own scrapbook. Even while he was still at school, Robert's clippings were prolific. He was, in his own way, the 'Best Boy of the Week'. Statistics proliferate, typed on my proudest possession, an

Olivetti typewriter given to me when I was thirteen, with its sensational red-and-black ribbon.

District clubs, aware of his potential, began to invite Robert to pre-season training, often adding the postscript 'Regards to Dad'. But it was always understood that Robert would play cricket—and football—for Collingwood. He went there in 1969 ('THE NAME'S ROSE...OF COLLINGWOOD'). He had left our school, Haileybury College, and was now working as a clerk. That year he was selected to play for the Victorian Cricket Association Colts, prompting the first of many floral headlines: 'A ROSE IN BLOOM'. By 1970—the year our Fler sofa broke—he was playing in the firsts, opening the batting with Keith Stackpole. That season Collingwood won its first District premiership since 1912/13. Jack Ryder, the only surviving member of that team, is photographed, capped and laughing, with the victors. State selection followed in 1971.

Robert clearly had his supporters in the media. Heading his story 'ROBERT RATES A CHANCE AT NZ', Rod Nicholson writes, 'Super-cool Victorian batsman, Robert Rose, 21, could be a surprise selection in the Australian team to meet New Zealand this month'. The BBC's Brian Johnston, touring Australia, nominated Robert as one of the most promising young Australian cricketers. A game against Queensland at the 'Gabba' brought Robert and Alan Sieler great success in both innings, including Robert's first Shield century and a record fifth-wicket partnership. At Victoria Park Robert faced the great English bowler John Snow, then playing for Carlton, and took eighteen off his first over.

27

I witnessed many of these milestones. I was there in 1972, when 'Sweet-hitting Rose' faced Dennis Lillee during a lively partnership with Ian Redpath. It was December. I had just finished school and was wondering what life held in store for me. District clubs weren't vying for my services. I wondered if my results, when announced, would prompt one of the universities to invite me down to training. I was sitting in the top tier of the Northern Stand at the MCG reading Norman Mailer when I became aware of the microscopic drama below. Lillee, who never enjoyed being clubbed, was bowling noticeably fast, only to be hooked repeatedly by Robert. This was before Lillee's back injury forced him to modify his technique and to temper his speed. Robert wasn't wearing a mouthguard or helmet. I loved Mailer, but I forgot his self-advertisements for half an hour. 'In 23 minutes before tea,' the cutting records, 'the pair hit the WA attack for 56 runs which had the crowd of almost 9000 roaring in delight.' Alone on the top tier, I was one of them.

And on it goes. There is talk of 'GRAND SLAM CRICKET!' along with images of Robert and his partner, a hairy and bear-like Max Walker, celebrating a win. 'Everything looks rosy for Robert,' writes one reporter.

Nor did Robert, an assiduous self-archivist, ignore his football career. Much seems to have been expected of him in 1969 when he began training with the Collingwood seniors. The aptly named Nicholas Columb gave him a puff at the start of the season in a piece duly headed 'ANOTHER ROSE BLOOMS FOR COLLINGWOOD'. It is full of information. Columb has clearly been sifting through the photo file. He too recalls Robert's little overalls. His style is wistful at times.

> The old-timers could not believe their eyes. It seemed incredible that it could happen all over again. But when 17-year-old Robert Rose snapped up the first kick of the practice game on Saturday then seconds later kicked the first goal, they were convinced. By now it's common knowledge that the sixth Rose had bloomed at Collingwood.

Robert—'the rage recruit'—is described as a natural ball-handler possessing the same tenacity as his father and uncles.

The last paragraph makes me sit up. Columb ends on a clairvoyant note. 'And apparently the Rose talents haven't finished blossoming. There's another budding champ in the family. Peter, 13, is already showing out in schoolboy football for Haileybury and will most likely don the black and white before long.'

My first clipping! Dad's thumbprint on this piece of journalistic whimsy is as palpable as the musty aroma rising from Robert's scrapbook. During my years at Haileybury I always played for the Ds, except once, when I made the Cs.

Then it is 1970 and I unfold a huge yellow newspaper banner: 'MAGPIES SELECT COACH'S SON'. Lou Richards, interviewing Robert after his first senior game, commiserates with him about his dual handicaps— 'lumbered with the same name as his famous sporting father' and 'copping him as coach'. Robert is more philosophical:

> 'Well, it's just a name like any other,' he said, 'and at
> least it's a lot better than being called Marmaduke or
> Archibald. But I don't like being called Bob—that's
> too close to home. Robert is the name and that's
> what I insist on being called. Even Dad does me this
> favour.'

I can't imagine Robert 'insisting' on being called anything,
and the closing phrase is uncharacteristic.

I was there when Robert made his football debut. He
had been selected on the bench. Dad kept us all waiting
until well into the final quarter. As Robert ran onto the
ground I turned to the person sitting next to me, an
Essendon supporter, and said, 'That's my brother'. Robert
promptly picked up the ball, ran towards goal—and kicked
it out of bounds.

By 1972, when his cricket was flourishing, his
football results were patchy. Dad was no longer coaching
Collingwood. He had resigned at the end of the 1971 season
and was now coaching Footscray. Robert played twenty
more games for Collingwood. He was often photographed
in skirmishes. In one dramatic image, Robert rips a St Kilda
player's jumper and appears to be head-butted by another,
while Don Jolley, who had umpired the 1970 grand final
controversially and who later became a paraplegic, runs in
to remonstrate.

In an article headed 'IT'S NO BED OF ROSES', a sports
writer asks Robert about taunts from the grandstand. Robert
admits that when he first started playing at Collingwood
people often yelled out that he was only getting a game

because his father was coach. 'It used to upset me a bit at the time. Now I don't take any notice.'

Robert didn't get on with the new coach, Neil Mann, who had played with my father. He wanted to leave Collingwood and join Dad at Footscray. He wasn't explicit about his reasons when interviewed. 'I would prefer not to say why I want to leave the Magpies,' he is quoted as saying, just like a politician. Collingwood refused to clear him to another League side, so Robert moved to Prahran, in another competition. There he was coached by Uncle Kevin, the third Rose brother. Kevin had played for Collingwood a few years after my father. He was the best player on the ground in the famous 1964 grand final, his opponent being Ron Barassi.

Midway through 1973, Collingwood relented and Robert became an 'Instant Bulldog'. One of the last items is a feature story with a photograph of Robert and his wife, Terry. She is holding their new baby. Salli pertly studies the camera. The story is headed 'CHANCE TO KILL DAD'S BOY TAG'. The interviewer writes, 'Rose knows that this could be the last chance to silence his critics...Rose, now a married man with a four-weeks-old daughter, is fast learning the meaning of responsibility.'

A few games with Footscray produced more newsprint. Then the football coverage ends. Botanical allusions and sporting genealogy make way, over the page, for a new kind of journalism and existential order. Sport yields to mangled metal, headlines such as 'WHEELCHAIR IN 6 MONTHS', and recycled photographs, one of which, as we know, is erroneous. No sooner is Robert cut from his Volkswagen than he is moved from the back page—his virile nirvana—to the front, which he never read. No longer seen or quoted, Robert becomes the subject of police statements and stark medical prognoses—and an editorial in the *Herald* titled 'The message of Robert Rose'.

I'm not in the habit of reading editorials. I only do so when a journalist friend tells me he or she has been co-opted into writing one—about some malingering billionaire absconder, or the tyranny of economic rationalism, or even, touchingly, the plight of poetry. I always read them with interest, but I never go back the following day. This indifference to editorials, known as leaders in the trade, strikes me as odd, given my addiction to newspapers, my inability to function without them.

No one likes to be thought leadable or suggestible, but in my case it's only half true. I belong to a family with a long record of allegiance. I too belong to that club, notorious or venerable, depending on your loyalties. My membership is purely nominal, quite unearned—vicarious and voyeuristic. I never sought conventional membership down that dangerous race, in those pungent rooms. Yet even in my forties I remain a member, irreversibly. Whatever I do, wherever I go, whatever I write, it is immutable—the sole constant in my life. I may change, but it does not. It is a kind of birthright, as strange to me today as it was when I was a boy.

I have no idea who wrote the *Herald* editorial. Whoever did was in an historical mood. He remembers a photograph of a handsome youth of seventeen. An impressionistic portrait takes shape: 'The file of pictures and stories on Robert Rose has become quite thick since then...brilliant Collingwood and Footscray footballer...Victorian State cricketer with a sure Test future...his famous footballer father, Bob, bursting with pride...Robert Rose happily married...daughter Salli born ten months ago...'

Then, inevitably, the transformation scene: 'Other pictures of Robert Rose have just been sadly filed. Paralysed in body and all four limbs, he lies in the spinal injuries unit at the Austin Hospital, his head pinned back with calipers and held in place by sandbags. His parents and his wife support his tremendous courage with their own. The one-time active lad of 17 is 22.' That 'lad' seems quaint, an anachronism, but the editorialist proceeds to his moral. 'All this transformation took was a driving accident—just another of our crashes—and a second or two in time. Robert Rose is well known. But there are 61 other beds in the spinal injuries unit at the Austin, and they are never empty long.' The author reminds his readers that tens of thousands of people are injured on our roads each year and that nine hundred people would die on Victorian roads in 1974. I am shocked by this figure, which is almost three times the current rate. How fast were they driving in those days? What on earth were they drinking? The editorial concludes on an urgent, emphatic note. 'Here surely is cause for pity, for anguish, for reflection—and for determination that the carnage on our roads must cease.'

Reading this a quarter of a century later, idle thoughts about lamentable road tolls surrender to reveries on a headlined theme. What exactly is the message of Robert Rose? One year after his death, twenty-six years after just another of our crashes, knowing the effect it had on his family and friends, and thousands of others who hardly knew him, I want to go back there, I want to examine my brother's life and reanimate him, despite those calipers and sandbags. Here, in my Adelaide eyrie, with my documents and my pent cathedral bells, I want to examine his achievement, what he symbolised, what he gave and what he withheld, what he divulged and what he never said, as a son, as a brother, as a husband, as a mate, above all as a tragic victim of that 'second or two in time'.

And so I hold on to the outsize scrapbook for a while longer. It is time to listen to my brother whose message, laconic but self-evident to many in his life, I somehow never fully heeded. If I am to overcome these eternities of maladjustment, as a friend put it when Robert died, I must try. Brothers so close yet so incongruous meet improbably in this shifting text.

Again I turn to the handsome lad, the vaunted youth, the rage recruit, and will him to speak to me.

2

ST VALENTINE'S DAY

My journal entry for Thursday 14 February 1974 is unusually brief. My mother and I were staying with old friends in Wangaratta. I was in the spare room at the back of the house where I had often slept as a boy.

> *After the many dull days I have spent recently, the trip to Wangaratta was a joy. (Now I sound like Margaret Whitlam in her much-publicised diary.) We lunched at Seymour, and were amazed by the millions of locusts covering the road and devouring the vegetation. We arrived at 2.30, found Uncle Hughie frail but well, and sat down for afternoon tea. It was good to see them both. Sammy wouldn't settle down.*

> *We had many visitors & a nice dinner, and went*
> *to bed at about 11.*

The previous entry, written in Melbourne and pompously titled 'A Short Note on America' (I was reading *Tom Jones*, with its ironic chapter headings), is much less contented. Being a dutiful Monash sophomore, I wrote about my disdain for Nixon's America. I was so indignant I ran out of space and had to colonise 12 February.

The allusion to 'many dull days' is representative of my—any?—adolescent diary. Mine, in its sixth year, was often churlish. Yet dull hardly describes that summer. Just three weeks earlier I had fallen out spectacularly—irreparably, I thought—with my soul mate, a boy whom I shall call A. He was eighteen. We had known each other since school. A. was my only male friend and my sharpest critic. He seemed to think it was his duty to upheave all my beliefs, cure me of bourgeois complacency and radicalise me in every way. He was good at it. This particular day he came over in the afternoon. My parents were away and I was at home minding the dog. We started drinking whisky. Later we moved on to other drugs. Things began to deteriorate. We sauntered to the nearby creek. I wanted to play a new game, a farce mixing personas and taunts. There was a swing above the creek, like the one in my favourite film, *Who's Afraid of Virginia Woolf?* A. misunderstood the game and became upset. 'I am destroyed,' he kept saying. Having been powerfully attracted to him for the first time, by the swing, I resented his overreaction and lambasted him. I was shocked by his vulnerability and despised him

36

for having the ignorance to say, 'You have been my god'. We parted bitterly, not expecting to see each other again. As he left, A. chanted George's abiding taunt in Edward Albee's great play: 'Who's afraid of Virginia Woolf, Virginia Woolf, Virginia Woolf?'

And yet…'many dull days'.

Nor had the previous week been uneventful. On the Saturday my parents and I had attended the wedding of an old friend of mine. We had known the bride's family since we lived in Wangaratta. Robert wasn't invited to the wedding. Perhaps Norelle had little in common with the distracted young sportsman, but the three of us had grown up together in Wangaratta, playing indefatigably in our other backyard, the Warby Ranges. On the day of the wedding I changed into my new flared beige suit. In the photographs Dad took I look radically thin and superfluously tall, as George Eliot would say. My hair is long and I am wearing those heavy tinted glasses that would make me look like a terrorist in my first passport later that year. Then we collected my date, Diane, the daughter of one of my father's business partners ('nice boy in suit picks up nice girl in long dress') and drove to the Dandenongs for the wedding. My diaristic tone remains mordant. 'Am I being too sarcastic?' I write hopefully at one point. 'I knew I was not going to like this or any other formal wedding.' I loathed the formality, the longueurs, the chauvinistic minister; I was even bitchy about the organist. I enjoyed dancing with Diane, but this was interrupted by Dad's speech and by the young couple's interminable withdrawal. Reluctantly I joined the ring of tearful onlookers and waited to congratulate them once again. 'Why does the bride cry? She has only gone to another suburb.'

I was that sort of eighteen-year-old.

By comparison, Robert's wedding, a year earlier, had been admirably quick, like an inoculation.

The day after Norelle's wedding Mum and I drove Dad to the airport. He was off to America and Europe with Diane's father. They would be away for a month. Perhaps it was the length of the trip that was unsettling. Mum seemed worried, and I wasn't looking forward to Dad's departure. He was edgy, possibly because he hadn't been to Europe before. He may not have relished the thought of being away for so long at the start of a new football season. In the car his unease became acute. Diane's brother was travelling with us, which made it even more embarrassing. Dad was very nervous. He hummed, he sang, he twitched, he even began speaking in a confused German accent. Finally, Mum had to tell him to stop, very politely.

At the airport I bought Dad several newspapers and a copy of *Papillon*. I drank a needed Scotch in the lounge. Then it was time to farewell Dad. 'He looked very quiet, gentle and fragile as he went away—nervous in a way that I have not seen before. I will never forget the way he looked,' I wrote in my journal.

Then we crammed onto the landing for a last glimpse of the plane. Robert wasn't present. There is no mention of him in the journal that weekend. He had played cricket for Collingwood on the day of Norelle's wedding, remaining not out at stumps. We had last seen him on 6 February, his twenty-second birthday—'an enjoyable

38

night, with much merriment & champagne. Terry was unusually quiet.'

After the wedding I hung around the house. The defection of A. had left me even more isolated than before. Now that Robert was married and living elsewhere with Terry, I saw less of him. I got up late, sunbaked, picked at some of the novels I would be studying that year at university and went to the movies, another passion. Mum and I decided to visit the Challmans in Wangaratta even before learning that Uncle Hughie was ill again. His old cardiac problem had returned, and he was said to be depressed. My journal for 7 February ends: 'That is, I imagine, how I shall feel when death is near—depressed. I must impress upon you the importance of this feeling of dread that I have.'

By the time Mum and I got to Wangaratta, Uncle Hughie had been discharged, 'frail but well'.

The Challmans were our oldest friends. My parents had known them since moving into the sports store on Johnston Street soon after marrying. Hughie owned the barber shop two doors down, with its exotic aromas and classy leadlighting. Older than Mum and Dad, the Challmans had two daughters who were already in their teens when Robert was born in 1952. Barbara and Marie doted on Robert, who was a beautiful child, wide-eyed, very blond, used to adult company. In those days there were few children on Johnston Street for him to play with. Robert would sit in the doorway of the shop, memorising the names of cars and their numberplates. One day, when the new Queen visited Melbourne during the 1954 tour, Barbara, always independent, asked if she could take Robert for a walk in his pusher. They were gone for hours. When Mum asked her what had happened, Barbara said they had gone into the city to see the Queen.

I don't recall Barbara and Marie in Collingwood. My parents moved to Wangaratta at the end of 1955, soon after I was born. My father had played his last game for Collingwood in the 1955 grand final, a bruising affair, as they say. Melbourne's Noel McMahen ironed him out in front of the members' stand. (He still boasts about it at reunions.) Twenty-five years later, when I worked in the bar at the Collingwood Social Club, collecting frothy beer glasses after the half-time swill, I often heard old-timers reliving McMahen's blow. I used this in an ironic poem called 'Operamanes', in which I juxtaposed football fervour and operamania, from which I also suffer:

> One went on to declare that
> only a monumental shirtfront
> stood between you and the '55 flag.
> Anyone else would have sagged on a stretcher,
> but not you—so the aria went.

Somehow my father got to his feet and stayed on the field, but he was concussed, not unlike Peter McKenna fifteen years later. Collingwood, which relied on Dad, lost to Norm Smith's brilliant young side. Dad, at twenty-seven, announced his retirement. He was Collingwood's most celebrated player and the first man to be dubbed 'Mr Football', but the money was woeful. In 1955 he was being paid ten pounds per game. John Wren's Monday morning visits weren't just welcome for sentimental reasons. Even more providential were his gifts of two hundred pounds each time Dad won the Copeland Trophy, Collingwood's highest award. When some Wangaratta businessmen offered him forty pounds a week to captain–coach the new rival to the Wangaratta Magpies, he accepted. I used to think this must have grieved him, but he told me recently that he never regretted his decision. Forty pounds was a fortune in those days. No other footballer earned that sort of money. Collingwood offered him the captaincy if he stayed, but no extra money. The board's attitude then, and later, was that it was enough to wear the famous black and white.

League football was everything to my father. As a boy in the Mallee he had dreamt about playing for Collingwood. The thought sustained him during years of Depression, a world war and successive years of drought. Dad still remembers driving around with an uncle and shooting the horses that were so starved they had begun to eat dirt. Then he went to Melbourne. He was amazed by the lushness of the grounds. In Nyah West the ground was so hard they hadn't been able to use football stops, just strips of leather. Nor had Dad's family always been able to afford a football. Instead, he and his brothers gorged on plum jam so that they could kick the empty tin around, thus accounting for Kevin Rose's bizarre kicking action.

Dad's family was large and poor. In addition to his parents, Bert and Millie, there were five boys and two sisters. They lived in a small four-room concrete house on Elizabeth Street, named after one of the little princesses but commonly known as Blowfly Flat. Uncle Rusty, a wheat-farming bachelor with a roll-your-own cough, occupied one makeshift sleep-out. A widowed grandmother squeezed into another. Bert and Millie had one cow but no fence. Every morning one of the boys was sent out to milk the cow. First he had to find it. It could be miles away. Beyond the sleep-outs, beyond Millie's springy lawn and tenacious rose garden, was a nothingness of wheat fields. There was one tree on the horizon, but the sunsets were spectacular. As the poet said, it was like walking on the sky's beach. Dust storms periodically swept across Blowfly Flat and blanketed the house.

Dad was the eldest child—a golden youth. Despite the plum jam and the missing stops, his sporting prowess made him famous in the district. He began playing seniors football at the age of twelve and helped Nyah West to win a premiership at the end of the war. When Harry Shaw started a gymnasium Dad became interested in boxing. He caught the bus to school in Swan Hill. Sometimes he drove it. After school he worked in the Linger Longer Café, his only acquaintance with a stove. He always liked a pun. He still laughs about the removalist's van with the sign that read *P. Overall, Nyah West*.

At Collingwood—the sporting acme for working-class and country boys—Dad seized his opportunity. Collingwood made him, he ardently believes. Pride, camaraderie, tribal loyalty don't explain it. My father has never outgrown his sense of good fortune at being embraced by Collingwood, that fierce, proud and, in those days, unrivalled football club. Something happened to my father when he began to flourish in the late 1940s under Jock McHale's tutelage. He became successful, but it went deeper than that. He was loved, watched, respected, *needed*. He belonged, utterly and irreversibly. Some singers talk about a similar visceral connection with their audience. Recently my father told a journalist, 'I still feel tremendously proud just to come into the club'.

Two episodes stand out for him. He recalls his astonishment when he ran on to the MCG to play Essendon in the 1946 second semi-final. It was his first final and only his fourth senior game. There were 90,000 people in the crowd. He never forgot the sound they made. He remembers everything about it: the precise score (it was a draw), whole passages of play. Twelve months earlier he had played in a grand final in the Mallee in front of 2000 fans, 'mostly relations'.

The second epiphany happened in 1948. Dad described it in another interview:

> It was a cold, wet day in the middle of winter. I arrived to watch the reserves and as I walked into the ground it really hit me. Every seat around the fence, right around the ground and wherever else you could get a seat—not too many of them were under cover in those days—was taken. The fans had arrived by 11 a.m. so they could watch the reserves and the seniors. It was a lesson for me about the faithful at Collingwood: they had come to watch the team, of which I was just one player. From that moment, I was determined never to give them less

43

than 100 per cent in every game. I don't know if such a thing had any impact on my team-mates, but it really affected me. I've never forgotten it. When I was coaching Collingwood, I used that sentiment.

When he was lured north to coach the Wangaratta Rovers, the newest team in the prosperous Ovens & Murray League, Dad was undoubtedly thinking about Elsie and his two young sons, but he must have known what he was abandoning—the stupendous crowds, the inner-city adulation, the unique roar in the coliseum, the adrenalin, a fifth or even sixth Copeland Trophy, more sobriquets and Saturdays, maybe a Brownlow.

I wonder if my mother felt a similar sense of loss when she gave up singing.

Not long after my parents left Melbourne, the Challmans followed. Uncle Hughie bought the barber's shop just around the corner from my parents' new sports store on Murphy Street. Eventually Marie and Barbara—striking young women, both adventurous—moved away and remained distant figures for ten years. Dad was busy coaching the Rovers, which he did with great success, winning premierships and Morris Medals. Robert was the team mascot and also helped with the statistics. One of Dad's players said they were more like brothers than father and son. Robert and I attended the primary school in Chisholm Street, with its mysteriously green swimming pool. One of Robert's teachers remembers him as a popular student. When Ian Blencowe joined the school in 1962, the other staff members were quick to point out who Robert's father was and predicted that their young pupil was sure to follow in his footsteps. Blencowe found Robert confident of his abilities yet neither brash nor boastful. He still remembers buying his first teacher's whistle in my parents' sports store and being introduced to Dad by Robert. That was a really special time for him, he told me recently. 'Bobby Rose was the first "really famous person" I ever met in real life.'

Dad resigned as coach of the Wangaratta Rovers in 1963 and we moved back to Melbourne. I was eight at the time. I vividly recall turning around as we set off and fixing Wangaratta in my mind. I had been happy there: it was a golden time. Dad was promptly appointed coach of Collingwood for the 1964 season. The club had just gone through one of its periodic upheavals. Newspaper photographers descended on our house in Lemana Crescent the next morning. We were all photographed on the verandah. Dad, Brylcreemed and besuited, looks remarkably like John F. Kennedy, who had just been shot. Deeply freckled, I am clutching a Magpie gnome with a chipped nose. Regrettably, my fly is undone. Later we went up to a nearby oval. Dad wore his Collingwood guernsey and Robert his school one. I'm still in my school uniform. They lope along, effortlessly bouncing footballs. I must have lost mine. I grin at them dementedly. The top button of my fly is still undone.

Dad says I had never looked happier than I did that morning.

Uncle Hughie and Auntie Chall remained in Wangaratta, but we still saw much of them. Our return journey in

February 1974 was just one of many we had made. By then Marie and Barbara were back in our lives. Upon their return from London in 1970 they had moved into a flat in inner Melbourne. I had never been inside a flat before. Theirs became a sort of mecca for me, the place where I spent most weekends, propped in front of the gas heater, drinking strong black coffee, listening to the talk about men and other follies, meeting their girlfriends who visited on Sunday afternoons to talk about their pursed or astonished hearts, inhaling the fug of Peter Stuyvesants.

I can't imagine what this acned adolescent offered these two sophisticates, but they seemed to welcome my company. Soon Barbara was introducing me to her friends as her stepbrother. While my schoolmates went off to the Bowl to hear Billy Thorpe or to discover sex on back beaches, I went to Elwood for superior female talk. Barbara, the more literary and political of the two, had come back from Europe with a library of strangers. It was she who introduced me to Norman Mailer, and Samuel Beckett, and James Baldwin, with his whiff of heterodox sex. Barbara even knew her way around *African* writers. At last I had someone to talk to about Conrad, whose *Lord Jim* had changed my life, as I thought ('In the destructive element immerse…To follow the dream, and again to follow the dream'). We stayed up all night talking about modish London, Franco's Spain and the vagaries of men. We joked endlessly about Barbra Streisand. Barbara told me about Paul Scofield's performance in *Uncle Vanya*. I thought I was in paradise. On Friday nights we often met in the city. I saw my first play, *Patate* (of all things), with Leo

46

McKern. They were there when I appeared in a production myself, Agatha Christie's decidedly un-Chekhovian *Murder at the Vicarage*, and later, in a conspicuously smaller role, *The Cherry Orchard*, when I had the consolation of becoming the first Haileyburian to smoke on stage.

Tutored by Robert's girlfriend Terry Yewers, I was also smoking off-stage. I had begun wearing scarves. Once, in Surfers Paradise, I was wearing a red piratical one when a street artist drew my portrait. Showing it to my father later, I pointed out the scarf, explaining that it hid my long neck. Quite correctly he criticised me for my vanity— a rare reprimand.

My friendship with Barbara was precious. Soon after she returned to Australia I wrote in my journal, 'Now I have met a person with whom I can forget my very wretchedness'. I was fifteen. Barbara was interested, opinionated and persuasive. As A. sagely observed, in her company one always felt compelled to modify one's thinking to suit hers. A little sheepishly, I confessed to Barbara that I had renounced socialism for anarchism.

Barbara introduced me to Pellegrini's, arthouse cinemas and the right bookshops. When Marie was away performing (like my mother she was a singer) Barbara and I often went to the movies. She took me to *Five Easy Pieces* and I held my breath during the fucking scene. I badly needed her to see my personal favourite, Visconti's *Death in Venice*, and saw it with her for the fourth time. When I wrote my first piece of fiction, a woeful story called 'Father to Son', she read it sympathetically and showed it to a visiting Englishman, the first writer I had ever met, with the exception of

47

Lou Richards, the title of whose autobiography, *Boots and All*, remains one of my all-time favourites.

Our talks, our endless talks, strike me now as curious and challenging. When I was sixteen Barbara predicted that neither of us would ever be happily married because we were too easily bored. She mocked me for wanting to go to university merely to satisfy my parents. She had graduated in other schools of life. When I told her that I would like to go back and live in Wangaratta, she laughed and said, 'You don't know where you're going'. I fumed at times, but I always went back. We stayed up late one night talking about our families and all the ambivalence therein. We agreed that Robert was overly dependent upon my father. Barbara said that I had a harder time than most because of my family situation, and predicted that I would cause my parents anguish, just as my larrikin brother was doing.

Introverted adolescents are easily flattered by such forebodings.

With my mother, we went to the football and the cricket—any contest, really, in which 'the boys' were appearing. I was proud of my glamorous and extended family and wondered what people made of it. At Victoria Park we sat with the players' wives and committee members in a kind of chook pen in the Ryder Stand. Collingwood, though still flagless, never lost at home, so those Saturdays were always fun—absurd and fanatical. When my father switched from Collingwood to Footscray and my mother, exhausted by football politics, decided to stay at home on Saturdays, I travelled to the unfamiliar western suburbs with Marie and Barbara in their white Volkswagen. Squashed in the back, I was hypnotised by the week's gossip and by the cloud of cigarette smoke.

Both sisters adored Robert. We were all there that sunny day in 1971 when Collingwood won the cricket premiership at the Albert Park Oval. When Robert and the other players appeared on the picturesque balcony Mum urged me to join the throng. She said it mightn't happen again. But I stayed on the grass with the ladies, listening to their talk. I felt sure there would be countless victories in the future. We left the revellers and saw *Sunday Bloody Sunday*, which elevated me to a new peak of sophistication: two men kissing in a hallway, instant coffee made directly from a tap, cigarette ash ground into the carpet.

On 14 February 1974—St Valentine's Day—Mum and I drove to Wangaratta. We were on our own except for the dachshund, Sammy, which travelled in the back, staring disapprovingly at haystacks and livestock. Being an innate nostalgist, I always wanted to hear about our original move to Wangaratta, back in 1955. I couldn't remember it, having been an infant at the time. Vague memories of putrid swaggies trudging along the Hume Highway were probably seeded much later, or dreamt. My mother, driving in her cautious way, reminisced. She told me she had dreaded the prospect of leaving Melbourne. Having left Tongala, with its ambiguous childhood memories, she probably disliked the thought of going back to the country. An astute woman, all too familiar with the intrigue and acrimony that beset football clubs, she must have known what awaited them in the recently polarised town, half of whose inhabitants

49

duly shunned their sports store, funded as it was by the interlopers, the Wang Rovers.

Mum was also a creature of the city. Postwar Melbourne was a vibrant place for someone like Elsie. As a young woman she had performed in countless theatres and moved in a large, stimulating circle. During the day she worked as a stenographer near the Victoria Market. Then she married into a gregarious sporting milieu. She frequented the legendary Rivoli and Mario's Restaurant. The last thing she desired was the claustrophobia of a small town, with a co-op for fashions and biannual visits from the Elizabethan Theatre Trust to look forward to ('*Rigoletto* in Myrtleford', as the old joke went).

But one thing solaced Mum as she set off for Wangaratta in 1955. She loved radio, then in its halcyon days. Radio was universal and inviolable. Even in Wangaratta she would be able to listen to her beloved 'Nicky' and his sidekick, Graham Kennedy. When she began to miss her old world she would be able to listen to a concert or serial or news broadcast. Elsie, whom I later dubbed 'Reuters' Rose, was addicted to the news. An hour without a bulletin was hollow, unfulfilled.

The first thing Mum did when she reached Wangaratta was to unpack the 'wireless' and switch it on. Silence and static greeted her. She had forgotten about the Great Dividing Range. There were no Melbourne radio stations: no 'Nicky', no Graham, no Jack Davey. The only station she could pick up was 3NE, the local one. It had just acquired a copy of 'The Black Hills of Dakota' to go with its other Doris Day records. It played them all day.

My mother sat on the kitchen floor and wept.

When we reached Wangaratta on St Valentine's Day, listening to the radio, of course, we went straight to the Challmans' house. Uncle Hughie, discharged from hospital, seemed cheerful, if weak. We sat in the kitchen drinking tea and eating Auntie Chall's immemorial Melting Moments. I always loved returning to Wangaratta. I loved being back in Auntie Chall's kitchen where the Roses and the Challmans had spent so many evenings together. I loved hearing about old friends, including a passing reference to a boy called Ross, the first boy I ever kissed. I loved the familiar dark cool of the Challmans' house, with its floral carpet and porcelain figurines and seductive Sammy Davis Junior and Judy Garland records, which Marie had added. I wished that she and Barbara were with us.

Throughout the day old friends kept arriving to say hello. I didn't recognise all of them. They knew me, though, and teased me about my height. They asked fondly about Dad and Robert. Within a few days some of them would be writing to us, using a different tone: those old, refractory phrases. We discussed a recent murder near Wangaratta. Murders are always gripping in country towns. This one was too stupid, too gratuitous, to be forgotten. It had happened a few summers ago. A fourteen-year-old girl— Ella was her name—was walking her Alsatian beside the Hume Highway one morning. Her family had stopped for a drink on their way north. Ella was mature for her age, blonde, leggy and attractive. A local, driving along the highway, spotted her, was 'reminded' of his estranged wife and shot her with his rifle. She died beside the road.

Mum and I remembered it well. We knew Ella. Her family, recent immigrants from Scandinavia, had lived near us in Lemana Crescent. I recalled the police arriving on Christmas morning to ask Dad a few questions. I had met Ella once or twice. Not long before her murder she had knocked on our door and politely warned my parents that she was organising a Christmas party. I was far too awed by Ella's beauty to speak to her. I was similarly dazzled by her handsome brother, Erik, and by the way his name was spelt. Both of them had the sort of classic good looks that always rendered me speechless with shyness. After the murder the family remained secluded, but now and then, around dusk, I saw Erik walking the Alsatian, profoundly sombre.

The insanity of Ella's murder riveted us in the cakey kitchen. Later Mum and I asked about friends, shopkeepers, the Wang Rovers. I kept looking at the high, exposed cabinet. Installed by some local carpenter, this rose to the ceiling and was full of Auntie Chall's impressive collection of teasets and dinner services—one for every occasion. It was like a mini-museum, florid and frangible. The cabinet was leaning over as mesmerisingly as ever. Ever since I was a boy I had been privately waiting for it to collapse. No one else commented on its Pisan tilt, so I said nothing. It was the slowest disaster in history.

Gingerly I removed some plates from the perilous tower. I have no idea what we ate for dinner, but Uncle Hughie no doubt spurned dessert and called for The Tasty Cheese. This aromatic rite had always fascinated me as a child, inured to processed cheddar. I thought Uncle Hughie sophisticated to the point of tetchiness.

Evidently people were tired and we all went to bed 'at about 11'.

Sammy woke me around two in the morning, wanting to be let in. Sammy was a highly intuitive dog, with a pedigree as long as a Remington ribbon, as Henry James said of his dachshund. Soon after—I didn't hear the telephone ring— Auntie Chall came into the room and said, 'Peter, you've got to get up. Robert's had an accident. You've got to go home.' Her voice was grave. She had never sounded like that before. I felt sure Robert was dead. It had happened, after all, the horror we are always half expecting in life. Now we had to hurry to its side.

Instantly there was terrible activity in the dark house. My mother was already up, dressing. She too had been awake when the call came. Perhaps it was the heat that woke her. But she had felt an odd premonition before leaving Melbourne. She had gone into Robert's old bedroom and looked at some mementoes. It occurred to her that if anything happened to me she would have ample memorabilia—all my silly cards and poems—but that if Robert were to die she wouldn't have anything to remember him by.

We packed our things, not speaking to each other. Weirdly, I washed my face. Mum told me to hurry up and we went out into the night. There was no light in the small garage at the end of the drive and Mum became frightened. I didn't know how to drive then (and would delay learning for another decade because of what happened), so Elsie, a nervous motorist at the best of times, had to drive back to

Melbourne. We squeezed into Dad's big powerful lime-green Ford. Reversing down the narrow drive we hit the wall twice. Uncle Hughie, in his dressing gown, had to scamper out of the way. Then we had to get out and clean the windscreen, which was encrusted with insects. We all moved around in silence, saying nothing. Finally, jerkily, Mum and I set off.

It was still hot. Locusts were everywhere. All night they rushed at us, smothering us. My mouth was dry. Mum wept occasionally but mostly we talked about the surprising volume of traffic on the Hume Highway and the suicidal locusts. Tacitly, we knew we had to maintain some sort of conversation. Mum sensed that I was nervous about her driving. Knowing that Robert might already be dead, she said to me, 'It's all right, I won't lose another son'.

We ticked off the familiar towns along the way: Glenrowan, Benalla, Euroa, Seymour. The bypasses we all take for granted hadn't been built yet, so we drove down the empty, flickering main streets. Away from the towns, the semitrailer drivers, as if knowing we were in a hurry, kept indicating to my mother when it was safe to overtake. Elsie had rarely overtaken anyone in her life. On the few occasions when she had, after much deliberation, overtaken a slowcoach, Robert and I, sitting in the back, would congratulate her and we would all breathe a sigh of relief.

My mother had been told to go straight to the Austin Hospital in Heidelberg. I was too callow to know what that might signify, though I did wonder why Robert had been moved from Bacchus Marsh, where the accident had happened, to the Austin. But Elsie knew where she was going, and why.

It was 4.30 a.m. when we arrived. As we neared the ugly hospital on the hill I decided that if Robert was dead I wanted to deliver the eulogy, possibly a strange wish for a young brother.

We left Sammy, oddly quiet, in the car and went to Casualty, where a pleasant nurse directed us further up the hill to Ward Seven. When we reached the waiting room Uncle Kevin was there to greet us. Terry or someone must have rung him, in Dad's absence. I was relieved by Kevin's facial expression. I knew immediately that Robert was still alive. But Kevin looked startled when the doctor, duly alerted, came out and spoke to us. Kevin's prominent jaw was quivering. He was obviously deeply shocked. The doctor introduced himself as David Burke, head of the spinal injuries unit. I seemed to be having trouble hearing or comprehending what was being said. Then my mother broke down and the doctor began consoling her. Kevin, a pragmatic man just like my father, said, 'He's all right *in himself*'—a phrase that would always fascinate me, one for the philosophers. Kevin told us that Robert had taken the news exceptionally bravely. Then I heard the words that Robert would never walk again, and I too started crying. I slumped on a bench away from the others. Mum remembers me sliding along the bench and cowering in a corner with my face averted. Fat unavailing tears fell on the polished floor.

But then my mother shocked me. 'It would have been better if he'd died,' she said. For the first time in my life I snapped at her. 'That's a terrible thing to say,' I reprimanded her. She looked at me benignly and said nothing. I was eighteen. I had no sons of my own. I had never nursed anyone. I had never been nursed. I had no idea what quadriplegia meant. I couldn't even spell it.

We never mentioned it again.

In the years that followed we all wished they had broken the news to us differently. Mum, as we would learn, had reason to. If only they had had more time or better resources. If only they had prepared us a little, sat us down, taken us into a private room, given us a drink after the journey. Mum had been driving all night. Almost forgotten in the crisis was the fact that she had had major surgery six weeks earlier and was still recovering.

Yet there were reasons for Dr Burke's sense of urgency and candour, however confronting. Apart from the fact that his main responsibility was not our equilibrium but keeping my brother alive (for Robert's survival was by no means assured that night), Dr Burke and many of his peers believed that directness was preferable to evasions or euphemisms. The relatively new director of the spinal injuries unit, then in his mid-thirties, had trained in Britain with a pioneering surgeon in the field who insisted on being frank with patients and their families, even at the outset. Dr Burke had previously worked in America where he was disturbed by the misleading promises made by some neurosurgeons, and by the dismay of quadriplegics and their families months later when they failed to regain the use of their limbs. He thought this deeply irresponsible. So Dr Burke was frank with Robert when he was admitted to the Austin, just as he was forthright with us.

When I visited Dr Burke in July 2000, he admitted that this policy was not without its critics. 'It's a bit controversial still,' he told me.

We were sitting in a small office near the reception desk at Ivanhoe Manor in Melbourne, where he helps road accident victims cope with quadriplegia and head injuries. I had sat outside for a few minutes, waiting to renew my acquaintance with Dr Burke, whom I hadn't seen since 1974 and by whom I had always been somewhat intimidated. The reception desk was clearly the busiest part of the hospital. It was almost five in the afternoon, always a hectic time in a hospital. Dinner was being served and patients put to bed. I watched a boy of eighteen or nineteen trying to use a public telephone, assisted by an aide, all his movements twisted, uncontrollable. I kept thinking about him during my interview with Dr Burke as sounds of laughter, coins being changed, patients chided or placated, penetrated the thin walls. I thought of Robert, who had spent more than half his life in institutions of this kind: frenetic, rackety, always vaguely hysterical.

Dr Burke elaborated: 'There are people who feel you shouldn't give people that sort of bad news straight off. I always believed, and it was taught to me by my predecessor, that it was more important to be honest with patients and with the relatives right from the start. Tell them the truth, as much as you can, but deliver it in a kind way, without being too blunt. But don't give them false hopes.'

I presumed that Robert, being the sort of laconic person he was, would have welcomed the truth. Dr Burke generalised in response: 'You don't necessarily give them the whole story first up. You've got to tailor it to suit individuals a bit. With some relatives you just know they're not ready to hear anything very much that first time. But you don't tell them untruths, you don't make false promises, and you don't tell them something you know is just not true—because you'll get found out and then you lose them forever.'

Cautiously I said that those interviews—imparting the terrible news to patients once or twice a week—must have been difficult, notwithstanding professional experience and exigencies. He must have done it hundreds, even thousands, of times. I wondered where Dr Burke was when he got the news in February 1974. He too must have been rung up that night, called away from dinner or the theatre or the *Lancet*, to be confronted by 'just another of our crashes', more maimed promise in the sixty-second bed, never empty for long. The director of the unit was always notified first.

Dr Burke agreed that it was a distressing role. He said it was one of the reasons why he had moved away from spinal cord injuries ten years after Robert's accident. 'I just felt that I was saying the same thing to the same people, the same families, time after time, and that it was time for a change. It gets to you after a while, even though it is a very important part of your work.'

He reminisced about his subsequent work in Armenia after the 1989 earthquake. This left many people with severe spinal cord injuries, but with few local specialists to treat them. Dr Burke was one of countless western doctors who volunteered. He spent three months in Armenia. ('Talk about a return to the good old days of spinal injuries! I mean, the sort of facilities we used to have at the Austin well before Robert's time—and even then the facilities were pretty basic.') Because none of the medicos spoke Armenian or Russian, they had to recruit university students to translate for them when they spoke to the victims and their families. The students, many in their teens, none au fait with quadriplegia, were the ones who had to tell the truth ('the talk I gave your family'), thus breaking people's hearts. Dr Burke was full of admiration for the way the students coped. Many wept after the first interview, 'but they were right from there on'.

I asked Dr Burke if he remembered how Robert reacted to the news. He doesn't recall anything unusual. He told Robert that he had sustained a serious injury to his spinal cord. He had broken a bone in his neck. His spinal cord was badly damaged, which was why he was paralysed. There was no feeling, no movement, and there was a real possibility that this might be permanent and that he might not walk again. He told him that if any recovery was going to take place it would happen during the next few weeks. He didn't go into further detail. As Dr Burke told me, 'It would have been something fairly straightforward, pretty much from the shoulder, but delivered in a friendly kind of way'.

My conversation with Dr Burke lasted for an hour. It was amicable, unreserved, at times gently rueful. When I told him about Robert's final illness he fell silent, clearly distressed and surprised that it had gone on as long as it did. He hadn't heard the details before. He asked about my work as a publisher at Oxford University Press and told me he was reading the book about James Murray and the mad American who helped him compile the *OED*. I thanked him and left him to his emergencies. As I passed the reception desk a fire alarm began to wail. Those patients able to walk and their visitors—haunted, exhausted mothers and sisters—poked their heads into the corridor, variously concerned or amused, wondering if they should evacuate the building, wondering if they could be bothered. A beleaguered nurse hurried along the corridor reassuring people that there was no need to worry, that it was only a false alarm, but the fire alarm continued to wail. It was still going when I reached my car. Fire engines pulled into the street as I reached the intersection.

I thought about that old dream of mine—the one with cemeteries and infernos—in which I belatedly recognised my young guide.

Mum and I, still in the waiting room, asked if we could see Robert. Dr Burke said we could as long as we composed ourselves. We did. We walked down a corridor, past tiny offices with nurses filling out graphs and rosters. Then we entered Ward Seven for the first of many times. It was in darkness, except for a space around Robert's bed. The newcomers usually arrive during the night, after their car or diving accidents. Some of the other patients in the long, crowded room must have been aware what was going on, but they said nothing. Nurses were leaning over Robert's bed, whispering. They were still working on him. I wondered why the bed had to be so high. It was like a bier.

Robert was lying on his back, looking rather beautiful. His head was shaved. They had already drilled holes in his skull and inserted calipers attached to eight-pound weights. Robert's head was pulled back, immovable. There was a tube in his mouth. Mum kissed him. His first words to her were, 'I'm in trouble'. Then he let out a profound sigh. She can hear it still. I too kissed Robert, the last time I would do so for twenty-four years. His brow was sweaty, feverish, but alive. Stupid or stupefied by now, I asked him how he was, how he was feeling. Then I think I said, 'I love you'. He smiled at us, quite calm. There were no howls, no complaints. When he spoke his voice was brave but unusually high-pitched and uneven. Later, remembering my Conrad, I wrote in my journal, 'There was a storm in it. He was brave, braver than I would be, but there was destruction of terror in his voice.'

Robert was clearly tiring. The nurses had sedated him. Reluctantly, we said goodbye and left. I thought about the terror Robert must have felt as they cut him from the car and drove him to Melbourne in the ambulance. I was unhappy about leaving him there alone, with the doctor's cruel words ringing in his ears, despite the drugs and devices.

We rejoined Uncle Kevin in the waiting room. He had just rung my father in Las Vegas and broken the news to him. Now Dad was hurrying to the airport. We decided that Kevin and I should convey the news to my maternal grandmother while Mum drove home on her own. It was light outside—bright, indifferent day. I didn't trust it any more. Kevin and I set off in one of his business vans. I was keen to speak to Nan as soon as possible. She, like her daughter, was a devotee of the wireless and an early riser. We didn't want her to hear about it on the news.

61

We drove to Prahran in silence. At one point Kevin ran over an unlucky dove. Normally squeamish about such things, I watched it happen without flinching, too numb to react.

When we got to Nan's flat she was sitting on the edge of her bed, as if waiting for someone.

My mother was right, of course. I didn't know it then, but I would learn. Whatever the consolations, and they were profound, she was right. No one deserves to suffer as Robert did.

3

RAMBLING ROSE

Mum had been waiting for that St Valentine's Day call for years. Robert, though only twenty-two, was a seasoned habitué of the night. He had been staying out ever since he went to Collingwood as the latest scion of the Roses. Men gravitated to the likeable all-rounder of whom so much was expected. Robert's affability and bone-dry sense of humour made him popular. He started behaving like a libertine before he got his L-plates. As a journalist wrote, he was 'a free spirit if ever there was one'. Robert became an authentically wild boy, the sort of youth who causes fond aunts to chuckle and sigh over their Melting Moments. A mate of Robert's nicknamed him 'Rambles' after the Nat King Cole song.

Along the way there had been countless midnight vigils as Mum wondered where Robert was, if he was safe—

always waiting for a Volkswagen to come spluttering along and stop outside their house. Robert was not responsibility incarnate. Fond of a drink and a party, he subjected Mum and later Terry to countless anxious nights. In my bedroom I used to listen to Mum moving around the house, tired and upset. One night, very late, she became frightened and came into my room and spoke to me. I feigned sleep. Somehow I couldn't bear this anguish. I didn't know what to do. Another time I was more forthright. Incensed by Robert's selfishness, I told Mum to forget about him. I said he wasn't worth it.

Dad too was often absent. After working during the day (all coaches had full-time jobs in those days) he spent several nights each week at the club, supervising training, selecting sides, attending board meetings, often fractious affairs at Victoria Park, as David Williamson astutely depicts in his play *The Club*, and drinking afterwards. God knows he must have needed a beer after those marathons. League coaches did everything in those days: there were no assistant coaches, no minders, no psychologists, no dietitians, no fitness experts, no skills coaches, no recruiting officers. Thursdays, when the team was selected, were epic affairs. One year we celebrated a birthday a day early, on the Wednesday, for, as I noted in my journal, 'Thursdays are non-events in the family'. Whole weeks went by with only brief glimpses of Dad. Football followed on Saturday—*all* Saturday—then *World of Sport* on Sunday.

For my mother it had been a twofold vigil.

But if she was dreading a telephone call, a car ride into uncertainty, no one could have predicted such an outcome.

Not even Elsie, innately fatalistic, suspected that it would end like this. Paralysis—especially quadriplegia—was foreign, inhuman, the last thing you expected. Death, yes—quick, unqualified—but not this. Everyone knew how unsafe the roads were in those days. People drove too fast, when they were drunk, and without seat belts. We had survived dozens of trips up the Hume Highway, a treacherous, two-lane war zone. But no one knew about quadriplegia.

Robert was an erratic driver. No sooner had he obtained his licence than he was involved in a crash and cut his head. My journal tells me he was lairising with six other chaps and waxes Presbyterian about his 'irresponsibility'. How did seven bucks cram into a Volkswagen? Two months later Robert was involved in a second accident. This time my journal is succinct, as if inured to risk. 'Robert had another crash. Everybody is worried about him.'

There had been other mishaps. As a boy, in Wangaratta, Robert was hit by a car and thrown from his borrowed bike. Pam Jakel, inspecting the mangled metal and ignoring her spread-eagled friend, wailed, 'My bike. My bike!'

In 1971 Robert almost missed the football finals after being badly scalded during a Collingwood visit to HMAS *Cerberus*. In the clippings, a smiling Robert is photographed resting his heavily bandaged kicking foot on our old green pouffe: 'Rose was walking past a gully trap when boiling water gushed out and sprayed his leg. He received immediate treatment from a navy officer…The accident could not have come at a worse time for Collingwood.'

Robert liked to carouse, and he very much liked women. Above all, he relished the company of men, their humour, their camaraderie, their hunger for excess. Women were attracted to him, not just because of his blond good looks and inherited fame, but I don't think he was fully content away from his mates: Steve Bernard and Trevor Laughlin among the cricketers, Peter McKenna and Ronnie Wearmouth at Collingwood, and Barry Round and Bernie Quinlan at Footscray.

In this regard I was doubtless a source of frustration or incomprehension. Three years younger than Robert, I obviously wasn't going to become a professional sportsman or to play for the club that had captivated nearly all my male relations since the war. ('I am not Bjorn Borg / nor alas was meant to be,' I later wrote in a poem called 'True Confessions'.) Fortunately I had highly civilised parents, and this was never an issue.

What decided me? Not just indifferent form. Boys will dream. Perhaps I had overheard my father talking about too many sacked or injured players whose lives had gone off the rails after their football careers were over. I sensed failure in the eyes of the has-beens, the wiry veterans of thirty games, many in the reserves, the brilliant recruits who 'did a cartilage' soon after their first headline. I had seen too many erstwhile idols with their ample girths and lopsided walks. I didn't want to end up at forty with arthritic knees and a future trophied with memories. There had to be more to life than that. Not for me the finite thrills of the afternoon hero, to borrow Alistair Cooke's phrase. In my more priggish moments I reminded myself that it was just a game with thirty-six grown men kicking a ball around a paddock.

Outsiders took more convincing. When I was young the first question strangers asked me was, 'And are *you* going to play for Collingwood?' Like all mantras it never changed: the wording, the intonation, the expectancy, the profoundly innocent goodwill. They cocked their heads and waited for an answer. How could I disabuse them?

While Dad was coaching Collingwood I went to each game. In those days they were all played in Melbourne, except for the annual pilgrimage to Geelong on a special train, with card games and drumsticks on the way down and, if we won, frequent songs from Des Tuddenham on the way back, including 'Click Go the Shears'. At first, I'm told, I was bored by those marathon Saturdays. Mum remembers my turning to her one day when the siren sounded at quarter-time in the reserves match and asking if we could go home yet. She pointed out that there were six more hours of football to go.

Even then it wasn't over. After the game the wives and children waited in the grandstand while the players and officials mingled in the rooms, drinking and smoking and eating excellent party pies—and doubtless singing 'Click Go the Shears'. This took a couple of hours. Families were never included. (Nowadays it's different, I'm pleased to say. The ladies sweep into 'Presidents' Luncheons' and 'Limelight Rooms' like nominees at the Academy Awards.) Often it grew dark before 'the men' emerged from the rooms. This vigil wasn't always pleasant. More than once we were targeted by rival supporters, incensed by some free kick or shirtfront. I never knew women could swear like that until I went to the Western Oval. Mum never swore.

Soon, though, I became a profane convert to the Collingwood cause. I began to love watching football. I enjoyed playing it too, however ineptly. I enjoyed the flux, the exuberance, the clumsy physicality of the game. One day at Trinity College I broke a boy's nose, quite by accident, and was audibly proud of myself.

As the coach's son, I was held in teasingly affectionate regard by the Collingwood players. Big men with huge hands, they ruffled my hair and called me 'Rosey', a variant on names I was getting at school. In a sense I was everyone's younger brother. Loyally, admiringly, I grew up amid this family of personable giants. They were like gods to me. When I grew tall myself they too were impressed and joked that they would have to start worrying about their place in the side.

Nearly all my memories of those days are footballing ones: our house full of players and their bouffant partners after spectacular victories or defeats; Nan's boarding house with its succession of shy recruits down from the bush; the Roman scene under the Ryder Stand after the inevitable win at Victoria Park; the reek of those crowded rooms; glimpses of naked players sharing jokes and tactics in murky baths; that week's bashful best-on-ground achingly hauling himself onto a bench, towel around his waist or vauntingly thrown over a grazed shoulder, to acknowledge the cheers of the open-mouthed supporters; aromatic heroes winking at me and wanting to talk while Alf King, older than LBJ, sterner than Arthur Calwell, massaged their shapely thighs and calves to bronze perfection.

They had their quirks, like characters in literature. One of Dad's captains psyched himself up by reading *Clockwork Orange* before a game. Des Tuddenham always entered the rooms at the last possible moment. Footballers are incorrigibly superstitious. Len Thompson, the ruckman who would overhaul my father's record number of Copeland Trophies, insisted on running onto the ground after all his team-mates. One day at Victoria Park a team-mate, determined to stymie 'Thommo', hid in the toilets while the others headed down the race. Nor was my father unsusceptible. He always put on his left sock and boot first, then his right.

Although Dad was absent much of the time, I was close to him. I liked having a father who gave interviews and coached sides into grand finals attended by more than 120,000 people. I liked the fact that he could take people off the field just like that, and that he was stopped by every second person on the street ('Bobby, Bobby, remember me...?' another longing mantra). When Dad moved to Footscray I cheerfully followed him—heresy, in football terms. After one stirring performance by his new team I went into the rooms and congratulated him and some of his young charges: a new breed of handsome warriors— Bernie Quinlan, Peter Welsh, Les Bartlett. The next day, in a Sinatra vein, Dad wrote me a note saying, 'I got a big kick out of your thoughts'.

Robert's allegiance was similarly shaken when Dad left Collingwood. This followed one last finals defeat, in 1971, further proof of the Rose jinx. Robert, recovered from his scalding, had played in that final. Before the game Dad sensed that Robert was nervous and told him not to worry about letting him down but just to go out there and play football. Dad paired Robert with Rex Hunt, the slowest Tiger, and told him to run Hunt all over the MCG. Unfortunately, Tom Hafey, Richmond's coach, switched Hunt and Francis Bourke, one of Richmond's greatest players. We still have a photograph of Robert soaring above Bourke and trying to punch the ball away. Kevin Sheedy, wearing white anklets and a Puckapunyal haircut, looks on bemusedly, as does a gentleman in Bay 12, who stands up, as if wondering, as indeed do I, why Robert didn't try to mark the bloody ball. Robert played a few more games for Collingwood under Neil Mann, Dad's successor, but he rarely left the bench. Robert was occupying it one day in 1972 when Dad led Footscray to its first victory at Victoria Park since the Holden was invented. Robert admitted later that he had quietly celebrated each Footscray goal and willed them to win. That, for all of us, was the most delicious day.

To encourage me, but also because he was genuinely interested, Dad always followed my sporting career, such as it was. He was there the day I elected to kick into a fifteen-goal gale and was relieved of the captaincy at quarter-time, and one summer's day when, fielding at third man (the only place they could hide me), I failed to stop a boundary because I happened to be executing a balletic handstand at the time. Gymnastics, I decided, were much more fun than fielding at third man. Both mishaps passed embarrassingly into family lore. Even when I was relegated to Haileybury's remedial Ds, Dad often watched me. The weakest side always played first thing in the morning, on the most distant oval. This was in the middle of winter. The standard of football was, shall we say, variable. The spirit may have been willing but the instep was weak. I put it succinctly in my journal: 'I can ruck and rove all right. I just can't mark over my head.' Our vice-principal, supervising one Saturday morning, spotted my father on the boundary of the oval known as Siberia, the walk to which took longer than the first quarter. The vice-principal, a bluff man known as Colonel Northcott (I was a cadet too), asked Dad what on earth he was doing there at eight-thirty in the morning. Dad was coaching Collingwood in a final that afternoon.

Maybe it was the 1970 grand final.

My status was different from Robert's, even before he was old enough to play football. Robert was the mascot. Robert knew what he was talking about. Robert actually watched and assessed the opposing players, who were quite invisible to me. Robert sat in the front row of the chook pen and helped a family friend, a corpulent detective with a trotter that always finished third, with the statistics. Robert knew the number, the nickname and the preferred kicking foot of every League player. Robert could mark over his head.

I, conversely, gravitated to the ladies because all lovers of conversation do. I sat with Mum, Barbara and Marie and knew all the other wives. I wondered how they felt going to the football year after year. I quietly followed the course of the players' romances. I peered into the pigeoned roofs of those old wooden grandstands and was reminded of galleons. I loved the fervour of the crowd, the way it could blossom into something tribal, invincible. I admired the outrage of the old-timers standing in front of the chook pen, incensed by some free kick or shirtfront, fists punching the air like a corps of angry emus. Once, when I was a boy, Graham Kennedy was ushered into the chook pen to watch St Kilda play and I was led up to him to shake his hand. I noted his stylish suit, of a kind rarely seen at Victoria Park, but thought him rather uncomfortable and strangely sad for a star. I looked beyond the facing R.T. Rush Stand and fantasised about people leading other lives, away from football, and television. Perhaps Kennedy did too. He was a reader, after all. I often took a book, just in case. Once I was accused of reading a history book during a boring match. This lapse, too, was often cited. I didn't tell them it was an historical novel, one of my romances about the Tudors or the Stuarts.

Apart from the bonhomie at Victoria Park and my Friday-night rendezvous with Marie and Barbara, I was a thoroughly insular teenager. I tended to exhaust my friends at Haileybury and to alienate others. I thought it was the responsibility of a Conradian youth to 'crash through', like Gough Whitlam. Boots and all, as it were. Crucial rebuffs at school cast me down for years. I hardly appealed to the jocks, and I was too weird and unworldly for the 'pseuds', who rolled joints during recess, pinned up their hair to escape detection and were rumoured to get sand in their genitals at the weekend. My relationship with A., still platonic, was a strange constant, but even this intimacy was tempestuous and ambivalent. 'A. is fighting something—it's not going to be me,' I wrote in my journal. Away from school and sporting venues, I was notably withdrawn. This produced a profound sense of abnormality or 'unsuitability', as I would put it in one of the many ghastly poems I was beginning to write. Rereading my journals, balder documents, I am struck by my agitation, my self-loathing, my sense of futility, my expectation of perpetual lovelessness and friendlessness— 'a sense of annihilation', to borrow a phrase.

> *What I am disgusts me but I can't stop it. If I could only help myself—if I wanted to live this life. Friends gone—a passage closed—my life disappearing. Help myself!*
>
> *Mixing with people, becoming more estranged from those I once sought—and yet there is an hysteria below the surface, like the tremulous fear of one close to death.*
>
> *I realise my voice is too high and suspicious, hence I intend to:*
> 1. *go deeper.*
> 2. *enunciate less clearly.*
> 3. *speak less.*
> 4. *speak softer.*
> *The noose can tighten. All the better.*

All journals, especially juvenile ones, exaggerate personal misery. Cynthia Ozick has described journals as 'vessels of discontent'. My diaristic staples were football, intimate dialogues with Barbara, and immitigable gloom. At fourteen I decided I would always be alone, a sort of outcast.

Eventually my parents must have acknowledged that something was wrong and that I was fast becoming an

73

oddity. Years later I recorded one grotesque experiment in fraternisation:

My parents, desperate to socialise their weird, unadventurous, isolated boy-child, sent me off to some youth club in Mount Waverley. What year was this? Perhaps 1969 or 1970. I recall my fierce embarrassment and resentment, my impatience with those ordeals of exposure, the dismal, paralysing games of basketball, by the end of which I was reduced to standing in a corner, incapable of conversation, or touch, or fluency, or dexterity, or speech, or gregariousness—all the things that came so automatically and charmingly to the fifteen and sixteen year olds who frequented the club and who, though tactful, surely regarded me as a freak. I remember my father's frustration and helplessness—did he stay one night to observe?—as he watched me avoiding the others in my nervousness and shyness. I remember his hopeless and unavailing pep talks, of a kind with which he was doubtless in the habit of inspiring gauche, recalcitrant football recruits. After a while those visits were suspended, but not before some warnings about the consequences of my wilful, abysmal solitude and friendlessness.

By the time I went to university—absurdly unready, at seventeen, for that adventure—I was killingly shy. During my first year at Monash, the year before Robert's accident,

I spoke to no one and eschewed clubs and activities. I seem to have been chronically and often suicidally depressed.

What had happened to the chirpy, outgoing child I was said to have been in Wangaratta, the boy who knocked on strangers' doors and spoke to anyone, the show-off who took over Nancy Cato's children's television programme and wouldn't shut up? What happened to the funny, stubborn little bugger, to borrow an old friend's colourful phrase?

Did I leave him in Wang?

Robert may have been repelled by my outcast state. I wasn't turning out to be the sort of younger brother he had anticipated. Rose boys weren't meant to be like that. Blessed with innumerable mates, Robert couldn't understand my signal lack of friends, my tastes, my inclinations. Did he too perhaps regard me as a freak?

Perhaps he remembered a bizarre phase I went through soon after our return to Melbourne, when I was about eight or nine. Somehow I got it into my head that my parents were going to be killed in a car accident. I could even picture it happening, though I told no one. I don't know what caused this phobia. I must have read something or had one of my dreams. Whenever my parents went out at night, which was often, I became distraught. I felt sure I would never see them again and that Robert and I would be orphaned. Sometimes my paranoia was so intense that Mum stayed at home, but other nights she had to accompany Dad. For Robert, those vigils must have been disturbing. I remember one night when I became almost deranged with fear. Sleepless and terrified, I stalked through the house. In hindsight, it was like a mini-breakdown. In the end Robert hugged me and told me to shut up because he too was becoming frightened.

My bookishness also mystified Robert. He mocked—and greatly exaggerated—my conscientiousness at school. He seemed surprised by the fact that when I wasn't seeing Marie and Barbara, I preferred to stay at home. The Rolling Stones' song 'Mother's Little Helper' gave him a new term of abuse.

Solitude, for Robert, was not an end in itself but a necessary interim. Like me, he spent hours in his bedroom, on the rare occasions when he was home, but those retreats were merely preparatory. With his transistor playing the latest hits, Robert tended his inchoate scrapbook or conjured up deeper statistical wizardry: those averages upon averages. Night after night, as summer approached, we heard that irritating little cluck in his throat as he practised cricket shots in the mirror, dispatching imaginary balls to boundaries of the future. This went on for hours and hours. Robert became a technically sound batsman by practising each shot thousands of times: the inviolate straight bat, the mellifluous cover drive, the ironic deflection off his legs. This glottal sound effect maddened me as I sat in the next room reading a history book—or historical novel. Why, I wondered, couldn't he just hit the bloody ball without pretending he had a constriction in his throat. But even I knew it wouldn't have been the same. The companionable cluck was an indispensable part of his apprenticeship in front of the mirror.

What Robert and I did have in common was sport and the competitive gene. My journal for the summer of

1971/72, when I was sixteen, records each score he made and charts his early progress as a State cricketer. Whenever he was free we played cricket in the backyard, just as we played football during winter. I recorded these contests in my journal. Apart from the novel I was ludicrously attempting to write, nothing else seems to have been happening in my life. The reliance on Robert to fill my cloistered days is striking:

Jan 21

A bitter-sweet day. Robert came home, but didn't want to play cricket. In the end I asked him—he laughed. What a moody bastard...The only thing worth the 24 bloody hours of life was a radio programme with Germaine Greer. I did 4 pages of the book.

Jan 22

I went to see Robert play cricket. Against the world's best bowler, John Snow, he hit 63—hooking him for four—and had two pictures in the paper. I am proud, loyal and nervous for my poor, sick brother. They were all out, so I watched All About Eve *with Bette Davis.*

Jan 23

I went with M & D to watch Robert play in a one-day match. He made 3, Collingwood won. Much good print for his 63...I stayed up late and wrote 8 pages of the book.

Jan 31
Monday, and little doing. Robert made 50, and I read.

Our cribbed Test matches on the L-shaped pitch were stirring affairs. Rumoured to chuck (I had been infuriatingly 'called' on my first day at Haileybury), I tore in like D.K. Lillee, straightened up on reaching the elbow in the pitch, purportedly bent my own, and hurled the ball at my first-class brother. A protruding root near the batsman's end offered accurate bowlers greater spin or decapitating bounce. I aimed at it as assiduously as an archer. When it was my turn to bat Robert gallantly gave me two innings to his one, thus ensuring a close result. We kept elaborate records (no Rose forgets a win) and Robert calculated the averages. Even after his elevation to the Victorian team we often played. Much later, when it was no longer possible, we reminisced about those panting, sterling days. After the accident I knew I was going to miss those contests most of all.

When it was too late or too wet for cricket we played cards or a complicated soccer-like game in Robert's bedroom, which involved adroit manoeuvres around the furniture. We Roses can play lawn bowls in a paddock. Wrestling I much preferred. This was serious sport: lawless, primitive, vigorous, a crude battle of wills, always thrilling, until one got pinned down, which was aggravating. We both flew at each other like cunning animals. Because I was suddenly sinewy and taller than Robert, I had my own raw advantage.

Then my parents built the new house in Crosby Drive

and Robert and I had a table-tennis table in the basement. The walls were hung with some of Dad's memorabilia: premiership souvenirs, thrilling marks by John Coleman, Dad's favourite player, and the inevitable photograph of the five Rose brothers in their guernseys, cross-armed to accentuate their biceps. Robert and I played table tennis at every opportunity. Matrimony and fatherhood didn't stop us. The minute Robert arrived with Terry and Salli he would say, 'Come on, thicko', as he motivatingly called me, and lead me downstairs. Whole evenings were devoted to ferocious series, which I usually won. Sometimes we were joined by Robert's new mates at Footscray, bulky men who seemed intimidated by the small wooden field. I was pleased to discover that footballers lack finesse at table tennis.

Invariably my contests with Robert ended badly. Whatever the sport, we pushed ourselves until one of us snapped. The ensuing rows were epic and vociferous. Sometimes we came to blows. Those backyard Test matches may have been viscerally satisfying—in a weird way, the best times we ever spent together—but they never ended happily or sportingly. Quarrelling seemed to be part of it: the real inexorable result. We trudged off into the house, spitting calumnies and complaining to our parents about some affront or illegality. Sometimes we didn't speak to each other until the battle was rejoined. Rejoined, though, it always was.

Mum once calmly observed that Robert and I had fought every day as children. I felt a kind of smug contrition at this—grateful for this spark of fraternal rivalry, sorry for Mum.

I remember one evening in particular. One of Dad's acquaintances had asked him if he would speak to his mildly delinquent son. The boy had been causing his parents grief and Dad, as Collingwood coach, was obviously well placed to counsel him. Dad led them to the other end of the living room and did his weary best. Robert and I were being uncommonly fractious. We went on squabbling over custody of the television. This led, with the animal implacability of youth, to taunts and insults and eventually blows. Finally, Dad, the model father, couldn't bear it any more. Apologising to his guests, he jumped out of his chair and loudly abused us. It was the only time we ever saw him really do his block. The surprised and ashen-faced acquaintance led his son from the house, saying that he would come back another time.

In retrospect, Robert seemed to welcome our contests, however bitterly they ended and despite his success in more public arenas. Perhaps those inconsequential marathons were a kind of respite from responsibility. As long as we were pummelling or hurling bumpers at each other, nothing else mattered.

By February 1974 Robert could no longer escape certain realities. He had his worries. Naturally cavalier about money, he was often short of cash. Upon signing with Footscray in the middle of 1973, he had received a lump sum $1000, plus $100 per game, but that didn't go far. Cricket paid much less. Shield cricketers earned $10 per day, a total of $40 for a match. This was three years before the players' rebellion and the lure of Packer money. After holding down various clerical positions in his teens, Robert was no longer guaranteed work. Not everyone welcomed an employee who needed so much time off for training. The Smorgon family, wealthy backers of Footscray, gave Robert a job in one of their abattoirs, but he was nauseated by the butchery and only lasted one day.

The cricket season of 1973/74, Robert's third with Victoria, had begun promisingly. In the first match, at the Gabba, Robert and Alan Sieler twice rescued the side with long fifth-wicket partnerships, the first of which held the State record until recently. Between them they compiled 468 of Victoria's 607 runs. Partisan scribes began pressing Robert's claim for Test selection. Never confident, even Mum thought his luck might be changing. When Victoria made 265 in three hours to defeat Ian Chappell's South Australia at the MCG, 'the crisis-proof Rose' remained not out.

But then Robert started going out too early and too easily. Like Chappell and his great mentor at Collingwood, Keith Stackpole, Robert loved to hook, but he executed it less competently and was often found out, dolloping the ball to some non-handstander on the boundary with a kind of sand-shovelling action, as one commentator put it, or snicking the ball to the wicketkeeper, as he had done to Rodney Marsh at the end of that exhilarating contest with Lillee the previous summer. Frank Tyson, the great English bowler, dubbed Robert one of the 'hapless hookers'. The nadir came at the MCG when Robert was twice given out first ball attempting to flick the ball off his pads. On neither occasion did he hit the ball, he told us. I believed him too: Robert was scrupulously fair as a sportsman. He never argued with an umpire. Robert became the first batsman to have a symbolic duck placed beside his name on the grand old manual scoreboard at the MCG.

There was something hubristic about these casual, if erroneous, dismissals. Robert's prospects were unravelling. He wasn't included in the Australian squad for the coming tour of New Zealand. As Peter McFarline, one of his backers, wrote, 'A mid-season slump did not help his cause'. Had Robert's form been more consistent, he may not have been in Ballarat on St Valentine's Day.

Robert's personal status had also changed. He was now a husband and a father. Robert had married Terry at the start of 1973. She was nineteen at the time. They had been together for a couple of years. It was a turbulent relationship, as I knew from my frequent chats with Terry, who confided in me. Ours was a close friendship, much more intimate than the one I enjoyed with Robert. Whenever he was absent, which was often, Terry and I went to the park and she let me smoke her Marlboros while she told me about the state of their relationship. I thought of her as my sister.

I had been performing this role—listening to women, that is—for years. I was quite accomplished at it. When I was about nine or ten, a family friend in her late twenties took me on similar walks and told me about her romantic adventures. I loved hearing about affairs. Intuitively, I knew I could trust women to divulge the heavy secrets of their hearts. Women needed to talk, and I was ready to serve. My youth and innocence made me an acceptable companion. Our peripatetic family friend even allowed me to participate in her toilette while she told me about her current and penultimate affairs. (One needed detailed accounts of the latter for a clearer sense of the former's durability.) Combing her long black lustrous hair, I discerned a pattern of *adultery* in her private life. I loved that word, so familiar from my reading about Tudor escapades. (The other word that fascinated me was *decapitation*, 'the long divorce of steel', as Buckingham calls it in Shakespeare's *Henry VIII*.) I was thrilled that this sexual malady was still rife. I may not have fully understood the meaning of the word adultery (was it hereditary? was it always punished by decapitation? was it only open to the young?), but I wanted to commit it as soon as I grew up. Emboldened, I broke off one night and proposed to my glamorous intimate. I remembered that Anne Boleyn, too, had raven hair. Accepting, she suggested a long betrothal. Years later we still joked about it, but even as I proposed to her I knew deep down that this wasn't my role. I was a confessor, even a go-between, but hardly Romeo and certainly not Lothario.

A few years ago I spent an evening in London with some friends, including Christine Porter, a Kleinian psychoanalyst. Listening to my maudlin panegyric about Maria Callas, Christine remarked: 'You're really a courtier'.

Even before their marriage, Robert and Terry's relationship was volatile. While powerfully attracted to each other, they often fought. Terry came from a large, assertive family in Heidelberg and was uninhibited by the coolness and reticence that were intermittent features of our family life. Terry spent a great deal of time at Lemana Crescent, occupying my bedroom while I moved in with Robert.

83

(This was a source of maternal anxiety and nocturnal migrations which I drowsily observed. I didn't mind being dispossessed, though I was glad when Robert crept off to my room like Paul Morel in *Sons and Lovers*, as this enabled me to duck into his much more comfortable bed.) Though fond of us all, Terry was frustrated by our reserve, our strategic silences. 'I wish you'd all shout a bit more,' she complained to me helplessly one brittle night. I pitied her. I knew it would take years of practice before she could compete with us.

Terry was unprepared for the chauvinistic world to which Robert introduced her. If she wanted to see her boyfriend she had to enter his alien sporting clique. Terry had no idea who Bob Rose was when she met Robert. She thought he must have been a trainer or something. After-match vigils in the Ryder Stand, followed by interminable nights in the Collingwood Social Club, bored Terry. Her Dutch mentor in the gift shop where she worked had introduced her to the notion of travel, fine things, a malleable future. Terry craved new experiences and destinies. Robert did not. Naturally conservative, despite his ebullient social life, he was profoundly indifferent to change. Change was foreign, even dubious, like wine and garlic and fussy greens around the affirming meat. Robert had always known what he wanted, ever since he kicked that shiny football around our backyard: now he was close to attaining his birthright. Part of the reason why I irked him was that he found me so *unplaceable*. I was turning out to be contrary to every expectation he must have had of me. It was as if I had risen without trace.

I understood his unease: I was bewildered myself.

Life near the young couple was always eventful. Sometimes Robert and Terry went to the movies. They invariably disliked my recommendations. Robert forever joked about my enthusiasm for *Death in Venice* and the subversive *Little Murders*. During one of their rows they took me to the drive-in to see *The Wild Bunch*, hardly a pacific choice. My role as intermediary appears to have been short-lived. My journal records one nicotined conversation with Terry, who admitted that Robert 'could be horrid because she and I get on so well'. Was Robert jealous of my friendship with Terry? Did he disapprove of this aspect of my personality—my fascination with women, their fondness for me? Did he fear that I would corrupt Terry with my talk of books and films and politics?

If Robert was perturbed by my cloudy sexual orientation, he never said so to me. Only once did it threaten to become an issue. The three of us were driving to football one Saturday. I told Robert and Terry that I had a surprise for them. 'You're turning gay,' said Robert brightly. It sounded more like an invitation than a threat, but I denied it, and we never mentioned it again.

Despite our differences, I was capable of sentimentality about our communal summers, as I wrote in 1972:

I went with Mum to the Vic–SA match. M & B came along and later we went home. I became reminiscent. What a funny bitter-sweet summer it has been. The cricket matches, and the talks on the 2nd tier of the Members' Stand with Terry, the cricket with Robert,

how I enjoyed it. The happiness in the Members'—
I believe it has gone. At home I was humorous and
not aloof—as I always seem to be now.

I saw Where Love Has Gone. *Is Bette Davis a*
dwarf? Robert–Terry freeze still frozen over. Oh
dear!

Despite this, Robert and Terry were eventually married at the Old Mint. This being the 1970s, no one looked his or her best. Robert wore a pink shirt and psychedelic tie under a new brown pinstriped suit. Very Yves Saint Laurent! With his long fluffy hair and sideburns he looked like a Bee Gee. The father of the bride wore a neck brace and lapels of formidable breadth. Fresh from university, I was in regulation black. My heavy shaded glasses made me look positively spectral. The exchange of vows and rings took about two minutes, of which I heartily approved. Did anyone present really believe that Robert and Terry were ready for this step? His voice was barely audible, soft and shy. It reminded me of his recent appearance on *World of Sport*—the most bashful interviewee in history. Terry, for her part, was so nervous she rocked during the vows. She had done something sophisticated to her hair, but otherwise she reminded me of a schoolgirl caught somewhere she shouldn't have been.

My parents and I were the glummest members of the wedding party. We must have seemed like a trio of lugubrious treasury officials overseeing a dubious lottery. The night before I had felt miserable as Robert prepared to leave home, though I rallied to defeat him at table tennis.

On the day itself I was stoical with Robert and the only person who didn't shake his hand when it was over. I felt incapable of showing emotion.

Robert, unemployed in early 1973, was spending a great deal of time at the club. He applied for one job that involved door-to-door selling on a commission basis, but failed to get it. He and Terry moved into a small flat in East Hawthorn. As I helped shift the furniture, I felt sorry for Robert.

Because we were no longer under each other's feet, relations between us improved. I visited them often. Another guest one night was the cricketer Trevor Laughlin, one of Robert's closest friends, not just because he came from Nyah West. We laughed all night and played charades, at which I was adept. We had to go out for more alcohol. I had rarely felt so happy or so confident with other people. I became seriously drunk for the first time in my life. It was one of our finest nights.

Salli Louise Rose was born in May, 1973. They changed the Y to I because the Carlton champion Alex Jesaulenko had recently named his daughter Sally and there was no way Robert was going to have a bar of that. Terry, too, inexplicably, sometimes preferred 'Terri'. When she and the baby left hospital Robert brought them back to Crosby Drive. Salli was a bright, wilful infant, very pretty, just like Robert as a child. The new father was unsettled. He adored Salli but clearly chafed at his new responsibilities. That weekend he went to the football and forgot to collect Terry and Salli after a function until it was very late. On the way home he drove too fast. When Terry complained, he drove faster. Not long after Salli's birth he took Terry to four football matches in five days. I babysat for them occasionally. When Robert transferred to Footscray I dutifully watched his first few games. After one match I sat in the car for hours waiting for him to drive me home. When I complained to my father he defended Robert, quoting Lou Richards: 'You're dead a long time'.

Every now and then Terry informed me that she hadn't seen Robert for a few days or that she had gone back to her parents in Heidelberg. In December there was talk of divorce, but I thought this unlikely. They were too young and impetuous for permanent solutions. They were also crazy about each other.

One of Robert's newer friends was Robert Bird, a Collingwood footballer. I knew most of my brother's friends, but not Bird. I don't think I'd even heard his name before the accident. Bird was eighteen, like me. At the start of 1973 he had come over from Tasmania with a big reputation. He soon started mixing with Robert and his cronies. Bird was studying metallurgy at university, so his hours were flexible. He would skip lectures and go and watch Robert play cricket. Afterwards they would celebrate in Robert's favourite watering holes.

During that summer the two Roberts became good mates. My brother now had a job. He was working for Boon Spa Cordials. He drove around Melbourne trying to interest hoteliers in sarsaparilla and lemon squash. Whenever Robert knew he was going to be on the road all day he rang up Bird and invited him along. Sometimes

Ron Wearmouth, Collingwood's flamboyant, fuzzy-haired rover, joined them. They went from one pub to another, flogging syrup and accepting free beers along the way. The two Roberts loved to gamble on the horses and often went to the races. Money was scarce, but somehow there was always enough for another beer and bet.

In early February they planned a trip to the Ballarat races. They had never been there before. No one can remember what drew them there, if there was a big race. Wearmouth was unavailable, so they invited Ken Lynch to join them. Lynch was a groundsman at Collingwood. He lived nearby with his mother, not far from Nan's old boarding house. Lynch was in his forties, much older than the two young sportsmen. The three of them often drank together.

It was agreed that Robert should drive. They met at Victoria Park. The two Roberts waited while Lynch finished watering the pitch. Collingwood had played there on Saturday, five days ago, Robert remaining not out at the close of play. His name was probably still up on the scoreboard. They then headed off to Ballarat. They stayed at the races all day. The horses were kind to them, and they weren't out of pocket at the end. After the races they went into Ballarat and had a few beers. At about 9 p.m. they bought some takeaway food, presumably pizza (Salli's first gummy name for me), then set off for Melbourne. The convivial and profitable day had left them in high spirits.

Robert Bird was travelling in the front seat next to Robert. They were near Bacchus Marsh when it happened. The highway was still narrow in those days, just two lanes. A few months later it would be considerably widened.

As they approached a bend in the road, a semitrailer travelling in the opposite direction appeared to drift across the double lines, as if the driver were intent on overtaking the car in front. Robert veered to the left and may have skidded before getting into gravel on the left-hand side. Later, all sorts of theories were advanced as to what happened. Certainly, the road itself was not in good condition. When Dad visited the site a few days later he found a drop of several inches between the edge of the bitumen and the gravel. It would be quietly repaired within a few days of the accident.

Robert seems to have reacted quickly. He had been drinking throughout the afternoon, but evidently not enough to impair his judgment. (When Dad investigated, a policeman told him that Robert was not drunk at the time.) After getting into the gravel, Robert promptly swung the Volkswagen back onto the road. He might have been all right but for a blow-out in his front left tyre. The car went into a spin and clipped the semitrailer. It rolled several times before coming to rest on the side of the road. The semitrailer continued on its way. Suddenly silence, followed by the faintest of night noises, and crickets. It was all over in a few seconds.

Robert Bird, who never wore seatbelts in those days, was thrown through the windscreen and onto the road. Somehow, miraculously, Ken Lynch, though squashed in the back, was flung out after him, uninjured apart from a cut leg which required stitches. Robert, who was wearing his seatbelt, was trapped in the car.

Fire brigades came from Bacchus Marsh and Myrniong, wherever that is. Using a portable saw, they cut Robert from the car. Ambulance officers stood by waiting to attend him. Robert lost consciousness briefly but otherwise remained alert during the long struggle. A passing motorist squeezed into the car and stayed with Robert for the ninety minutes it took them to free him. She had been travelling in the opposite direction and stopped, unlike the semitrailer. Subsequently, we heard from this woman—Mrs Scott was her name. She remarked on Robert's composure. He talked about his family and his eight-month-old daughter. He asked her why he couldn't move his feet. But even then he stayed calm. She said he was exceptionally brave.

The *Herald*'s egregious front-page story quotes a police officer as saying that Robert appeared to be in severe pain. This seems unlikely, given what had happened. Later the policeman amends his statement: 'I think it was more shock than anything'. That seems more probable. A tow-truck driver from Ballan describes the scene. Was this the man photographed the next morning beside the decapitated Volkswagen, gazing blankly into the wrecked cabin, with its detritus of a day at the Ballarat races?

The press found out quickly. They were probably tuned in to the police or ambulance radar. They reached the Bacchus Marsh and District War Hospital before Robert was admitted. The press knew about the accident long before anyone did at the Austin Hospital. Dr David Burke told me that it was the only time during his long directorship that journalists alerted him to an imminent admission rather than doctors or the police. The press were waiting for Robert when he reached the Austin four hours after the accident.

The records show that Robert was admitted at 0100 hours. Sammy hadn't yet woken me up in Wangaratta. It was the middle of the night in Las Vegas, where Dad was sleeping in his hotel room. Dr Burke read the letter from the doctor at the Bacchus Marsh Hospital, who had officially reported complete paralysis and decided that Robert should be moved to the Austin immediately. Dr Burke interviewed Robert and ascertained a few facts. Robert couldn't remember the accident itself—one mercy. Nor could he remember the lead-up to it. An examination revealed severe quadriplegia. He had flickers of movement only in the shoulder and elbow flexor muscles but no other movement in his upper limbs, trunk or lower limbs. His sensation was normal over his head and neck as far as the tip of his shoulder. He was areflexic in the muscles of his arms and legs. Areflexia is typical of spinal shock.

X-rays revealed a bilateral dislocation of the fourth and fifth cervical vertebrae. Dr Burke inferred that a major forward flexion force on his head had caused the neck to dislocate. This bony injury was entirely consistent with severe quadriplegia. It was a very high fracture, dangerously so. Robert couldn't have survived it a few years earlier, before certain medical advances. Now they knew how to keep such people alive.

Dr Burke treated Robert in consultation with Mr Bromberger, an orthopaedic surgeon. (I met or rather served Mr Bromberger ten years later when I was managing a medical bookshop at another major public hospital, one of the weirder chapters in my life.) Calipers were inserted in Robert's skull and attempts were made to reduce the dislocation by traction on the neck. When this failed they decided to anaesthetise him the following day and to manipulate his neck back into place. Traction, no longer practised in this manner nowadays, would be maintained for eight weeks. Robert also required intravenous fluids, nasogastric aspiration and a catheter for his paralysed bladder.

Dr Burke had no illusions about Robert's outlook. The prognosis for any chance of neurological recovery was deemed to be very poor.

There wasn't a mark on his body.

Robert Bird, meanwhile, was taken to a local hospital, probably the one in Bacchus Marsh. Like Robert, he is hazy about that night. We talked about the accident during a recent conversation. It was the first time we had spoken. Somehow our paths had never crossed. My only recollection was a newspaper item showing Bird in hospital a few days after the accident. 'I was thrown from the car,' he is quoted as saying. Powerfully built, with long dark hair, he is strikingly good-looking, like a young Alain Delon. His right eye is bruised. He looks absolutely desolate.

Robert Bird was amazed when I told him about this article. He had no recollection of being interviewed and no idea which hospital he was moved to in Melbourne. He had forgotten where the accident happened. Like an historian, I told him what had transpired.

Bird now lives in Townsville where he manages a big transport company with a fleet of trucks around the country. Their contract with the military requires them to move personnel to East Timor, so they are busy. We spoke for an hour one morning after he got his trucks on the road. Bird moved to Queensland in 1977, soon after leaving Collingwood. In his own words, he didn't really crack it, despite all the expectations he brought with him from Tasmania.

I was very keen to speak to someone who was involved in the accident. For some reason I wanted to know who was sitting where in the car, how they had spent the day. Ken Lynch, the former groundsman, chose not to be interviewed. Now seventy and living in a hotel in Collingwood, he told my father that he just wanted to forget about it. Bird, fortunately, agreed to speak to me, but during our conversation I became surprised that he had, for it emerged that he had never discussed the accident with another soul. 'I've kept it to myself,' he volunteered. 'I'm a fairly private sort of person.'

Bird doesn't blame the driver of the semitrailer. He thinks it likely that the Volkswagen hit the middle or rear of the trailer, not the prime mover. 'I don't believe that truckie knew that we hit him. It's conceivable that the driver didn't feel the impact. We may have just hit a tyre.'

Bird's surmise is vindicated by the newspapers. Although the article on Bird refers to 'a hit-and-run driver', there is no evidence of any vicious intent or negligence. The truck was flagged down in Ballarat and the driver interviewed, but no charges were ever laid.

After being thrown from the car, Bird woke up on the gravel, obviously concussed. He had double vision and couldn't focus on anything. He remembers Robert crying out for help. 'Oh Birdy, Birdy,' he kept saying. Then Ken Lynch asked Bird if he was all right. 'Ken never even mentioned how he got out. All I know is that I was on the gravel and Ken was standing next to me. How on earth it happened is a mystery. I've never thought about it before. Unless he got thrown out behind me. He wasn't hurt. He was okay.'

The next thing Bird recalls is being placed in an ambulance. Eventually he was transferred to another hospital in Melbourne. His right eye had been damaged internally. 'They stuck it back in,' he told me nonchalantly. He had double vision for a couple of months but no long-term damage. He passed over his own medical condition as quickly as possible.

Bird remained in hospital 'for about ten days'. He became very anxious about Robert. The doctors asked his visitors not to tell him how bad his friend was. He quizzed Ron Wearmouth, who admitted that there was something wrong with Robert's back. Bird realised that it was 'deadly serious'. Then my father, whom Bird hardly knew, visited him and he got it out of him.

'Your father was fantastic,' Bird remembered. 'The impression I got was that he was concerned about my welfare and my health, and that's the only reason he came to see me. It made me emotional. That really got me in a bad way.'

Indeed, how characteristic of Dad to think about the eighteen-year-old boy from Tasmania who was on his own. It meant another hospital visit. Another long drive. Another pep talk.

As soon as Bird left hospital he visited Robert in the Austin. Bill Lawry, Robert's first captain when he played for Victoria, was there. I may have been present that day, for I clearly remember one visit from Lawry. A Test match was being played; naturally, Robert was listening. When Doug Walters went out Lawry became animated and gesticulated excitedly, repeating the news several times. It was all, apparently, happening. I remember being quite amused by his performance. I wondered what the other patients thought.

Robert Bird behaved differently. He vividly recalls the traction, as we all do. 'It was just terrible. He took it so well. Naturally I broke down. I think I held myself together while I was looking at him eye to eye, but I didn't handle it at all well. Because I loved Rob. Unbeknownst to a lot of people we were really, really good mates. It shattered... I mean, my life was in tatters. I just couldn't come to grips with it. You've got all these feelings of guilt, all that comes through. People would say to me you've got nothing to feel guilty about. Probably I didn't—I don't know—but I did.'

Scuttlebutt didn't help. Collingwood is rife with intrigue at the best of times. After Robert's accident the gossips went to town.

'And then you had innuendo,' Bird told me. 'It was a football club, with a high-profile sportsman like Rob. The innuendo was very strong about what may have happened—

who was driving even—all that sort of thing. Lots of people…' He hesitated. 'Somehow a rumour got out that I was driving. All that sort of stuff was happening.'

There was no respite, no social escape.

'Another thing that used to irk me was that twelve months, two years, three years after the event, you'd go to a barbecue somewhere and you'd get introduced to somebody as the person who was in the car with Robert Rose. All that sort of crap.' He was silent for a moment. 'I've never ever…I've kept a relationship with Robert and myself in my own mind, in my own life.'

Listening to Bird, feeling guilty about putting him through this, moved by his tribute and by his personal ordeal, I wasn't at all surprised that his football had suffered, that he had 'never really cracked it', or that he had gone to Far North Queensland as soon as it was over. He too had been marked by that day.

I asked him about Robert's mood before the accident. He didn't think that Robert was under pressure because of his mid-season slump. 'He wasn't concerned about his form. He wasn't hitting the panic button or anything like that. He knew he was having a bad trot, but it wasn't really affecting him. It didn't send him off. He took it on the chin.'

Bird mentioned Robert's domestic problems. 'He was troubled about his home life. Things weren't good at home. He loved Salli, but he was living a single man's life. Terry was young too.' He paused before going on. 'I don't think he wanted out. I knew he was having troubles, but he thought it would just go on the way it was.'

Robert obviously confided in his young friend. Bird knew, for instance, that Terry had gone back to her parents just before the accident. 'Robert thought they'd be all right. She'd be back. It was a volatile relationship. He never indicated to me that he thought he'd be better off out of there.'

In later years Robert Bird saw my brother whenever he came to Melbourne. They never discussed the accident. We agreed that Robert had managed to have a rich life, with his sport, his family and his friendships.

'I'm fortunate that I've been part of it,' Bird declared. 'We were best mates, although we didn't grow up together or knock about together during our adult lives. What we had was very special. I'm sure Rob would say the same.'

He last saw Robert in 1992, after a football game. 'He was in good nick. He could still smoke. I didn't see him at his worst, that's for sure.' Robert left his other companions to speak to Bird. 'He made a point of having a good yarn with me.' At one point Robert asked him to take him to the toilet and empty his catheter. It was as if they had never been separated by gravel or a major forward flexion force. 'He was quite forthright about this. I took it as being a strong friendship.'

I thanked Bird for speaking to me so openly. He said it had been good for him—'therapeutic'.

'It's happened,' he concluded. 'It's a part of my life. It's always been there. Despite the fact that Robert has passed away nothing has really changed in my relationship with him. Our mateship never changed. I just remember the good times and I remember how lucky I was and how unlucky he was. That's the bane of it. It could have been either of us, it could have been both of us, it could have been all of us. I didn't turn to God or anything like that, but I've got my own things to live with about it.' He hesitated. 'It's the most terrible thing. It's been with me all the time. And so has Rob. And I know how strong he is, how strong he was. He's a bloody marvel. The way he handled it is just extraordinary.'

As we would all, each in his or her own time and way, discover.

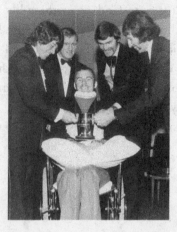

Mum and I returned to the hospital later in the morning. Robert was conscious, his manner unchanged. Everyone was waiting for Dad to get home. How Robert must have longed to see the old chap, as he called him. At midday he was anaesthetised and his neck gently manipulated back into place. The dislocation was greatly reduced. Nevertheless, Robert was still in danger. The risk of respiratory failure was heightened because he was a smoker.

We spent the rest of the day at Crosby Drive. Family friends and neighbours kept dropping in. The telephone rang constantly. No one expected good news. I took most of the calls so that Mum wouldn't have to talk to people. Our Mallee relations rang, disbelieving. When Marie and Barbara arrived, the three of us talked quietly in the kitchen while making endless pots of tea for the visitors. Norelle's mother slumped on to a sofa with mine, both crying. She told us that Norelle had just rung from the country where she was honeymooning. The newlyweds had panicked after spotting a newspaper banner that read 'ROSE TRAGEDY'. Throughout the day journalists kept ringing up to find out how Robert was and when Dad was due back. We heard from an unidentified journalist at Maxwell Newton's dubious *Sunday Observer*. Mum told him that no one wanted to be interviewed, and thought no more of it.

Our cousin Tom Rose arranged a visit from the local minister. My parents were nominally Christian, but none of us had worshipped in a church for years. Robert's religion was innocent as willow and shaped like a cricket ball. Our churchgoing didn't revive after the accident.

We asked Marie and Barbara to stay the night. The four of us went to bed early. I remember laughing with Barbara as we all took it in turns using the bathroom. I felt a thin bat's squeak of guilt about this levity. How could we joke while Robert lay on the other side of town, with 'destruction of terror in his voice'? How could we ever laugh or gossip or forget what had happened? It was the first twinge of guilt about my own unfettered state.

I slept badly. Tranquil nights were a thing of the past. My dreams were horrible, violent. Morning brought no drowsy insouciance before the killing realisation. I thought about Robert the moment I woke up. It was as if the accident had happened weeks ago and I had accepted it. Later in the morning we drove to Tullamarine where we joined Kevin and Ralph Rose. Ralph, my youngest uncle, was due to become a father again that afternoon. His wife had already gone into labour. Dad's plane was delayed. Everyone felt nervous about seeing him again. Pressmen were there but didn't harass us.

Then the gates opened and Dad rushed over to us. He cried bitterly as he embraced Mum. When he came over to me he tapped me on the back and said, 'Bad luck, Pete'. I recalled my uneasiness the previous Sunday when he had left to go overseas. We walked briskly to the car and Dad began to calm down. He said he felt better now that he could talk to someone. He had flown home alone. The long journey had been particularly hard.

All Dad knew was what his brother had told him. Kevin, direct as Dr Burke, had said that Robert would never walk again. Dad refused to believe him. We drove straight to the hospital and walked up the hill to Ward Seven. The *Herald* devoted another front page to Dad's homecoming. He is photographed striding into the spinal injuries unit with that purposeful, arm-waving gait of his. 'Bob Rose, one of football's all-time greats, came home from the US today, tired and unshaved.' It must have been the first time Dad, normally well-groomed, had gone out without a shave.

Dad wanted to speak to Dr Burke before seeing Robert. He asked him about the outlook. Dr Burke was just as frank as Kevin. Dad was flabbergasted. Paralysis is anathema to all of us, but especially to athletes. Dad found it incredible that it could be irreversible from the outset. My father is an intrepid man. As a footballer he was renowned for his tenacity. Not tall, he attacked the ball and anyone in his path with a ferocity that galvanised less talented team-mates and that still makes people shudder. Winning, overcoming, never squibbing were moral necessities. Writing in 1955,

Alf Brown said, 'He seems to glory in heavy clashes'. He often played with serious injuries, because the restful alternative went against his code. Persistence had never let him down. How, therefore, could he digest Dr Burke's terse prognosis? How could he accept that a mishap in the night, a millisecond on a country road, couldn't be fixed by slog and guts and will power? It was inhuman. It was against nature.

Dad thanked Dr Burke and walked into Ward Seven. Robert was perfectly composed. His first words to Dad were, 'I don't want to go on living if it means spending my life in bed'. Dad reassured him that the doctors expected him to be in a wheelchair within six months. Robert didn't believe him. Like everyone, Dad remembers 'the spikes'. The sight of the calipers 'shook him to pieces'. He was astonished by Robert's self-control.

Afterwards, we went into Dr Burke's office and Dad briefed him about Robert's reaction. Apropos of nothing, I said that the accident should have happened to me. Dr Burke remembered this when I interviewed him at Ivanhoe Manor. 'You made the comment—I don't know if you recall this—that it would have been better if the accident had happened to you because you could have coped with it better, being the academic one of the two and Robert the physical one.' When I remarked that this was the sort of callow thing any teenage brother would have said, Dr Burke disagreed. 'I thought it was a very poignant comment for a young brother to make. And you meant it.'

Outside, Dad spoke to reporters, including Ian McDonald, who would become a friend of Robert's. Next to his story, titled 'HOUR OF AGONY FOR A FATHER', is a close-up photograph of my father. Dad's eyes are dark and deep-set. They could have been gouged out by what he has seen and heard. His brow is furrowed, his mouth grim, almost angry. He is forty-five, my age now. McDonald writes: 'Rose, haggard and unshaven…had just given Robert a pep talk…"I told him the family team would be fighting for him, but the future is up to how he fights… It's a hell of a shock, but I was pleased to see that Robert is 100 per cent mentally."' Dad repeated this for the *Herald*. 'Mentally Robert is 100 per cent alert.' Mental impairment is what Dad had feared most during the '32-hour sleepless trip'.

We drove to the Yewers' house in West Heidelberg. As always, this was full of people. Salli was naturally the centre of attention, even more so that day. A precocious child, she had a new trick to show us. She had begun to walk the day Robert stopped.

I was unnerved by the clamour, the exuberance. The men were drinking beer. They asked Dad about his trip. I felt uneasy and said nothing. Terry was still in a state of shock. She hadn't slept since the accident. She talked about that night. She was staying with her parents when she got the news. It was a doctor at the Bacchus Marsh Hospital who rang, perhaps the same one who diagnosed quadriplegia. At first Terry refused to believe his story. She was used to hoax calls from Robert's friends, who would ring in the early hours of the morning and invent bizarre excuses as to why he couldn't come home. Terry thought it must have been another prank. Eventually the doctor, no doubt deeply mystified, convinced Terry that he was serious. She and her mother hurried to the Austin and saw Robert. He was quite calm. Terry was horrified by the bricks hanging from his shaven head. Dr Burke asked her how she was going to handle the press. Terry, inexperienced in this regard, said she would need help from Robert's family. She telephoned Uncle Kevin.

Mum and Dad and I drove home from the Yewers' in silence. The journey took about forty minutes. We were getting used to it. Sammy, perplexed by now, rotated on her little legs like a stumpy ballerina and hinted that she was hungry. Dad shaved and changed, then we decided to revisit Robert. As we left the house two men got out of a car on the street. They introduced themselves unctuously as journalists from the *Sunday Observer* and asked about Robert. Mum said we didn't know any more than they did. The chatty one asked Dad if he could get them into Ward Seven so that they could get a photograph of Robert. Dad refused and we got into the car. They continued to pester us, leaning into the car, holding the doors open. I pushed the photographer and nearly broke his camera.

As we drove to the hospital we thought no more of this, though we knew the *Sunday Observer* had a vile reputation. Dad was used to media molestation. Before a grand final, or during one of Collingwood's regular coups, our telephone would ring constantly with journalists desperate for a story. Most of them respected Dad and treated him decently; a few couldn't be trusted to quote him accurately. Dad was polite and rarely impatient. Being a master of publicity, he knew that great caution was needed when dealing with journalists.

Fortunately, we were able to stay with Robert for as long as we liked. He was in a corner of the long bright malodorous ward. He was quiet that afternoon. The tubes in his throat made it painful for him to swallow, so we removed the saliva and mucus in tissues. Robert's bed was high and his neck utterly rigid, so he couldn't look at us directly. A tilted mirror above his bed enabled him to see us. He smiled occasionally; he even made a joke. We told him about Ralph's new son, his umpteenth cousin. Robert asked about the result of the two-day game between Collingwood and South Melbourne, the one he had played in the previous Saturday. We told him that Collingwood had collapsed to be all out for 121. We didn't tell him that many of the players, distraught at what had happened during the week and playing without heart, as one reporter wrote, felt that the game should have been abandoned. Robert wouldn't have approved of that.

It was apparent that the full impact of the accident hadn't sunk in yet. Dr Burke had warned us that this kind of bravado can last for several weeks, especially if the patient is under intense scrutiny.

Needing a cigarette, I left the three of them and went outside. Terry was sitting on a bench, crying. When I went over and asked her what was wrong—another of my cogent questions—she said, 'He'll never make love to me again'. That was the first thing Robert said to her. Like many of us, Terry had no idea what quadriplegia meant. She had no experience with handicapped people, no knowledge of spinal injuries. Terry's first interview had appeared that morning. 'I don't know what the future holds,' she told

Peter McFarline of the *Age*. 'All I know is that I will be looking after Robert for a long, long time.'

I didn't know what to say, how to console her. Terry was still tearful as the four of us walked down the steep road. None of us was aware of spies. As we got into the car one of the journalists from the *Sunday Observer* reappeared with his photographer. They had followed us to the hospital. This time they were less oily, more adamant. Elsie, normally the politest of women, slammed the door and told them to get away.

That evening Kevin and Pat Rose joined us, followed by Terry and Salli. We picked at some of the casseroles that neighbours had dropped in throughout the day. Mum was very upset. I took Sammy for a walk in the park and wept uncontrollably. Back at Crosby Drive, Terry broke down completely. The extreme days had begun—days of futility, days of grief. I couldn't foresee an end to them. I kept wondering how we would have felt if Robert had been killed in the accident, if he hadn't been granted this spiked extension—if it had all been over.

The next day my parents wanted to read all the newspapers. This troubled me. I couldn't understand why they needed to look at grotesque images of the roofless Volkswagen or innocent photographs of their mobile son. What were they looking for? What further proof did they need?

The story in the *Sunday Observer* was dreadful. One glance at the headline told us how appalling it was going to be. Subtlety was never a feature of Maxwell Newton's final, creepy editorship. It was a kind of gutter journalism rarely practised in Australia. When Rupert Murdoch started his national newspaper, the *Australian*, in 1964, Newton was the founding editor. Like several holders of that position, he didn't last long. Some people still regard him as one of our most brilliant journalists. By the early 1970s any genius had begun to degenerate. He moved to Melbourne and started the *Sunday Observer* in opposition to David Syme and the Herald & Weekly Times. Its tabloid style soon became notorious. 'MY BILL'S NOT A HOMO,' screamed one headline, announcing an 'exclusive interview' with the wife of former Prime Minister William McMahon. To pay the printer, Newton was also publishing soft porn. Later, he turned to sex aids and pornographic books. His drug and alcohol consumption was ruinous. A few months before Robert's accident he somehow survived an overdose of a hundred Mandrax and six bottles of Scotch.

While writing this book I had to hunt for a copy of the *Observer* article. It wasn't in any of the scrapbooks. Mum had never looked at it again. Finally, Salli produced a copy. The front page is dominated by a plangent headline, 'OUR AGONY—MUM TELLS', next to a surreptitious photograph, taken with a telephoto lens, of Terry getting into the car after our walk through the hospital grounds. Worse follows on page three. There is a photograph of Mum comforting her distraught daughter-in-law. Next to this are two 'exclusive stories', supposedly written by my parents, with a cameo from Terry. It's a wonder they didn't drag in Millie! My mother's fictitious story is the biggest. I won't bother quoting much of it. The opening sentences will suffice: 'Today I'll be praying for my son Robert.

I'll ask God to give him the strength to fight and overcome his terrible injuries. I couldn't keep the tears from my eyes when I saw Robert...' And so it goes.

The other two stories are no better. It is maudlin, mediocre newsprint cribbed from earlier newspaper stories. None of it is true. A tiny box in the corner tells us that 'Bob and Elsie Rose were interviewed by Mike Worner'. We were pleased that Mr Worner identified himself, however modestly, as the author of this fanciful prose.

There was also room on page three for a succinct editorial, presumably written by Maxwell Newton. He instructed us that Robert's tragedy should be a warning to us all and hoped that it would highlight the plight of people crippled in accidents. (Robert as victim, or symbol, or white knight?) More needed to be done for such people; more funds should be found; public money shouldn't be squandered on distasteful paintings by Jackson Pollock. 'We need less spending on things like the Blue Poles painting at $1.4 million—and more on medical research.'

Subsequently, my parents sought legal advice but were told there was no point in seeking a retraction or suing the *Observer*. Newton had no money, the tabloid wasn't expected to survive much longer, and such an action would only dignify this trash. Besides, my parents had other things to worry about. Our only consolation was that no one who really knew them would believe that they were capable of uttering such bilge or selling their stories. But those unacquainted with them or naïve about the tabloid's mendacity may have wondered. My parents found that disturbing.

Even now the audacity of what the *Observer* did to my parents and to Terry—two days after their lives were shattered—outrages me. Part of me, the revenant of 1974, wants to rail before posterity's Press Council and to expose the perpetrators. His alter ego, inured to the way of the world, is more resigned.

Janet Malcolm, the fine New York journalist, puts it neatly in her book on Sylvia Plath: 'The freedom to be cruel is one of journalism's uncontested privileges, and the rendering of subjects as if they were characters in bad novels is one of its widely accepted conventions'.

Not all journalists were prepared to sacrifice my parents. One senior writer, working for a rival newspaper, later told them he had incensed his editor by refusing to write something to match the *Observer*'s fabrications. He told the editor that he wouldn't do that to my parents.

This miserable affair had a pathetic but telling postlude three years later. It happened at the MCG. Dad had taken Robert into the rooms after stumps so that he could speak to his old team-mates. The journalist from the *Observer* was there too. Dad had seen him before, in the distance, but in the past the sleuth had always vanished. This time there was no escape. Tears in his eyes, he said to Dad, 'Bob, if you want to hit me, you deserve to'. Dad looked at him and walked away.

The next few days were anxious, blurry. Robert's respiratory system adapted to its new precariousness, pneumonia (always the greatest risk) didn't set in, and the immediate crisis passed, but his body was reacting to all the therapies

110

that were necessary to keep him alive. He detested the tube in his throat and never adjusted to it. He brought up a great deal of phlegm. Expelling this, in his strengthless state, exhausted him. He felt sweaty and nauseous. His shaved scalp began to itch. Every few hours he was turned a few inches to rest his back and avert pressure sores. These turns were awkward and distressing. His jaw became swollen from resting on the pillow. Five days after the accident he developed acute peptic ulceration, a common complication after spinal cord injuries. The following day he had his first bowel movement since the accident. Although this was overdue and a good sign, I was glad I wasn't there to witness Robert's first experience of being nursed in that way in an open ward. His old acne came back virulently, just to spite him. As a teenager Robert had had one of the worst cases doctors had seen. Now his face and back became ulcerated again.

Robert began to have basic physiotherapy. It was bizarre watching the physiotherapist bending his long tanned muscular legs. Any minute, surely, she would find the spot to revivify his broken frame. How could such a robust body suddenly freeze? Were we all just potential boy-puppets, bits of string and bone, ready to snap? If it could happen to a flawless youth, what about other people's spinal cords, encased and sinuous, as yet unmutilated? When would it happen again?

Robert enjoyed listening to his chatty physiotherapist, whose long black hair drifted over his chest as she manipulated him. Afterwards his neck became sore, but morphine restored him. He began to complain about pains in his abdomen and left leg, but these were dismissed as phantom pains, again quite common after paralysis.

We got to know the nurses and the orderlies. Gregarious as ever, Robert joked with them about Australia's form in the Test matches, and wanted to know which football teams they supported so that he could tease them during winter. Most of the nurses were expert and solicitous. The tactlessness of one agency nurse, who asked Robert if he saw any reason to go on living, was atypical. He was distraught about that when Mum saw him the next morning.

Robert didn't look forward to the nights. He was learning to share with five dozen other people who were all learning to cope with paralysis. Robert had always slept on his stomach like a proud pagan: now he was pinned on his back with tubes down his throat. He was kept awake by the ward's endless nocturnal disturbances: regular turns, urgent conversations between nurses and doctors, early-morning admissions, accidental bowel movements. He never talked about his dreams, but morphine and existential terror must have warped them. One day he said he thought he might be able to sleep if Mum and I stayed with him, but this wasn't possible in Ward Seven. There were no empty beds.

'Night is when the patient imagines dying,' says Robert McCrum, the Englishman who wrote a book about the severe stroke that paralysed him when he was forty-two.

Robert's morale during those first couple of weeks was surprisingly positive. We visited him every day for several hours. We staggered our visits, so that Robert wasn't alone for long. Dad went back to work but was still able to spend long periods with him, reading to him from the sporting

112

pages or telling him about developments at Footscray. Mum, meanwhile, stood by that high bed like a sentry, in spite of the discomfort she must have felt from her recent, forgotten surgery. She found it terribly difficult to leave. I too felt hopelessly depressed whenever I left Ward Seven.

Extreme days spelt extreme emotions, from listlessness to panic to a desperate altruism. A fortnight after the accident, just before the start of my second year at university, I wrote: 'I must get down to work soon, because the knowledge that I must become a professional something-or-other consumes me. My responsibility to Robert is total.' During this phase there was no improvement in Robert's condition, no lessening of his paralysis. He refused to accept that he would spend the rest of his life in a wheelchair, but the outlook wasn't promising. I began to dread what would happen when he left hospital.

Yet Robert's mood continued to surprise us. Some days he was positively chirpy, a word I often used in my journal. A week after his accident he wanted to discuss his injuries. He struck me as being strangely ignorant of the ramifications. He asked about the difference between quadriplegia and paraplegia—which was worse, which description fitted him. He wanted to know if it was better to lose your legs or to be paralysed. Two days later he was talkative and nostalgic. He was learning to rely on memory, mining it to forget the boredom and despair. He reminisced about our Test matches in the backyard. When I reminded him about his celebrated feats for Victoria he said he wouldn't be repeating them. He wanted to talk about the accident. He remembered being trapped and calling for help. He had

113

no memory of Mrs Scott, who had stayed with him in the Volkswagen.

Our long visits led to a curtailment of our visiting rights, which upset everyone, especially Robert. He was no longer the latest incomer. Those sixty-two beds were never empty long. Every few days, when we entered Ward Seven, we would pass another freshly calipered patient, another pair of ashen parents hovering over their son (for they were usually boys) like premature mourners over a high grave. Robert was just one of them now; he had joined the ranks of invalids.

On 25 February the wretched tube was removed. Robert joked that it was almost as good as making a century. We all laughed about his daredevil days. I predicted that even in a wheelchair Robert would find a way. He was now permitted a light diet. While Mum delightedly fed him I stroked his itchy brow. He said it was beautiful. He could express affection now. Extreme days produced a new familial order, very tender but also very exposed. The old self-sufficiency was no longer tenable, desperate moods no longer disguisable, except in Ward Seven. The four of us were gropingly revising our emotional lives. Robert's bed, his condition, its fluctuations, were the focus of our devastated universe. Watching him, charting his progress, noting each flicker of improvement, it was possible to forget other certainties and to believe, however innocently, in some sort of rehabilitated meaning. His illness was our cause, our cosmology. We were beginning to orbit him, needful and responsive, just like him.

Robert McCrum wrote about this mutual reliance in

114

My Year Off. A celebrated publisher, he had the support, like Robert, of a large circle of friends and admirers, including some of the most celebrated writers of the day, but his greatest consolation was much more primitive:

> The longer I stayed helpless in hospital, the more
> I came to understand why it is our blood relations
> who will respond, instinctively and without ques-
> tion, to the claims of family. I had lived in a world
> seemingly outside family, but there were moments
> during those first hospital days when it seemed that
> family was the only world that mattered...If I were
> now to reduce my experience in hospital to two key
> words they would be 'family' and 'love'.

Relations between Robert and Terry were tense during those first few weeks after the accident. Whatever had provoked their last row hadn't been resolved. Ward Seven wasn't the best place for détente. At times I was mystified by Terry's manner towards Robert in hospital. She was already planning for a modified future. A return to the upstairs flat was out of the question. Robert would need 24-hour nursing and at least two people to lift him. Terry and my parents began discussing ways of modifying the basement at Crosby Drive. There was even talk of an elevator. I wondered what it would be like when we were all living together.

After a fortnight Robert was allowed other visitors. Many former team-mates asked if they could see him. A few, conspicuously, stayed away, unable to face him. Robert's bed was usually surrounded by Rose relations and prominent sportsmen. Many of the younger men had never been in a hospital before. Nor had Robert. They were nervous and sometimes overtly upset. Robert became adept at relaxing people. He quickly made a joke when they arrived. Trevor Grant, a friend and journalist, saw him around this time. 'It's happened, mate,' Robert chuckled. 'I've just got to get runs in the next dig.' My brother was becoming quite a psychologist—or had he always been one? I often saw him coax a distressed or speechless visitor into conversation.

I got to know some of the other patients. I remember one boy who was admitted not long after Robert. We all became friendly with Paul and his family. He was eighteen. A soldier, he had been stationed in Queensland. One day he was practising on the pommel horse and forgot to put his hands out. He landed on his head. Each week produced similar horrors. One new admission had been shot in the back by her husband. A young man was paralysed after diving into a treacherous river. A week later a boy of sixteen was crippled at exactly the same spot. The same ambulance officer attended both times; he couldn't believe it. Only then did the local authorities erect a warning sign.

I enjoyed the patients' sardonic humour. One day—the last day of that putrid summer—a northerly was blowing outside. I relished this exchange between two veteran patients, both cynical about their visitors' motives. Harold Pinter couldn't have phrased it more beautifully.

Ian: It's hot today. We'll have a lot of visitors, all
    here for the air-conditioning, making us hot.

Jan: And they'll say, 'You're so lucky to be here in the cool'.

Ian: Should we ask them to join us?

Meanwhile, Robert and my parents were inundated with cards, letters and telegrams. Entire classes of school-children wrote to Terry, who was photographed lying on the floor amid their polite messages. My parents received many official messages of regret from public figures and organisations. The Collingwood Town Clerk assured them of the distinction their son had brought to the municipality. Robert was no evangelist, but the Commissioner of the Salvation Army expressed his sympathy and remembered Robert in his prayers. Humorous cards were mercifully few. The Fitzroy players signed one urging Robert to hurry up and get back in the swim, while an old school mate offered this variation on the same salutary theme: 'Hurry up and get well because the sooner you get out of bed the sooner you can get back to your favourite pastime...back in bed'.

Robert received letters from the same cricket clubs that had written to him a few years before inviting him to train with them. An old friend at the Waverley Cricket Club portended a coaching career for Robert and said the club would welcome his services. A sonorous broadcaster and Collingwood diehard wrote to my mother suggesting a career in radio. One stranger urged Robert to become a sports writer ('I'm a nutty old mum writing letters and offering gratuitous advice...although you obviously don't need it—you seem to have resources within yourself of strength and intelligence'). Bill Jacobs wrote to Robert

117

commending his fortitude. He had nominated Robert for MCC membership the day he was born. Many years after the accident, he told Dad that every morning when he woke up he thought about Robert.

In another letter, one of Robert's younger teachers at Haileybury spoke of the enduring bond between teacher and student, and reminisced about an infamous economics class. Peter Harris taught me too. When I spoke to him recently—he is now a headmaster—he remembered Robert as a shy boy who wasn't one of his finest scholars. Robert sat in the fourth row, by the window. (Why did I know it would be by the window?) Robert always daydreamed in class, staring at the oval. Harris would ask him if he intended doing any work. He also remembered a wart on Robert's hand, perhaps because he had one in the same place and, like everyone with warts, tried to hide it. For Harris, a young migrant working-class teacher, drawn to Haileybury because he thought he was joining a social and cultural elite, attracted by the blazer, the colours, the military tradition, Robert seemed like one of the gods, a golden youth.

The legendary Ted Whitten, whom Dad had replaced as coach of Footscray, sent Robert an extraordinary motivational card. Deeply underscored, the message reads: 'A quitter never Wins / And a Winner never Quits'. Dad told me that this annoyed Robert. Whitten's subsequent letter was similarly inspirational:

You have inherited a Body that's full of Fight Courage and 'Will to Win' & to know that the whole

118

Sporting <u>Fraternity</u> of <u>Australia</u> is pulling for you,
must make you want to <u>fight harder</u> than <u>Ever</u>...
Robert there is an old saying in life which says '<u>A</u>
<u>Winner never Quits</u>'...you Robert have enough <u>Fight</u>
to prove <u>Medical Science</u> Wrong.

The most prescient commiserator of all was Jean
Sherrin, wife of Collingwood's long-time president. Dad—a
distant relative—had known the Sherrins since coming to
Melbourne. His first job was at the Sherrin football factory,
stitching balls. Tom Sherrin, a small courteous beady-eyed
man, had assumed the presidency not long before Dad
became coach in 1963. Jean Sherrin, too, was short, polite,
curious-eyed. In her letter to my parents she wrote, 'What
a challenge you have this time Bob! To help if possible the
boy back to health and strength and in so doing to inspire
all the other young injured ones to get up and go. Perhaps
this is your purpose in life.'

Rereading her eloquent letter now, I wonder how
Dad felt when he read that prophesy in 1974. What a
calling, what a raison d'être for this sunny man approaching
middle age.

Thankfully, all Robert's medical costs were covered
by Victorian legislation just enacted by the Hamer Government. But for that sole bit of luck my family would have been
bankrupted. Because no one was deemed to be culpable in
the accident, there was no prospect of a separate financial
claim. Within days of the accident, two major appeals were
launched to raise funds for Robert and his young family.
Proceeds from several cricket contests were donated to the

appeals. The Forest Hills Lions' Club organised a sportsmen's night, which raised $7000. The Australian cricket team, still in New Zealand, sent a sizeable donation. Robert received dozens of letters from schoolchildren and pensioners who enclosed a few dollars. One girl sent him her pocket money and recalled seeing him play at the MCG. 'I also think you are very handsome...I still and always think you are the best.' We held up these letters and Robert read them slowly, rarely commenting.

Dad's moratorium on interviews had caused Dr Burke some problems. There was still considerable interest in Robert's story. Finally, three weeks after the accident, Dad told him that Robert was ready to face the press. They both knew it had to be done sooner or later. On 6 March about thirty journalists from newspapers, radio and television descended on the Austin. Dr Burke briefed them before they were led into Ward Seven. He remembers this with some amusement. They were most uneasy about seeing Robert. Several of them asked Dr Burke what they should say to him. He found this surprising coming from seasoned journalists. He advised them to speak normally and predicted that Robert wouldn't bite their heads off. 'They were really quite frightened,' he told me at Ivanhoe Manor.

Since Robert couldn't be moved, the interview took place around his bed. My parents stood beside him. Terry was there too. (I had gone back to university, so pleased to miss this conference that I didn't mention it in my journal.) There are several photographs of Robert, with his head still pulled back and those penetrating tongs. His hair is growing back, much darker than before. He sports a weedy moustache, which will soon be replaced by a more convenient beard. Old friends in the press noted other changes during the '45-minute ordeal' (ordeal for whom, I wonder). 'His voice was high-pitched through reduced breathing capacity,' wrote Peter McFarline, 'but Rose answered all questions calmly—and at times happily.' *Happily?* Dad had helped Robert to prepare for the interview. Knowing Dad, he would have pre-empted most of their questions. It would have been like preparing for a crucial game, anticipating the opponents' moves.

Robert set out to relax the nervous thirty. 'A cigarette, a glass of beer and a feed of potato cakes wouldn't go astray,' he told the *Sun*. They all ran with *that*. Robert denied being bitter, praised the medical staff and said he hadn't thought about the future. He pointed out that other people were in the same boat. 'Life isn't too bad. Anyway, there isn't much I can do about it.' All he complained about were those awful tubes. Of his many sporting visitors he said, 'I love them all. I knew I could count on them.' He said he would have to start an entirely new life and talked about becoming a scorer again. Later, in a final briefing with the reporters, Dr Burke cast doubt on this. He held out little hope that Robert would regain the use of his arms, though he didn't rule out the possibility of his being employed in the future—selling insurance over the phone, of all things, or commentating for radio or television. Dr Burke admitted that he would have liked to see some form of recovery by now.

Dr Burke was pleased with the way the conference went. 'Robert coped very well,' he told me at Ivanhoe Manor. 'He was on top of it. He was comfortable, and they weren't.'

It had also given Dr Burke an opportunity to apprise the public of the meaning of quadriplegia—as well as correcting a few journalists' spelling. One of them quotes Dr Burke as saying that the spinal unit had admitted twenty-four new patients since Christmas. Robert, in his laconic and self-deprecating way, was fast becoming a useful symbol for the disabled and their carers.

Within days of the press conference Robert became depressed—very depressed—just as the doctors had predicted. Perhaps the media scrum and the resulting headlines ('ROBERT ROSE FACES LIFE AS A CRIPPLE') demoralised him. He still had the calipers in his skull. Nausea, acne and phantom pains wore him down. On 6 March he began to get some reflex movements back in his legs, but there was no evidence of voluntary return. Twelve days later he regained flickers of motor control in his shoulder and elbow flexor muscles, but they were barely perceptible. On 27 March, the six-week mark, X-rays showed some bony union, so the doctors decided to persist with traction for another fortnight. When Dr Burke attempted to discuss Robert's prognosis with him he strongly rejected the possibility of permanent paralysis. During case conferences the doctors noted that Robert was depressed and refractory.

Robert was no longer 'chirpy'. Sometimes he cheered up during visits; sometimes he didn't. His relations with Terry were volatile. I found their squabbles disturbing. Usually Robert remained composed with my parents, but one day he became upset, crying for the first time and saying over and over again, 'Why did it have to happen?' Such breakdowns were almost as traumatic for my parents as they were for him. What could they say? How could they console him? His silences were even worse. I began to realise that nothing compares with the sorrow and impotence parents feel when their child suffers acutely.

Extreme times—nakedest of days. It was dangerous now. Death had to be preferable, you sometimes thought. We hung on while we were with Robert, but everyone was failing. It was like a slow collapse of the nerves and the heart. One evening Dad got home after a solo visit and sobbed in my mother's arms. There was nothing anyone could say. Then he composed himself and ate his warmed-up meal. (We ate in shifts, half-heartedly.) He was back at work and coaching a football side—both full-time jobs. He had to go on. I began to notice how unwell he looked: puffy, grey, dispirited.

Around that time I wrote in my journal: 'We spent the afternoon in the hospital. We managed to laugh, but all was sadness. Why? Life has stopped, but I haven't energy to explain. Dad told me that Mum said to him that we were all dead now. I agreed.'

At least once, I think, everyone in that position contemplates flight. My turn came one day when Ian Chappell sent Robert a message on television. This upset me tremendously. I thought of quitting the house forever—my family, my friends. I thought of old sick dogs that just head off into the bush and die.

I stayed, of course.

The next day I returned to the hospital and was struck by Robert's haggardness and by the frailty of his spirits.

123

I told him about Chappell's message. Sore and drugged, he fell asleep. While he dozed I rubbed his head and looked out the window at autumnal life. I thought of Philip Larkin's great line, 'Dead leaves desert in thousands'. I thought about my new honours course in philosophy and wondered how I could possibly codify or dignify my thoughts while this person lay crippled in bed. I mused on how quickly I had accepted Robert's fate, how deciduously I had forgotten his thrusting youth. They seemed like two different people: one helpless, sparring with Terry, appeasing her, eager for our company, gentle, forbearing; and the other, the absent brother, my eternal adversary, so recklessly impatient to realise his manhood—'a free spirit if ever there was one'— impish, vexing and endearing.

One evening I attended a fundraising dinner in a nearby restaurant. Footballers from both of Robert's old clubs attended. I was dismayed by people's gaiety and seeming indifference. I often thought about people's capriciousness during those first few weeks. How could they enjoy themselves while Robert suffered? I felt out of place in that rowdy throng. Watching my erstwhile idols with their women, I felt profoundly loveless. That night I wrote in a conciliatory vein to A., my anti-hero. We hadn't spoken to each other since the incident by the creek. Agonised but unbending as ever, A. had refrained from contacting me after the accident. Cautiously I proposed a meeting so that we could resume our 'dialogue'. Thus, tentatively at first, it began again.

A few days later I ran into A. at Monash. I had just attended an election meeting addressed by Don Chipp. This was interrupted by a streaker with a hypothetical penis who ran onto the stage and covered the then Liberal politician in flour. I took A. to the 'caf' where we discussed fin-de-siècle aesthetes, an unlikely rapprochement. A. offered to drive me home. He wanted to show me his new car. It was a white Volkswagen. I sat there reading Shakespeare aloud while he drove in that militant way of his. Did we even talk about Robert?

Relations at home were tense. 'We are a sickening clan,' I noted in my journal. No one was in good shape. Mum had various ailments, one of them serious. Weeks after the accident she realised that she was automatically moving the telephone receiver from her right ear to her left because she couldn't hear anything. Typically, she didn't tell anyone. There was no time for a consultation. No time, no point. Then her sister came over from New Zealand and noticed that Mum, in her mid-forties, was going deaf. The only person in the world who could command my mother, my aunt insisted that she have her hearing tested. The specialist confirmed her fears and asked Mum if she had had a profound shock recently. He put two and two together and diagnosed nerve deafness, which is incurable. It must have happened in the waiting room at the Austin when we got the news, so great was the shock, so harmful the brief cessation of oxygen to the brain. Had she been suitably warned, prepared, it might not have happened.

I developed a rash on my legs and a peculiar hernia-like pain in my side, doubtless psychosomatic but acute enough to wake me at night. Dad had never seemed so edgy. He often stayed late at the club. Footscray, like Collingwood, was not without its malcontents. There was talk of a putsch if Dad didn't get the side in the finals. He knew he had to perform.

Driving home one night after visiting Robert, Dad and I had one of our frank conversations. He seemed impatient with my bleak outlook. He said that as a family we had had a comparatively lucky run. Surely I agreed with that? I didn't. My anarchic mood got worse and Dad became upset. He said I believed he cared more for Robert than he did for me. He had said this once before. I had denied it then, as I did now. Although I knew that Dad and Robert had much more in common than we did, and although I had long thought of myself as a redundant and confusing son, I never felt that Dad favoured Robert. Nor was I conscious of harbouring resentment. Dad spent more time with Robert, but that was perfectly understandable, especially now. They had lots of things to talk about, but we weren't exactly tongue-tied together. Had he preferred Robert, I wouldn't have been particularly affronted. But it wasn't Dad's form. I often thought him the fairest man I knew. He loved both his sons.

I placated Dad as best I could.

Three days later—this was 20 April—Robert thrilled us by moving his right arm. Within days he could almost turn over his hand when it was lying palm down on the sheet. I was suffused with memories and hope. 'Seeing him move,' I wrote in my journal, 'actually showing signs of human activity, after the pessimism I have learned, is so glorious I cannot express it. It is like a dream when he moves.'

By the end of the month Robert had regained some power—still considerably less than normal—in the paralysed muscles around his shoulder and elbow flexors. The doctors had introduced him to his wheelchair on April 11 as soon as the calipers were removed. It was disturbing to see him being lifted onto the chair, proof, as if it were needed, of his limpness. Mum was shocked by that sight, that confirmation. Sitting in the wheelchair made Robert giddy at first. Greatly weakened after ten weeks in bed, he fainted and had to be lifted back onto the bed. But gradually he became accustomed to his new sedentary life. By the beginning of May he was staying up for longer periods: half an hour, then an hour. This made reading easier, and he could greet his friends face to face. Very tentatively, reassuring him every inch of the way, we pushed him around the ward and took him outside.

Reports of his new mobility prompted more letters. A schoolboy in Braybrook wrote to him: 'One day Mrs Barnes came into the class for our Religious period. Mrs Barnes told us that she had been reading the news paper and found some very good news. It said that you were sitting up in a chair. All the class were over joyed when she read the news to us...'

Robert was temporarily moved into a small room off Ward Seven. This had a television and was more private. Robert seemed happy when I saw him there. The Victorian Cricket Association had invited him to a dinner on 31 May to celebrate Victoria's victory in the Sheffield Shield, to which he had contributed so notably. This would be his first public appearance—if he was well enough.

On 12 May Robert was moved into a bigger ward with a range of paraplegics and quadriplegics. There we celebrated Salli's first birthday. Robert continued to make good progress. He exercised daily and could now lift his arms off the floor while lying on his back. Such was his improvement that we were told he would be able to feed himself with the aid of a brace around his wrist. There was even talk of finding him a job when he left hospital. Robert's doldrums were less frequent now. One night when Mum briefly left the ward, he told me that being in hospital all the time drove him mad, but that was a rare admission.

Five days before the VCA dinner Robert was ready for a trial outing. Crosby Drive being too far away, Terry's parents' house was chosen. Terry had just got her licence. She still has some lurid super-8 footage of their arrival. Several men struggle to extract Robert from the car while Salli capers about like a heedless sprite. Terry looks on with a new driver's amazement that they have arrived in one piece. The ceremony of pillows has begun. Myriad are produced from the small car like props in a slapstick movie: pillows for his back, pillows for his wrist, pillows for between his legs to prevent chafing. From now on, wherever we went, the pillows went with us.

I had stayed home to finish a typically overdue essay. When I rang Robert to congratulate him Mum held up the receiver for him. His first words were, 'Hello, thicko'. He was recovering nicely.

Throughout the six-hour furlough Robert's mood remained euphoric, but it changed when it came time for him to go back to the Austin. My mother remembers his terror as they negotiated a major intersection near the hospital. He kept saying how dangerous it was. When they got him into bed he broke down. He loathed the thought of being back at the Austin. He was learning to hate hospitals.

But Robert had passed the test and was judged to be strong enough to attend the dinner. In later years, with exquisitely perverse timing, illnesses and relapses often prevented him from attending special functions, but this time he wasn't thwarted. The VCA had postponed the dinner for some weeks so that Robert could attend. There was another, smaller press conference prior to the event. Under a headline reading 'ROSE'S BIG NIGHT OUT...WITH THE BOYS', the *Herald*'s medical reporter found Robert much changed. 'Much of the earlier hesitation in Rose's speech has gone... so are the calipers which braced his head. Even his hair is thickening.' Robert told him how much he was looking forward to getting together with 'the fellows' and described the Shield win as the greatest thrill of his sporting career.

When Dad pushed his wheelchair into the members' dining room at the MCG Robert received a standing ovation from the guests and officials. In the many photographs taken that night he looks marvellous: bright-eyed, round-faced, spiky-haired, and indescribably happy. He alone is not in black tie. Instead he wears a turtleneck jumper over his neck brace. He still has the cheeky grin. He beams at Max Walker, whose raffish moustache is much more frightening than Robert's thin one. 'I'm bloody glad to be here,' Robert told one journalist. Although terribly hot and perspiring freely, he stayed until midnight. Rupert Hamer, the then

Victorian premier, presented him with an inscribed silver ice bucket, which I still borrow for dinner parties. A young Eric Beecher, writing for a cricket magazine, said of Robert, 'He smiled and he took it all in'.

Robert was also photographed between Dad and Paul Sheahan. Only Dad is unmaimed. Robert is wearing a thick white belt around his stomach to stop him from falling onto the regal carpet, and his hands are resting on a large pillow. Paul Sheahan stands beside him on crutches, his right foot in plaster. He had ruptured ligaments in his ankle playing football. What on earth prompted Paul Sheahan, the most elegant of cricketers and certainly the finest fieldsman I have ever seen, to play football? More congruously, he is wearing a black velvet suit. He looks like the next James Bond.

I spoke to Sheahan while researching this book. I visited him at Melbourne Grammar School, where he is the headmaster. We met in his salubrious office in a nineteenth-century bluestone building overlooking an oval where I once played football. This time the headmaster wasn't wearing velvet. Tall, slim, still impressive, he wore navy blue trousers, a check shirt and a reefer jacket. Generously, he gave me an hour.

Like many of my interviewees, Sheahan began by saying how astonishing my parents were. He described my father as a great man, regardless of his sporting achievements. He said he was always struck by Dad's modesty, and speculated that Robert's self-deprecating humour was hereditary.

Sheahan couldn't recall the VCA dinner in 1974. He barely recalled hurting his ankle. Apologetically, he said he doesn't keep a scrapbook or a diary, adding that future

130

historians of his school won't thank him for the latter omission. He was hazy about his own sporting career. He told me that, unlike many former athletes, he doesn't live in the past and rarely attends sporting reunions, which have become something of an industry. (This year, during grand final week, my father was out every night attending football functions, many of them nostalgic or valedictory.) Sheahan always made it clear in the press that he was a teacher who played cricket, not a cricketer who taught. As with Robert, that VCA dinner was his swansong. Although Keith Stackpole, during his speech, predicted that Sheahan would succeed him as Victorian captain, he retired soon after and never played first-class cricket again.

Nevertheless, Sheahan remembers one partnership with Robert. This was in 1972, in Adelaide. South Australia was always kind to Sheahan, he said wryly. 'There was South Australia and the rest!' Many of his centuries came against the side that included the Chappell brothers and Ashley Mallett. He made another one that day in 1972, during a second-innings fightback with Robert. Sheahan, 'batting with absolute arrogance', according to one reporter, made 154. When I asked him if this was his highest score he hesitated for a moment before saying that he once made about 170. Checking this later, I discovered that Sheahan made 202 against South Australia in 1966/67. Has any other cricketer in history ever forgotten his highest score or making a double century? I liked him more and more.

It was during this four-hour opening partnership that Sheahan was struck by Robert for the first time. Hitherto

Sheahan, six years older than Robert, was hardly aware of him. They had little in common. As Sheahan put it, they liked different books and different parties. But as the innings wore on he had a chance to appraise Robert's style. He was more impressed by his temperament than he was by his technique. 'He wasn't the finest player in terms of fluency,' Sheahan observed. This surprised me a little. Defensively, I remembered all those mirrored boundaries of the future. 'Technique will take you only so far,' Sheahan added. What struck him was Robert's determination. It certainly must have been a dogged innings. Robert took five hours to make 94. Fast bowling didn't intimidate him. 'He was pretty fearless,' said Sheahan. 'He was the sort of person you wanted to have in the trenches with you.'

Sheahan told me that after this match he and Robert 'found a friendship', a nice way of describing these arbitrary bonds. He liked Robert's sense of humour. 'Because of his impishness you almost felt paternal towards him.' There was 'nothing malicious, nothing evil. He had a real innocence.' Without really knowing why, Sheahan wanted to help Robert. He was the sort of person you wanted to 'take under your wing' later on.

I asked Sheahan how Robert's accident affected his peers. 'It unnerved a lot of us,' he admitted. Even if people chose not to temper their behaviour, they suddenly understood one of the risks. I remembered a letter that Sheahan wrote to my parents in 1999, in which he recalled 'feeling devastated, along with many others, at the news of his car accident and its consequences. He was a lively young bloke and he always "pushed the envelope" which

132

in some ways might have led to his accident, but who of us can honestly say that we have not done things that might have left us in the same condition.'

I thanked Sheahan for giving me so much of his time. Before leaving I asked about one of his students whom I had read about the previous year. Just sixteen at the time, he had become a quadriplegic in a rugby accident. Sheahan told me about his slow recovery. We agreed that it must have been a terrible time for his family. Many of the students were greatly affected, too. I told Sheahan about the Robert Rose Foundation, which had just been launched to help people with spinal injuries.

Before visiting Melbourne Grammar I had discussed this boy's plight with a friend who has a son there. A brilliant organiser, she belongs to a school committee which the headmaster periodically addresses. At first she found Sheahan charming but intractable, a smooth and single-minded politician. One day he came to a meeting and told the mothers about the young quadriplegic's progress. As he spoke tears began running down his face. He made no attempt to check them and spoke with great feeling. My friend immediately respected him. For the first time she realised he was 'one of us'.

Two days after the celebratory dinner Robert came home for the first time since the accident. Getting him out of the car was an awkward, even traumatic business. We had to bend his neck to free him. It felt incredibly stiff. Never having lifted Robert before, I was shocked by the sensation of those inert limbs.

Everyone was there that day. Mum made Robert's favourite dishes for lunch. Afterwards we sat on the terrace overlooking the creek. Dad set up a portable television so that Robert could watch the football. Visitors kept arriving. Eventually Robert became sore and we laid him on the sofa in the living room. I took photographs of him. He is propped up on his side, facing the camera. He smiles at us wonderfully, encouraging us all. Terry, seated behind him, balances Salli on more pillows. Terry's expression swings from relief to resignation. Salli is innocent of all the consequences.

It was only after we lifted Robert back into the car and they set off for the hospital that I surrendered to some new phase of sorrow and tenderness. I went inside and wept. No amount of congenial Sundays would ever mitigate the horrors of Robert's condition. Thinking about his helplessness, I wondered if he would be able to bear it. I felt sure I couldn't.

Even Sammy, the doting dachshund, seemed to feel it. From that day on, the minute Robert was driven away after one of his visits, this most companionable of dogs would move promptly to the back door and insist on being let out. We could never lure her from the kennel on those Sundays.

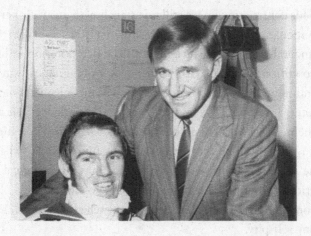

After the VCA dinner Robert's life began to change appreciably. As his health improved he gained more freedom. With daily physiotherapy he could almost lift his left hand to his mouth, while his right arm got halfway up his chest. Although he never regained movement in his hands, soon, with the aid of a brace, he could feed himself, smoke a cigarette and turn the pages of a newspaper.

Unbeknown to Dr Burke, Dad had engaged the services of a chiropractor. Everyone was becoming frustrated with the Austin's conservative methods and their effect on Robert's morale. The young chiropractor used a spoon to gauge Robert's reflexes and seemed impressed by the results. I noticed that even while the chiropractor examined him and speculated about his future mobility, Robert went on watching the football on television.

The following Saturday, Dad took Robert to training. There is a photograph of him sitting near the boundary. This confronting image still takes my breath away. Robert, wincing in the sunlight, is thin, twisted and clearly uncomfortable in his neck brace. The deterioration in his condition is graphic. A few diehards (only fanatics watch training) talk among themselves. Dad brought Robert home later. I was amazed by his courage and patience. 'He is the master of his condition. It does not seem to upset him any more. I often think it must attack him at night, when he is alone, but he betrays no sign of this.' We watched a cricket programme containing footage of some of his old companions. Robert chuckled as he watched them, without any self-pity.

One month after his first outing, Robert was permitted to stay overnight at Crosby Drive. We had never put him to bed before. This was a complicated procedure and everyone was involved. The old bedroom, with its countless trophies and photographs of Robert, was full. It was like putting a French monarch to bed: the entire court was present. Even Sammy crept around, engrossed. I had never seen so many pillows. It took us a while to get used to dressing and undressing Robert. Being inanimate, he was difficult to manoeuvre. We were all frightened of dropping him. Finally we got him onto the bed and propped him on his side. I hated having to bend his legs and expected them to snap. Ensuring that he was comfortable and that there was no risk of pressure sores was a complicated business, though we had watched orderlies do it a hundred times. Dad, strong as a bullock, was patience itself, puffing away conscientiously.

But it would take years of practice before we got it right.

Robert now had a catheter in his bladder. By day he wore a leg bag. We disconnected this at night and let the catheter drain into a bucket beside the bed. I emptied the urine into the toilet, noting the colour for any sign of infection, then sterilised the bag. In those days Robert had to be turned during the night to prevent chafing. Terry and I were meant to turn him at 2 a.m. Unfortunately I slept through the alarm and Robert remained on his side for six hours. This was dangerous, as he already had some red marks—constant stigmata in his new life. We all laughed about it in the morning. 'Sleep well, thicko?' Robert inquired.

Then there were suppositories. Robert no longer had control over his bowel movements. Every second day suppositories were inserted in his rectum to generate a movement. This could take one or two hours. When it was about time we sat him on a commode with a towel around his waist. Robert hated this and felt intensely uncomfortable. The whole household waited. 'Any action yet?' someone would call out from the kitchen. 'No—false alarm,' came the response. This was the bit we had all tacitly dreaded, Robert probably more than anyone. Sometimes people had to leave the room for a few deep breaths. But my parents handled this unpleasant chore superbly, going about their work briskly and cheerfully, never betraying impatience or squeamishness. Twenty years after rearing him, they were nursing their first-born again. After it was over, we showered Robert on his commode, cleaning his bottom, shampooing his hair.

We quickly learned what Robert could and couldn't wear. Anything tight-fitting was forbidden: belts, collars, ties, underwear. Denim was too harsh on his skin: soft, baggy trousers were desirable. Shoelaces had to be loose, otherwise the circulation in his feet was reduced. Even on non-suppository days it took a couple of hours to get Robert up, from the awakening slice of toast to the final lift into his chair. Some days things didn't go according to plan: no sooner had he arisen than his bowels would work and the ritual would start all over again.

Robert went to the chiropractor's office for more X-rays. Consulting the Austin's set was out of the question. Dad began investigating other types of therapy. Any lead, and there were many, was explored. Robert remained hopeful but passive. I was more sceptical about chiropractic in those days and doubted the value of these weekend manipulations. One day the chiropractor brought along a colleague and I became uneasy as they fiddled with Robert's neck. Later Robert told me that one of them had said there was a remote chance that he might walk again. I thought this encouragement was tactless.

One evening these desperate remedies caused a scene. There was a gathering at Crosby Drive. Robert wasn't there. One of the guests was Tony Capes, the Footscray vice-president. Capes was witty and urbane. He and my mother, both passionate about music, were fast friends. Capes began to rhapsodise about his greatest passion—Wagner. 'Who are *they*?' I asked. I thought that Wagner must have been one of Robert's bands, like Marmalade or Cream. Capes's derisive expression taught me the meaning of the term faux pas.

Capes was also a doctor. When Dad told him about the X-rays he became upset. He defended the Austin and said it was the best place for Robert. Quackish distractions would only harm Robert. I don't think we used the word denial in 1974, but Capes said that my parents were resorting to chiropractors because they hadn't accepted Robert's condition and were still deceiving themselves that he might walk again. Robert had regained some movement because the bruising around his spinal cord had receded, but there was no chance of a full recovery.

Strangely enough, I had never nursed any such delusions. Ever since the accident I had accepted that Robert's paralysis was irrevocable. Full recovery was a physical, even an ontological impossibility. It was as if we were talking about two different people—the athlete and the cripple. The former was dead, unrevivable. That's what haunted me.

People became terribly upset, Tony Capes included. My parents broke down, as if they were receiving the news all over again. I had seen this coming. Our emotional lives were volatile, ungovernable. There were waves of acceptance, even optimism, followed by rejection and despair. People rallied, then grieved. One night—it may have been after Capes's outburst—I went out into the garden to get away from the others and wept so convulsively I became frightened. I knew I had reached the nadir of sadness. Battling to control myself, I focussed on the night noises, the banter from nearby households, happily unaware of our dilemmas, the occasional whimper from my attentive dachshund, mystified by my vigil in the garden. It was cold out there, but I knew I had to outstare this mood—confront it, survive it. In order to live I would have to accept Robert's affliction. But how to cope after a morbid adolescence? How to survive with this unshakeable sense of annihilation?

Gradually I composed myself and in doing so crossed an emotional Rubicon. At some deep, inexpressive level, I resolved never to allow myself to become that upset again. I would never collapse. I would never futilely suffer in the garden. Hysteria didn't help Robert or my parents. Someone had to stay calm and objective and I was going to be it. I would try to be strong. I would even try to be good, god help me. Even if people thought me a bastard, a monster of detachment, I would never weep like that again. I would cope.

My father was exhausted. Footscray was doing well and seemed likely to reach the final five, as it was then configured, but Dad wasn't in good shape. Other people must have been worried about him too, for it was decided that the two of us should go away for a few days. Friends lent us their house by the sea. We played tennis each day. I can still remember the exact scores. I won each contest, including a 4-6, 6-4, 10-8 marathon. Dad must have been worn out! As always, I relished each victory and replayed crisp forehands and rare aces in my head until the next game. At night we drank unaccustomed liqueurs and I smoked cigars. Dad started one of our intimate conversations. He was worried about my unsociability, my lack of a girlfriend. He said he would have to take me away on a footy trip. I let that one go through to the keeper, to mix my metaphors.

June, seismic already, ended eventfully. Robert became

a journalist with the *Sunday Press*, a new tabloid. The *Age* and the *Herald* had finally relented and formed an alliance to combat the *Sunday Observer*. Sales of Newton's rag had continued to rise since February. Evidently headlines like 'MY BILL'S NOT A HOMO' appealed to the burghers of Melbourne as they prepared for Sunday worship.

Ian McDonald, sports editor of the *Sunday Press*, hired Robert to write a story about his accident, followed by a weekly column on cricket and football. 'My Story' was compelling. Robert's natural candour and lack of pretension made him a winning subject. Possibly surprised, I noted in my journal: 'It was quite neat, personal'. Robert talked about the accident, as much as he could remember of it, and about his first night in hospital. He described his daily regimen and said he felt stronger all the time. He cited the sudden improvement in his right arm, aided by twice-daily sessions in the gymnasium. He was typically self-deprecating. 'Last week I put my finger in my mouth accidentally. As an achievement it was a little difficult to swallow, but it represented a small milestone.' He said he had enjoyed going to a training session and a subsequent game, but not the attention that went with it. 'I went into the dressing rooms after the game and the feeling was tremendous. I would have preferred to stay in the background, but they pushed me forward and clapped and all that. Dad couldn't believe I was still there—he thought I would have been back in bed by then.'

I well remember Robert's reluctance to encroach on the players' limelight—I can almost feel the traction of his modesty—for I was the one pushing him.

Robert was looking forward to getting out of hospital and to spending more time with Salli. 'I find it upsetting that I can't even pick her up. That hurts a lot. It'll be better when I get home. She's good, Salli. Already she seems to be used to the wheelchair and everything.' Speculating about a future career, he said he would make a good runner for Dad. He would have been faster than Uncle Colin, Dad's slightly portly runner at Collingwood, whose profane interpretations of the coach's messages were legendary among the players.

I was particularly struck by one passage, which I recorded in my journal:

> My greatest task lay in staying happy. It becomes a deliberate task and you must work at it. Not because you don't mean it but just because it needs a hell of a lot of concentration and effort. It's funny, but at some point there's a changeover of responsibilities. Suddenly you find you are responsible in a way to the people caring for you and you have to look after their morale almost as much as they care for you. Your family is caring for you so much they become pretty vulnerable themselves, while you are learning to cope better each day. So it means I have as much of an obligation to them as to myself to keep up my morale.

I was moved by his compassion, his intuition. I realised there was something formidable about what Robert was becoming.

As always, these developments were offset by physical complications. Predictions that Robert would be out of hospital in two months proved illusory. He wouldn't leave hospital until the end of November, nine and a half months after the accident. In the meantime, he was beset by new problems. He began taking medication for postural hypotension. Most paraplegics and quadriplegics suffer from spasms—involuntary movements that occur when they are lifted or turned and that can propel them from their wheelchairs. With Robert, these spasms were particularly acute, perhaps because of his sporting past: a frame that had been used to constant exercise. He likened them to severe cramp. He was especially vulnerable in bed. Spasms often happened while he was being dressed or undressed. These tremors locked his limbs, making it impossible to continue. The danger was that he would be thrown to the floor, breaking a leg or a hip. He soon required massive doses of Valium—as much as 90 milligrams per day. Later this was reduced to 60 milligrams, still a phenomenal amount. I once took 20 milligrams and slept for twenty-four hours.

Valium was just one of the drugs Robert needed to go on functioning. I forget most of the other names. Brands came and went, but not Robert's reliance on drugs. Four times a day we heaped a dozen pills onto a spoon and held it up for his approval. Robert knew every drug in his pharmacopoeia and would often point out a rogue pill. When he was convinced, he gulped them all down at once with a huge draught of water.

Urinary infection was a constant risk. Robert drank

copious amounts of water as a matter of course—several litres daily. Nevertheless, he began to suffer bladder infections. His catheter would block, stopping the flow of urine and causing great discomfort. Flushes and spasms heralded these attacks. They happened at any hour of the day or night. Often we had to rush him back to hospital so that his catheter could be changed. A sphincterotomy, in which the sphincter of the bladder is partly severed to ensure better emptying, was recommended, but Robert rejected this. Dr Burke believes that he feared a loss of his residual sexual function if he had the operation. Robert, in his quiet way, was beginning to manage his own health and to keep his own counsel.

In July the phantom pains in Robert's paralysed limbs were succeeded by real pain in his thumbs. With the new movement in his hands came acute discomfort. Dressing Robert or slipping on the wrist brace was an anxious business. Robert recoiled in agony whenever we touched his thumbs. His cries and recriminations were unnerving.

While we waited for his release, work started at Crosby Drive. The games room underneath my parents' house was converted into a small flat. Uncle Kevin removed the old table-tennis table in his van. Meanwhile, Robert's weekly articles began appearing in the *Sunday Press*. He got on well with his collaborator, Joe Fairhurst, a seasoned sports writer from England. Joe visited Robert during the week then went away and wrote up the story. Robert loved the challenge, and the diversion. His own connections and regular hospital visits from leading sportsmen, complemented by Dad's contacts, gave Robert an advantage over other sports writers. This inside knowledge resulted in several scoops. But there was more to his journalism than just headlines. Robert had real sporting acumen, an older man's understanding of the athlete's psyche. Hospitalisation had also sharpened his encyclopedic memory and zeal.

In hindsight, Robert's articles were punchy. At times they were downright provocative. I wonder now, rereading them, how his old team-mates reacted. Robert didn't shirk controversy or soften his criticisms because of old allegiances. He was quick to suggest that a certain player should be rested or cajoled or promoted, and another one cleared to Coventry. He was impressed by courage and flair, and scornful of lapses or timidity. I like his acid tone, typified by this verdict on his old coach Neil Mann: 'Neil's a good coach in certain respects, but he wouldn't be the best speaker in the world. Neil doesn't go in much for tactical talk during a final. When I played he left us very much to our own designs.' Robert 'couldn't suppress a smile' when Murray Weideman, never known for his exuberance at training while playing for Collingwood, succeeded Mann as coach and began laying down the law. 'A little bird tells me the Magpies won't take too kindly to the six-day plan, or to Murray Weideman for that matter.' One week Robert attended a function for sports writers. The article begins, 'A funny thing happened to me on the way to the Victorian Football Writers' Soiree the other night'. He is photographed next to Kevin Sheedy, who had just won an award. Lou Richards compered the show, as Robert noted: 'I must say I've enjoyed Lou's quips, jibes and witticisms more since the accident, because I can assure you while I was playing footy he always got on my pip.'

Robert was prepared, or encouraged, to write about personal subjects. He devotes one article to our father. 'I've a lot of time for Bob Rose. He's the man I always hoped I'd grow up to be. Ours has always been more of a friendship than the usual father and son relationship.' Robert also wrote about his old mate Trevor Laughlin, a deliberate, and successful, attempt to bring him to the notice of the Victorian selectors. Celebrating Trevor's loyalty, he talked about 'a different kind of love...the bond existing between two blokes that some may call queer, some unhealthy and most will hide with embarrassed smiles'.

The rest of us muddled along. The pattern of hospital visits and weekend outings was unchanged. We saw more of Salli, who was growing up precociously. I enjoyed my new avuncular role. 'What's that?' Salli demanded like a staccato doll. I named things for her and watched her fascinated reactions. She was delighted by her first moon and by her debut on my old recorder. I thought I would like to have a child of my own one day. Sometimes I wondered how Robert reacted to my being able to frolic with Salli while he was immobile.

Barbara married an academic and promptly announced that they were moving to the United States. I knew I would miss her immensely and decided to visit them at the end of the year. One of our last outings as an unconventional family was to a fundraising benefit for Robert. I was unnerved by one of the acts, a drag queen named Stan Munro, but I did

146

enjoy one pouting line: 'You don't really think Mick Jagger got those lips sucking strawberries!'

Footscray, with a late surge, made the finals for the first time in many years, only to be quietly eliminated by Collingwood. Encouraged by their late-season form and by the likely recruitment of the South Australian champion Neil Sachse, Dad decided to stay on as coach. Mum, as before, would have preferred him to stop.

Our emotional instability produced moments of strain and euphoria. One morning Robert and I were joking with each other as I gave him breakfast in bed. I said he had a cheek expecting to be fed just because he was a cripple. It was one of those stupid jests that die on your lips, staining them. We looked at each other, then went on talking, but that silence was terrible. Why did the word 'cripple' intimidate us so? Robert understood the innocence of my remark, but also the everlasting tragedy of it. Later Terry told me he had cried all the previous night, and I felt even worse. Robert didn't get up that day. He told me he was going through a silly period and decided not to attend a family function he had been looking forward to for some time. But everyone's mood improved next day. Robert had a visit from Jack Ryder, simply 'The King', still ramrod and immaculate at eighty-five. Ryder had played in Collingwood's first district match in 1906 and had made 295 in 245 minutes when Victoria hit 1107 against New South Wales twenty years later. I took photographs of him with Robert.

That evening, about to take Robert back to the hospital, Terry accidentally put the car into reverse and slammed into a brick wall. Anyone standing behind her, as we often did when seeing them off, would have been killed. No one was hurt, but Terry became distraught and Salli howled in her harness. Robert stayed amazingly calm. I began to hate cars and all the misery they caused. Some nights, when A. drove me home late, often stoned, in his white Volkswagen, I became petrified and fully expected to be paralysed in an accident. I hyperventilated, but said nothing.

My mood fluctuated, like Terry's driving. I often became morose at night: the old death wish. I was reading Conrad again, including the incomparable *Nostromo*, and was much affected by Martin Decoud's nihilism. I often quoted Conrad's 'We, living, are out of life'.

Nor was I alone in my despondency. One day Mum and I agreed, innocuously enough, that the year was flashing by. Then she said she wished that time would go even faster. The casual bleakness of it haunted me. Nevertheless, Mum returned to work for the first time since December.

Robert somehow rose above it all. Terry and I took him to one of the last games of the year and sat with him inside the fence. I wrote in my journal, 'I felt very close to him, but was saddened as I watched him. But then, he is stronger than anyone.'

Still, there were lifelines of sorts. A. and I continued to circle each other warily. After a woefully anonymous year and a half at university—'always slightly veiled'— I began making new friends, largely because of a riotous ethics tutorial on Tuesdays. My studies were shambolic. I read all the wrong texts and had the deductive skills of an ant. Why didn't someone advise me to suspend my course until the next year? (Perhaps because they didn't know what had happened.) Why didn't I think of it myself? Logic, so liberating the previous year, addled my brain, but I loved reading the Greeks and thinking about ethics. I was seduced by Hamlet's indecision and often quoted the sweet prince on Tuesday afternoons—'There is nothing either good or bad, but thinking makes it so'. My new friends also wearied of my other motto, one picked up from Tolstoy: 'If man must die, what even is truth?'

We were a lively if undisciplined bunch. Whole days were spent in the dopey 'caf'. We would meet at breakfast, stay for lunch, then move on to our hotel in the afternoon. We often missed lectures; sometimes we forgot exams. Assessment was a controversial issue that year at Monash—why, I can't remember. By a large majority the students sought its abolition. The vice-chancellor, not surprisingly, demurred. Agitators promptly occupied the administration building. It stayed occupied for more than a week. Sir John Monash's bust acquired Mickey Mouse ears, and portraits of Che Guevara replaced those of the obstinate vice-chancellor. Mum woke me one morning and inquired if I intended to go rabble-rousing today, and how would I like my eggs. After rare lectures and tutorials we visited the siege for thin coffee and revolutionary gossip. Never, perhaps, has so much fornication happened in a vice-chancellor's office. I felt terribly grown up. Finally, inevitably, the police appeared and seventy-four students were arrested.

Throughout all this I never mentioned Robert or his illness. None of my comrades knew about my family. I preferred to uphold my alien status. When I took my new friends home there would be a surprised thud of recognition, that is if they knew anything about sport, which many of them didn't. (I marvelled at the thought of a life without sport.) Fanatical or not, my female friends all adored Dad, the most charming of men.

As the year wore on, and exams and essays loomed, my lassitude increased. I found it impossible to study in our new, noisy household. I began to hate the tyranny of sport—the endless broadcasts, the idiotic commentaries and post-match analyses. Robert, naturally, could watch whatever he liked. Sometimes two or three televisions and radios were going simultaneously. I hated being shushed during horse races. I loathed the jockeys, the contest—I even hated the bloody horses. I withdrew and played Velvet Underground very loud to block out the hysterical commentators. Other times, when Robert was confined to bed, I knew I should go in and see him, but often I didn't. What on earth would we talk about? One of my English tutors, a snooty Blakean, told us that all undergraduates should live away from home. She was of course right. But flight, even if I had been ready for it, would have been indefensibly selfish.

So I began to feel guilty and resentful at the same time. Robert, especially when morose, was demanding. Always anxious about the next lift or dosage, he could be quite tetchy. We were all doing far too much lifting in those days. Hoists, now mandatory, weren't available then. By October I had permanently damaged my back. Because I was still wary of chiropractic—especially the final neck adjustment, which would surely be paralysing—I tried to conceal my injury. It would also have been outrageous to complain. My back ached, but not as keenly as Robert's thumbs. His comfort was paramount. We all knew we were close to an affliction we couldn't comprehend. We circled this ordinary and extraordinary force-field. It was centripetal, irresistible. Robert sat there in his wheelchair and even when he was comfortable, even when there was no crisis, even when the wretched nags were turning into the straight and everyone was willing them on, all our thoughts somehow veered towards him. Living on like that, bizarrely, sufferingly, Robert alone mattered.

I was becoming aware of the creeping ambivalence, the feelings of unease and inadequacy that arise when you care for someone as seriously disabled as Robert. You start to feel unworthy just because you move freely, or loathe the trots, or want to drift. I wasn't alone in this, but I probably thought I was, for we never discussed it as a family. Perhaps 1974 wasn't the right year for me to ponder philosophical notions of duty and altruism, egoism and responsibility. Then again, maybe it was.

Minor things irritated me. John Bayley, in one of his books about his wife, Iris Murdoch, stated that, unlike the many disagreeable tasks he had to perform when caring for the senile novelist, feeding her was always enjoyable. He said it gave him pleasure. This surprised me. Mum liked feeding Robert (it was the most overt way of nourishing him), but I always found it vaguely repellent spooning soup or sausage and mash into his waiting mouth. Fortunately Robert was able to feed himself with the aid of a wrist brace, but it was obviously quicker for us to feed him and we often did. I was always glad when it was over. I'm sure Robert didn't enjoy being fed either. He ate far too quickly as a consequence, gulping down the soup—sighing if I was too slow, even sucking it through a straw if it was thin enough—and swallowing whole biscuits or sandwiches rather than biting them in half. I used to worry about it. 'You'll choke,' I'd warn him. 'Just like good old Mama Cass,' he'd quip. He went on masticating and never choked. He always thanked us at the end of each course, just as he did when we emptied his urine bag or removed his faeces. He never forgot.

Bayley's first book impressed me as a study in eccentric devotion. The second one I found more troubling. I still wonder about the propriety of writing such a book about a living spouse, however famous or senile. Isn't it otiose, even gratuitous? I have no intention of writing a second book about Robert. I'm not even sure I should be writing the first. What would Robert have made of my essay in fraternal juxtaposition? Would he have liked my tentative portrait? Would he have approved? Would he have tried to stop me? And how would Iris Murdoch have reacted had she suddenly, miraculously, recovered from Alzheimer's disease? Would she have resented her spouse's affectionate promulgation of her descent into infantilism? And what of Bayley's motives? Did the writing comfort him as Iris sank into vacancy?

And what is *my* true motive (if I can be said to have formulated one)? Am I perpetuating my brother's memory, which is what our father believes and perhaps why he is so enthusiastic about my book? Am I writing it for Salli, and

152

Lachlan Robert, the grandson Robert didn't live to see? Am I trying to reveal the essential Robert, the latent messenger in the *Herald* editorial? Or am I trying to impose a version of him on the public, unconsciously distorting what really happened? Do I still need to recognise my brother, as in the dream? Do I crave *his* recognition? Is it atonement for things left unsaid and undone?

In all likelihood Robert would have ignored my book, while politely asking about the reviews. His interest in my career was genuine, but the writing itself never interested him. We never talked about my work, other writers, or the books I published at Oxford University Press, excepting two companions to cricket and sport in which he and my father featured.

Yet while I was writing this book a family friend told me something that gave me pause. Laurie Adamson got to know Robert well after the accident. They shared a passion for parties and a sardonic sense of humour. When I asked Laurie for some general impressions, he said that Robert was proud of my poetry but couldn't understand it. He added that Robert was distressed by my poem 'I Recognise My Brother in a Dream'. This surprised me. I don't recall us ever discussing my poem, although I dedicated it to Robert and gave him a copy of my first collection, in which it appeared. Should I be touched or contrite?

In October 1974 Robert developed his first serious bedsore, the quadriplegic's curse, or one of them. It kept him in bed for several weeks, delaying his departure from hospital. The only way to get rid of pressure sores is to stay off the affected

153

area, usually the buttocks. Finally, on 29 November, Robert was discharged from the Austin. Again he went straight to West Heidelberg, a much shorter drive.

Three days later I flew to Greece. In hindsight, it was one of the best things I have ever done. In my green and cloistered state, the challenge was overdue. Although I had always regarded myself as self-reliant, this isolation was entirely new. There I was on a chilly Monday morning, standing in the middle of Syntagma Square with no map, no Greek, no contacts, no itinerary, no reservation, just an outsize suitcase full of novels by Henry James and Tobias Smollett. I was on my own at last. But I loved the deracination: the not knowing and the not being known. I found a hostel and went straight to the Acropolis. In those days you could still wander through the Parthenon. Behind the Erechtheum an urchin was nonchalantly kicking a feral cat to death. I suddenly felt very foreign. Otherwise, it was a thrilling time to be in Greece. The tyrannical colonels had just been overthrown. Near the Athens Polytechnic, where eighty students had been gunned down during the uprising, walls and pavements were still pocked with bullet marks. Five days after my arrival, Greeks overwhelmingly supported the abolition of the monarchy in a referendum. Like the Athenians, I stayed up all night, drifting from one packed square to another, excited by the republican euphoria.

This exposure to Greek sculpture and architecture, at the Acropolis and the National Archaeological Museum, was seminal. I had come late to art. Before going to Europe I had never been inside a gallery. Although I would go on to title one of my poetry collections *Donatello in Wangaratta*, after an equally formative experience when I was six, the title poem—about a chance glimpse of a reproduction of Donatello's sculpture of David in an encyclopedia, which occasioned a shock of sexual recognition, however furtive— was accidental. (A few readers, struck by my unlikely title, expressed surprise that Wangaratta owned a Donatello. I didn't like to tell them that it didn't even possess an art gallery when I lived there.)

After Greece I went to Italy, where I formed a passion for painters such as Titian, Poussin, Raphael, della Francesca and the incomparable Giovanni Bellini. Somehow, mystifyingly, they changed my godless life. I would never be so content as when looking at a Bellini.

In Paris I pounced on my first English newspaper in four weeks. Arrested by *The Times*'s headline— 'CYCLONE DESTROYS AUSTRALIAN CITY'—I phoned home to find out if Melbourne was still intact. Reuters Rose was predictably informative, and I heard all about Gough Whitlam's summer of discontent. Mum also told me about Robert's belated arrival at Crosby Drive a few days before Christmas. Still prostrated with bedsores, he had been driven home on a mattress in Uncle Kevin's van. It sounded ghastly, but at least he was home. There was talk of taking him to Sydney in the new year to consult some American doctors.

Mum's ordeal wasn't over yet. In January her beloved sister died during a seemingly minor operation. I was staying with Barbara and her husband, Leo, in Columbus, Ohio, when I received the letter. I wondered how Mum

155

would endure this further loss. My aunt's death and the impending anniversary of Robert's accident weighed on me. I had inherited my mother's dismalness about certain dates. In Mexico I became acutely homesick, despite my thrilled response to the great revolutionary mural art of Diego Rivera and his school.

Earlier, in Venice, I had ruminated about Robert. One chilly evening I sat in St Mark's Square writing in my journal during the *passeggiata*. Guiltily, I thought about how different 1974 had been for both of us. For me it was turning out to be the boldest year of my life; for Robert it had been catastrophic. I questioned my seeming acceptance of what had happened after those first few terrible months. I regretted the intermittent tension between us and was troubled by my ambiguous relations with Robert. I spoke of 'the disease of detachment'. I also recorded a typical dream I had had about Robert, in which he died horribly after an epic ordeal.

I was back in Ohio on St Valentine's Day. It was freezing outside, and Barbara was heavily pregnant, so we stayed inside talking and drinking coffee. Whenever we turned on a chat show Truman Capote seemed to be on, puffy and incoherent. Turning the tables on Barbara, I told her about all the theatre I had seen in London, another wonderful discovery. We discussed Terry's new life with Robert and the challenge of staying with a seriously disabled partner. One weekend Leo drove us to Washington and we talked incessantly. Leo's small car filled with cigarette smoke, which made me nostalgic. Then it was time for a final rapt week alone in New York.

I still remember my powerful feelings of ambivalence as I flew over Melbourne and all the remembered suburbs. Helen Garner put it neatly in a recent essay about returning to Melbourne after several years in Sydney: 'And had it really always been so...flat?' Again I felt guilty, but immediately began planning my next escape.

Back home I read Robert's 'Black Valentine' article in the *Sunday Press* in which he talked frankly about his marriage, not fathering more children, and his gratitude to his family and friends. Referring to Terry, he wrote:

> Our love must wait in the shadows, waiting, needing but with only a glimmer of hope of fulfilment. I've often looked at Terry during these impossible 12 months in sheer admiration. If any woman's love for her man has been put to the test it is hers. She has nursed me, dressed me, comforted me and completely belied her 21 years in showing a maturity and utter understanding of the situation. I long to hold her, to feel her love, to show her my devotion and appreciation, but of course I can't. And I must confess that has to be the worst part of my being confined to a wheelchair. That and the knowledge that I will never be able to pick up my daughter.

He tries but fails to remember the accident:

> I suppose the brain blocks out moments of severe suffering. I do remember the doctor telling me I

would never walk again, but I didn't believe him and even now I won't fully accept that kind of thinking. I can't quite describe those first awful months in the Austin Hospital...Since the accident my emotional senses have become more acute and I find myself falling into pits of depression. Not that I'm grumbling. On the contrary, it has taken this accident to make me realise the importance of my family and my true friends.

Without his friends, he said, he would have gone mad and thrown in the towel—'like a few of those blokes at the Austin who asked to die rather than live with hell'. Robert was already aware of the measures that some quadriplegics take to end their suffering. He never mentioned this to the rest of us, but he told Dad about the suicides, usually by starvation, one of the few available methods.

In the accompanying photograph, taken in the courtyard outside their new flat, Robert looks as cheerful as ever but much more healthy. His hair is long and dark, and he has a lush beard. Salli, almost two, perches on his knees, while Sammy occupies her usual spot by Robert's left wheel, within patting distance. Robert concludes: 'In any event I am lucky...which is more than I thought possible on St Valentine's Day, 1974'.

The flat, known as the bunker, was small but functional. The aim had been to create a private space for the young family. They had their own entrance and could come and go as they wished. The flat comprised a tiny kitchen, formerly the bar. The bathroom was large enough for Robert to be showered on his commode. A partition divided the living area from the bedroom, which was directly beneath mine. There wasn't enough room for Salli, so she slept in Robert's old bedroom upstairs. I often minded her and took her to Monash. I taught Robert how to play chess. He rapidly mastered it, being quick-witted, but our games never had the élan of earlier boisterous contests. An old family friend dropped in for a weekly game to alleviate the pressure on Terry. In April there was a party to celebrate her twenty-first birthday. 'Happy Majority!' I wrote on the card.

Once a week Terry loaded her brood into the car and drove to Berwick so that the persistent chiropractor could attempt to 'unkink' Robert's spinal cord. This was unavailing. The pain in his thumbs remained acute. Eventually a surgeon would divide a nerve in his right thumb to lessen the pain, but this was still eighteen months away. Otherwise Robert's health continued to stabilise. A district nurse called every morning to assist Terry. Robert grew fond of Ruth, who struck me as very perceptive. There were other visitors. Robert's old mates stayed loyal, with a couple of notable exceptions. Two of his closest friends, both prominent sportsmen, began to stay away and eventually disappeared forever. We all thought this unforgivable, but Robert never mentioned it. When I criticised one of them, Robert shut me up decisively. I don't recall him ever impugning anyone for not visiting him. He was always delighted to see or hear from people, but I don't think he took it for granted.

Joe Fairhurst visited Robert every Wednesday to research their next article. The two of them sat in the courtyard swapping ideas. Their partnership was proving fruitful. Because sportsmen trusted Robert and because he spoke their language, he was able to break several major stories, including Bill Lawry's retirement from cricket and the renewed strife at Collingwood.

Worse followed in April 1975, resulting in Robert's saddest scoop. The football season had commenced. Robert had already devoted one article to Dad's star recruit, Neil Sachse. In mid-April, Robert and Joe Fairhurst chose, not altogether wisely, to write an article called 'War of the Roses' about the forthcoming match between Footscray and Fitzroy, now coached by Kevin Rose. This was only the second time that brothers had coached opposing League sides. Beneath a photograph of a delighted Robert separating his sparring elders, Dad and Uncle Kevin ham it up relentlessly:

Kevin: Defeat? I'm not sure what that word means. It's not in my dictionary, but you might be able to tell me something about it.

Bob: Yes, I notice you don't like losing when we play tennis.

Kevin: You can't remember the last time you beat me at tennis. You're on dodgy ground there, better stick to football.

I was at the Western Oval the following Saturday, sitting with the Footscray wives; Robert and Terry were elsewhere in the grandstand, in a separate enclosure. I have no idea who won the game. It didn't matter in the end. Neil

Sachse had starred in his first few games. This particular day he was dominant, especially in the third quarter. I can still see him lowering his head and charging into a pack near the boundary just below us. He seemed to lose his footing and ran straight into a Fitzroy defender's hip. He fell to the ground. I can still recall the silence that followed—the sort of eerie, slightly bewildered calm that descends on a football crowd when a player is knocked out. The trainers started waving for a stretcher. Neil's wife, Janyne, a nurse, got up and moved purposefully towards the rooms. I think we all knew that something terrible had happened. After the game word reached us that Neil had been paralysed in the collision and was now a quadriplegic. Someone pointed out that it had never happened to a League player before.

The atmosphere in the social club was desperate. Dad broke the news to Robert, who became distraught. Dad asked Terry to take him home in a cab. I have no idea if I accompanied them, for my journal contains no reference to the accident or its aftermath. This I find astonishing, but telling. I don't think I could write it down again. When Robert arrived home, he broke down completely. Mum hadn't seen him so upset since the unthinking nursing aide questioned his will to live. He said it was as if it had happened to him. They had to put him to bed and sedate him.

Dad, meanwhile, returned to the Austin. Dr David Burke, still in charge of the spinal injuries unit, recalled his arrival when I spoke to him at Ivanhoe Manor. 'I can remember your father coming in with a face as long as a barn door and saying, "Well, Dr Burke, here we go again".

They're the very words he said to me. And I thought, my god, poor man, he's been through it so recently.'

The irony that Neil Sachse's tragedy should also involve my father, less than a year after Robert's accident, wasn't lost on people. (Uncle Kevin's feelings, visiting Sachse in hospital after seeing Robert in that condition, but also as the coach of the guiltless Fitzroy player who had collided with Sachse, were equally keen.) Caringly, the *Sunday Observer* ran a story about the 'Rose Curse' in which an astrologer speculated about my father's malevolent stars.

We hadn't heard the last of that atrocious rag. A fortnight after the accident Robert sought permission to visit Sachse in Ward Seven. Dr Burke agreed, knowing that an interview had been arranged before the accident. On the Saturday night after the interview, Dr Burke received a late telephone call at home. It was Maxwell Newton. 'Dr Burke,' he blustered, 'I've been *scooped*!' He was furious that Robert had been given an exclusive interview. Manically, he accused Dr Burke of favouring the *Press* because he had once played amateur football with its editor. 'He went on and on about it,' Dr Burke remembers. He knew better than to retaliate. 'I had learned enough about the press over the years to know that you don't hang up on them, because that's the worst thing you can do. They'll crucify you. So I tried to argue with him reasonably. He went on for about an hour.'

Newton was desperate. Sales of the *Observer* had peaked and its finances were disastrous. It eventually folded in 1977 amid risible scenes. After a brief flutter with sex aids, Newton emigrated to the United States where he became a syndicated columnist and a financial adviser to the great and the good. Milton Friedman, the father of economic rationalism, much admired his business acumen.

Robert's article on Neil Sachse is affecting. On the front page there is a large photograph of Sachse in calipers above a smaller one showing Robert in the same posture the previous year. Robert, in the unaccustomed role of visitor, is sitting beside the bed. He quotes Sachse as saying, 'I've got no wrists...nothing at all...they just wobble around on the end of my arms'. Robert interviews both Neil and Janyne. They compare their experiences in the Austin. Robert notices that Neil has a television, which he wasn't permitted. He mentions the Sachses' two infant sons. Neil is philosophical about the accident. 'It was just one of those things...He came through...his hip and my head... And that was the end.' He dreams of getting out of bed and playing football again. His fracture was lower than Robert's. Already he had regained some movement in his arms, much earlier than Robert. He could even move one finger slightly.

What wasn't yet apparent was how much mobility Neil would regain. In time he returned to South Australia, achieved full independence with steadfast help from Janyne, and held several senior positions with charities. I saw the Sachses again recently, when Collingwood and Footscray contested the first Robert Rose Cup at Colonial Stadium. I sat with them at the dinner and heard about their grown-up sons' careers. Briskly, efficiently, almost imperceptibly, Janyne cut up the inevitable chicken breast for Neil. Dad had visited them a few weeks earlier to invite them to the function. Dad told me that Neil had wanted him to see a video of the collision at the Western Oval. I wondered how many times the Sachses had watched it since 1975.

A few weeks later Robert's career as a newspaperman came to an end. Incomprehensibly, some genius at the *Sunday Press* decided that they couldn't afford to pay two salaries for one weekly article. Robert joked about being sacked, but it was a blow to his morale. Having a job and income, regaining status, mixing with journalists, had transformed him. He thrived. Looking back, I am astonished that no other newspaper recruited him. Old stigmas and meanness had thwarted him, in the most heartless way.

Robert thought about becoming a commentator, and diligently practised during football games, but nothing came of this. His voice was too soft. Unlike the American actor Christopher Reeve, Robert never needed a respirator—at least not until he became ill—but he had very little lung-power. His cough was like a whisper.

Joe Fairhurst vividly recalled his visits to the bunker at Crosby Drive when I contacted him recently in England, where he now writes plays. He too was eventually discarded by the Murdoch press. He spoke of Robert and Terry with great affection and described Robert as one of the gutsiest blokes he had met during forty years of journalism. He rated my father as 'the greatest Australian I met in thirty years of living and working in Oz'.

Everything fell away after Neil Sachse's accident. The Footscray players, many of whom had followed Robert's progress closely, were traumatised by what had happened to Sachse. Some of them required sedatives before the next game. Dad recalls the toll it took. Laurie Sandilands, the captain, a close friend of Sachse, was particularly affected. Injuries were also a problem, but it was the Sachse factor that proved conclusive. The team's early good form faded. Midway through the season it was apparent that they wouldn't make the finals. Dad announced that he would resign at the end of the year. He wondered privately what he would do after coaching.

Morale at home was low. Everyone seemed unwell. The pressure on Dad, already enormous before Sachse's accident, was almost intolerable. His back was giving him trouble, though he would never admit this. In his thirties and forties he had twice had major spinal surgery, a legacy of a football injury. (One day, playing for the Wang Rovers, he had flown for a mark and landed on an inadequately covered concrete cricket pitch. The damage to his lower vertebrae was serious, almost crippling.) The constant lifting exacerbated his old injury. One way of coping was to stay out late from time to time. Terry fell off a pony, of all things, and broke her arm. We all joked that it was one way of avoiding a lift. Mum began to have chest pains. One night, very upset, she said to me that if I had any sense I would get away and move into a flat. A year after hurting my back, unable to straighten up, I relented and saw a chiropractor. Robert was still having periodic treatment.

At times it felt as though we were all crippled.

The situation seemed irreparable. I began to feel trapped—morally trapped. I turned to A., my Monash circle of friends, and poetry. Enspelled by Wordsworth,

165

I began writing mountains of nature poetry of unalleviated awfulness. During the winter of 1975 I wrote eighty-one poems—all bad. It must be some sort of a record. Befogged, I discovered St John of the Cross. One day in November I spent hours in the Medley Library reading his ecstatic poetry. On leaving the library I discovered that the entire campus was empty. Gough Whitlam had been dismissed during my reverie and everyone had decamped to the City Square.

The situation at home was deteriorating. Relations between Terry and Robert were precarious. I found his manner vexing: he was withdrawn and querulous. He went back to the Austin for a fortnight because of bladder infections, but also to afford Terry some relief. She was obviously depressed, at times hysterical. After one midnight altercation she drove off in her pyjamas. She came back, but Dad expected her to leave eventually. He and Mum began to prepare for life after the seemingly inevitable separation. Mum pointedly told me they were not including me in their plans.

In late November Robert and Terry flew to Brisbane as guests of the National Paraplegic and Quadriplegic Games Committee to help promote the forthcoming games. Their visit coincided with the first Test between Australia and the West Indies. Robert returned to the 'Gabba', where he had starred two years earlier. On the final day, accompanied by Ian Chappell, he was pushed onto the ground during the drinks break. As the crowd applauded him, Ian Redpath introduced him to the West Indies side. Robert and Terry stayed at the same hotel as the West Indians and spent a great deal of time with them. One photograph shows Robert relaxing with Michael Holding and a superbly sleek Gordon Greenidge. Robert, beardless now at Terry's behest, looks about eighteen.

We celebrated Christmas together. After a massive lunch I sunbaked and smoked my new pipe while reading *War and Peace*. Those were the days! Later I took Salli for a long walk to the park where we fed the horses. Two and a half years old, she had just had her first perm. She looked like a prize-winning Botticelli angel. I watched her romping around in the grass and knew that one phase of my life was coming to an end.

I had decided to share a house with A. We found one in East Hawthorn, just around the corner from Robert and Terry's old flat. Life, I would discover, is a small neighbourhood. My parents encouraged me at every turn. Dad helped me to move my few bits of furniture in Uncle Kevin's van. Salli went with us, excited at first. When it came time for them to leave she stared at me as I waved goodbye.

Where did I think I was going?

6

THE BUNKER

One of the things that surprised me about Robert's disability was the lack of change in his interests or outlook. His obsession with sport intensified, if anything. Having been imbued with the Rose ethos as a toddler, he now pushed it to the limit. Nothing else seemed to matter. Cricket, football, racing, golf—whatever was available, really—absorbed him. His dependence on sport was total. It fired his mind and filled his days. We had no choice but to indulge his addiction. Other forms of discourse felt unreal or elitist.

The only type of sport he avoided was that involving disabled people.

Robert looked forward to the weekend more than anything. Dad, keen for him to maintain his old friendships, always took him to a match. Before long, the sight of Dad pushing Robert through the crowd was very familiar. Robert's excitement before these outings was palpable, the anticipation intense and week-long. The mood when he got home, if Collingwood lost, was deathly. Victory, by contrast, induced a kind of boyish stream of consciousness. Robert would watch a replay of the entire match he had just seen. When it was over he wanted to relive highlights, umpiring anomalies and freakish statistics. In the end we all shut up and just let him talk. Even while we fed him pizza or put him to bed, he went on extolling the victors. Who were my top three players, he would ask me, even if I hadn't been there.

This cult of sport seemed to preclude other interests. Robert wasn't acquiring new skills or hobbies. Interviewed soon after the accident, he had mused, doubtless tongue-in-cheek, about learning to paint with his mouth, but he showed no interest in pursuing any of the activities suggested by occupational therapists. I often marvelled at how fundamentally unaltered he was by his new situation. It baffled me. How could anyone endure such torment and not be changed?

I mentioned this to Dr Burke at Ivanhoe Manor. Was he, too, surprised by Robert's abiding preoccupation with sport and his indifference to new pursuits?

Dr Burke became defensive and responded a little inconsequently, as if I had underestimated Robert's difficulties. He spoke about the courage it took to revisit the scene of his sporting successes. He said it demanded great character, especially in the early days. I agreed wholeheartedly. Dr Burke often saw his former patient at the MCG, pushed by Dad or myself. (The rest of us weren't members, so sometimes three or four of us would attach ourselves to Robert's wheelchair like benevolent barnacles. We were never stopped.)

I remembered those early forays: the gawking recognition of onlookers, the unmistakable suspicions about Robert's mental condition, the artless wonderment of children at the sight of his wheelchair, the silent helpfulness of others as we negotiated crowded spaces or lifted him up stairs. One day at the MCG, Senator John Button, then a federal minister, crouched down and took up some of the considerable weight, then moved on without a word. Most annoying to Robert were the clumsier expressions of compassion, such as when strangers, presuming that he was too imbecilic to speak, would peer at him and then ask Dad how he was—in himself. Robert always told them, emphatically. He had never suffered fools and he wasn't about to change. Now that Dad was no longer coaching, they started following Collingwood again. At Victoria Park every second fan wanted to commiserate with Robert or to ask about his health. He knew they meant well, but he saw no reason why he should tolerate inane or mawkish monologues, let alone people obscuring his view of the game. Crisply, curtly, he cut them off or told them to get out of the way. He became adept at ignoring people, and his withering looks were legendary. 'Let's get away from these peanuts,' he would mutter out of the corner of his mouth. Accustomed to Dad's unfailing courteousness, I was embarrassed by Robert's brusqueness. Dr Burke laughed when I mentioned Robert's temper. 'Oh yes, I know,' he said. 'I copped that a few times myself.'

Eventually Dr Burke addressed my earlier question.

'I don't think people who suffer a major disability with spinal cord injury really change as persons. Their interests remain much the same. There's no reason for them to change. Temporarily, yes. People do become depressed. People do change in the short-term. But that's a short-term issue. We usually say that it takes about two years for people to come to terms with their disability. You can be fooled by somebody who seems to be coping well after three months. They're not. They're hiding it. They're putting on a front.'

He was right of course. It was foolish of me to expect Robert to transform himself. Why should he? What did I expect him to become—a seer, a sociologist, a *poet*? Was I waiting for him to peer into the abyss and divine a cure for my own sense of futility and discontent?

Changing the subject, I told Dr Burke I had always assumed that Robert's adaptation to life in a wheelchair was aided by his robust physical condition before the accident. Dr Burke agreed, with one qualification: 'That sporting background, that ability to overcome pain and to get through something that's difficult physically, does help people who become disabled. There's no question about that. There's some sort of drive that other people perhaps don't have. But it can also be detrimental, because they realise how much they've lost.'

Dr Burke had a chance to assess Robert's recovery first-hand. In April 1976 Robert was readmitted to the Austin because of urinary complications. Again he declined to have a sphincterotomy.

I still saw much of my family after leaving home. Often I was glad to get away from my new and increasingly turbulent household. It was clear that relations between Robert and Terry were hopelessly strained. In retrospect, I'm amazed they didn't receive professional counselling. During those eighteen months no one suggested they should see a psychologist, a psychiatrist, a marriage counsellor or a sexual therapist. The weekly visit to the chiropractor was about it. It was up to them to smooth the myriad other kinks in their lives.

Years later I remarked on this deficiency to my mother. Why hadn't the authorities recognised Robert's plight and encouraged him to talk about his fears, his frustrations, his longings, even his dreams? Something, anyway. I now understand that a few years after Robert's accident, during a sojourn at the Austin, a psychiatrist did see him, only to conclude that he couldn't help him. I don't doubt that my brother would have been a stubborn patient, but surely something could have been done to break down that masochistic reserve. How could a young person in his condition be expected to go away and get on with his life without professional guidance? Normally wary of such analogies, I likened Robert's condition to that of a survivor of psychological torture or prolonged incarceration in a concentration camp. I wasn't trying to be melodramatic. It is impossible to exaggerate my brother's—any quadriplegic's—misery during the first few years after the accident. The grief was indescribable. We weren't psychologists. We couldn't play that role. We were far too close. Besides which, none of us was in very good shape either.

Mum agreed. She said we should *all* have been counselled. She remembered a pathetic session at the Austin shortly before Robert's discharge. A couple of young nurses tried to explain to her and Terry the rudiments of the daily care that would be required. One of them started giggling and nudged the other saying, 'Oh, we can't tell them that!'

One evening in late May 1976, Robert and Terry joined me and A. and some friends of ours for an evening of overconsumption and merriment. The Rose boys shared a joint and then led the dance. But the tension back in the bunker was insufferable. Four days later I was told that Robert and Terry were planning to separate. Dr Burke had written to Robert about a new hostel (the first of its kind in Australia) for paraplegics and quadriplegics, to be opened later in the year. Robert was invited to move in if he wished.

Few of us are good at the endgame. One week later, two days before my twenty-first birthday party, there was another row. Terry, in a desperate state, picked up Salli and left the bunker. When Mum got home from work hours later she found Robert sitting in his wheelchair on his own. Very alarmed, she asked where Terry was. He wouldn't say. He kept on reassuring her. He said everything was all right and told her not to worry.

That's when my mother realised how phenomenally brave he was.

In July 2000 I drove to Kangaroo Ground to visit my former sister-in-law. I had forgotten how long it takes. I must have driven for an hour. The roads were narrow and winding, the weather vile. Finally I reached the unmade road that Terry had told me about. As I approached the property, electronic gates opened silently. Terry greeted me at the front door, quite unchanged, warm, affable, and pretty as ever. I hadn't seen her since her most recent misadventure, a car accident. I was relieved to see her looking so well, and unscarred. She told me that apart from residual double vision and a crook ankle she was on the mend. Arthritis was a possibility, but the specialists were sanguine. She hoped to start driving again soon.

We enthused about her grandson, now a fortnight old. I had met my great-nephew the day before, so was able to contribute to the traditional guessing game about his dominant looks and the eventual colour of his eyes. I thought he looked uncannily like Salli and Robert as children.

After a cursory tour of the renovated house, we moved outside. I admired the pool on the hilltop with its massive, electronic umbrella. The view from the terrace was equally impressive. The property is hilly and heavily wooded. This is serious equestrian country. I noticed several horses, including Salli's thoroughbred, which she stables at Kangaroo Ground. Four fat geese mooched around the dam. Terry told me that a rogue fox was slowly picking them off. She pointed out a troop of kangaroos in a distant gully, including the albino that appeared each afternoon. We agreed that it would be most unfortunate if anything was allowed to spoil this idyll.

My contact with Terry had been reasonably frequent during the previous two decades. Soon after she left Robert, I began seeing her and Salli. Terry, understandably, didn't attend my twenty-first birthday party—a small and overwrought affair—but she often visited my house in

East Hawthorn and subsequent communal abodes. In those early days Terry, still in her early twenties, was looking for distractions. She went to parties with me. Finally, in her late twenties, she met Darryl Butler, and they married soon after. Three more daughters followed. Salli is eighteen years older than her youngest half-sister.

I liked Darryl. So did the rest of my family. He was good to Terry after a very unhappy time, and he proved to be an exemplary stepfather to Salli—every bit as generous to her as he was to his own children, and never seeking to muddy the roles of father and stepfather. He and Terry both ensured that Salli went on seeing Robert during those early, difficult years, and there was never any doubt that Robert was 'Dad'. Soon after marrying Terry, Darryl started his own printing company. The hectares, the gates, the thoroughbreds, the luxurious pool attested to his success. Darryl used to print catalogues for me at OUP before I switched from marketing to publishing. During winter he would sit in my office and bemoan Collingwood's fortunes. He struck me as being as rabid as Robert. When his company began to prosper he became a Collingwood sponsor. Dad was still vice-president (Kevin Rose became president in the 1990s), so I often attended lunches and ran into Darryl. Terry sometimes went along, but never watched the football. We would stay inside, drinking the sponsor's wine, reminiscing. 'Is it over yet?' she would wail at quarter-time, just as I had done as a child.

Although Robert had a standing invitation, he never attended these functions, which are much sought after by corporations, former players and ambitious politicians.

You often find yourself sitting next to cabinet ministers or media barons. When the social club was officially named after my father in 1989, Prime Minister Hawke flew down for the afternoon and Premier Cain did the honours, welcoming 'Comrade Prime Minister'. During his typically emotional speech Dad mentioned some impenetrable poems of mine that had just appeared in a newspaper. Later, Hawke asked me about my poetry. He wanted to know about my background, but broke off at one point to listen to a horse-race in which he had a vested interest. It was a bizarre experience watching the prime minister and Mum with their ears pressed up against his pink tranny, urging on the favoured nag, to no avail. Putting away his tranny and his disappointment, Hawke turned to me and said, 'Now where were we, Rosey?'

Robert may have approved of betting, but he disliked the atmosphere upstairs. That was for 'the toffs'. For him the general frivolity was almost sacrilegious, as was the audacity of people who went on chatting long after the game had commenced. Missing a single kick was anathema to Robert. He preferred to sit among the true believers. He took a small box in the rickety Ryder Stand, near the old chook pen, and sat there agonising over the outcome with his mate 'Butch' Canobie. Butch, like his brother Rod, was superb to my brother and equally avid. They were indistinguishable studies in anxiety—fretful, chainsmoking, always fearing the worst, even when Collingwood was five goals up with fewer minutes to go. The fates could always rob you; 1970 might happen again. One day, years after their divorce, Terry crossed to the Ryder Stand to sit with Robert, only to return a few minutes later chuckling bemusedly at his engrossment in the game. He had completely ignored her, as if his life depended on the game. Terry should have known better than to expect civilities during a game. Did Robert even *recognise* us in that state?

After admiring the Kangaroo Ground fauna, Terry and I moved inside and she made herself comfortable on a sofa. I hadn't seen her since Robert's funeral in May 1999. Much had happened in my life too. At the end of that year I became ill for the first time in my life. Abdominal problems, not unrelated to Mum's, required emergency surgery. I went out to my parents' house to convalesce. For several days I lay in Robert's bed, unable to do anything but reflect. One morning, staring at his old trophies and thinking about my frenetic life, I suddenly decided to leave OUP, to spend more time writing, and to be with my partner who lived in Adelaide. I moved there in the new year. Illness, in a sense, had freed me.

Terry and I discussed the accident—her own, not Robert's. This had happened in May 2000, just a few days before the first anniversary of Robert's death. The coincidences were almost as stark as the consequences. Terry was driving along a busy road near their property. As she approached a roundabout a car travelling at great speed in the opposite direction veered out of control and hurtled across the roundabout straight into her path. It happened so quickly Terry didn't have time to brake. The cars collided head-on. Even the Butlers' tank-like Range Rover was crushed and had to be written off. The young man in the other car died instantly. He was twenty-two, just like Robert. He also came from Wangaratta. A few days earlier he and a mate had been reported to the police for tailgating other motorists in the area. This particular day they were playing possum at the roundabout.

Terry cannot remember the accident, so great was the impact. She was lucky to survive. It left her with broken ribs and a fractured ankle and cheekbone. She was profoundly concussed for several days. Her vision was shot, and one side of her face collapsed. Ironically, Terry was admitted to the Austin. I groaned when Mum told me this. I thought about poor Salli, heavily pregnant and preparing for the anniversary, having to go back to that place. Terry remembered a remark of mine during our long vigil by Robert's deathbed: 'It would have to be a very close friend to bring me back to the Austin'.

Terry's recovery was slow and uncertain. After several weeks in Intensive Care she was finally moved to Ivanhoe Manor for rehabilitation, where Dr Burke attended her. Terry hated the atmosphere in the rehabilitation hospital. She was surrounded by paraplegics and quadriplegics, mostly young men, with major head injuries and tragic futures. She watched the sleepless parents and bewildered girlfriends who sat with the victims all day, watching, listening, sponging them, murmuring encouragement. The old associations must have been powerful. Terry saw no point in this suffering, these life sentences. She loathed every minute of it and discharged herself as soon as possible.

By the time I saw Terry in July 2000 she had made a good recovery. She showed me photographs of the battered

178

Range Rover and of herself in Intensive Care. Darryl, a keen family documenter, had taken them. Looking at the wrecked car, Terry said she was increasingly troubled by the fact that a young man, however foolish or self-destructive, had died in the accident. But for the sturdiness of her Range Rover he might be alive today. (But for it, we knew, she would almost certainly be dead.) She had survived, but somewhere his uncomprehending parents were sonless, grieving.

When I told Terry about my book she was interested and agreed to help. Clumsily, I set up my little tape recorder and we both laughed at the absurdity of it all. Terry's jovial cackle filled the spacious house. Even during the gloomiest days after Robert's accident we had always made each other laugh.

Terry warned me that her memory wasn't good. During the first few weeks after her accident it was positively useless. Like Robert, she couldn't recall the collision or the hour leading up to it. Her memory was slowly improving as the massive concussion receded, but she still had difficulty with names and dates.

We talked briefly about the period leading up to Robert's accident. Terry was unsentimental about the vagaries of her early life with Robert. 'It was terrible. I mean, Robert was a pain really. He was a real chauvinist, an ocker—I don't know how you describe it. I had no idea what a sportsman's life was like.' She remembers ringing my mother one evening soon after Salli's birth. Robert was missing, and Terry had no money. Desperate, she insisted that something be done. She laughed as she recalled Mum's

179

response: '"Well, you wanted him, love! You've got him now." Poor Elsie, she must have hated me.' Both of us knew this was never the case. Mum and Terry remain very fond of each other.

'Robert wasn't ready for marriage or commitment,' Terry admitted. 'He just wanted to play sport and to be with the boys. It was all immaturity and lack of experience, a lot of it on my part.'

We talked about the night of Robert's accident and about Terry's general unpreparedness, before discussing her eighteen months at Crosby Drive. Interestingly, Terry focussed on Mum's feelings about the domestic disruption. She felt guilty about invading Mum's new house. 'I often think how terrible it must have been for your Mum to have Robert and me move in there. Being a mature woman now, I just know how awful it must have been to have another woman there all of a sudden.' Elsie was famously meticulous, whereas Terry had a laissez-faire attitude towards housekeeping. 'I do appreciate that more than ever now—how hard it must have been for Elsie. I didn't at that stage.' Things are different now, she told me. With her own daughters she insists upon things being done in a certain way or not at all. She said her long convalescence on the sofa after her own accident, when she was completely dependent on others, had been trying for Darryl and the girls.

This emphasis surprised me. It's curious what people choose to regret. Given everything else that was going on, I don't think Mum was particularly concerned about lint in the washing machine or dirt rings in the bath.

Amusedly, Terry recalled her culinary deficiencies. 'Elsie must have wondered what I was feeding her poor sick son every night.' Mum used to invite them upstairs for a meal, 'to make sure Robert was getting some nutrition'. We laughed about Dad's huffing and puffing as he lifted Robert, and about the prevailing moodiness. 'I wouldn't have been easy to get along with, because of my inexperience,' Terry admitted.

Her memories of life in the bunker are mostly grinding and unhappy. Not surprisingly, she remembers the physical details. 'I have vivid memories of having to insert suppositories into Robert's bottom every second day and then clean up what came out of it. I was doing catheterisations—without any nursing training—and I had to put these tubes inside him. It was a very sterile procedure. I can't imagine how I did those things. It's hard to imagine now. But you just did them, I suppose, because you were told that's what you had to do.'

Terry, too, regrets the lack of counselling. She does remember one rare exception prior to Robert's release from the Austin, when Dr Burke talked to them candidly about the possibility of a sexual relationship. 'He did his darnedest to get us going in that area,' Terry laughed, 'but it had no effect.'

By now Georgia, Terry's youngest daughter, aged nine, had come home from school and was cooking fish fingers in the microwave. We began to speak in euphemisms and lowered voices.

Sexual tensions were at the crux of Robert and Terry's mounting difficulties. Robert desired physical intimacy,

181

Terry didn't. 'Robert wanted me in bed with him, but to me it smelt like a hospital—a hospital bed. I couldn't do that. And he became bitter about that—that I wouldn't lie with him. It was all quite revolting to me. It put a terrible strain on things.'

This became acute in 1976. Each night was an ordeal, each morning brought recriminations. By early June the situation was untenable. 'In the end,' Terry went on, 'that's what caused that terrible day when I left. And thinking about it, it's all because we didn't have this long, happy, mature love. We were only young. We were very much infatuated with each before the accident, and then for all that to come to an end, if you know what I mean.'

I nodded. Georgia watched us over her pungent snack. No one listens quite as intently as a child. And no one is more conservative.

'I just remember how dreadfully difficult it was being a young girl and having a quadriplegic husband,' Terry continued softly. 'And I often think that if we'd been married for ten years—twenty years—maybe our love would have been more mature and I would have been able to stay and look after Robert. But I was too young and still infatuated with him as he was. He eventually became my patient and my brother, rather than my lover or my husband.'

I began to wonder how many young couples in similar circumstances are defeated by sexual differences. Intimacy is of course still possible, with a degree of trust, openness and ingenuity. Quadriplegics are by no means sexless. Many such marriages survive paralysis. But Terry was right about hers. Their youthfulness, the brevity of their relationship,

182

hindered the exploration and compromises needed to forge a new kind of partnership.

Terry concluded by saying, 'I just had no understanding at that stage how Robert was feeling and how bitter and frustrating it must have been for him. Now I can think back and imagine how awful it was. I suppose I was a bit selfish—and, well, young.'

By now the Butler household was stirring with all the usual late-afternoon adolescent activity. Georgia's sister Casey came home from high school, similarly ravenous. Terry needed to visit the local medical clinic. I offered to drive her there. We set off through the magisterial gates. As we approached one of those vast outer-suburban round-abouts Terry mentioned that it was the site of her accident. We negotiated it in silence, very carefully. Then Terry wanted to talk about the mishaps that had dotted her adult life. This surprised me. I had never known her to dwell on past misfortunes. Indeed, I had always marvelled at her resilience, her sunny temperament, her refusal to mope. She listed the five trials and tragedies. Her first husband was crippled when she was nineteen, nine months after the birth of their child. Just prior to the birth of her second child, her new husband, Darryl, developed cancer and for some weeks his survival hung in the balance. Their next child was stillborn. At the age of three, their third child was diagnosed with a rare heart condition that could have killed her at any moment, especially in infancy. Georgia required open-heart surgery but made a full recovery. Then came the accident at the roundabout.

I remembered something an old friend of mine used

to say about the crumminess of life. I am often amazed by what human beings are expected to endure—and do.

'It's left me feeling very pessimistic about the future,' Terry said as we pulled up outside the clinic. This was uncharacteristic, like a crack in a sturdy bowl. I couldn't think of anything to say. But I knew Terry would cope, in her own way, with her daughters, and her devoted husband, and her slightly unreal view of affluent slopes and an albino kangaroo.

After the separation the mood at Crosby Drive was oddly tranquil. There was relief that the tensions of the past two years had been resolved, albeit in dissolution. I don't think anyone—not even Robert—had expected Terry to stay indefinitely. It was too hard.

It was clear that Robert couldn't stay in the bunker on his own. Even with an elevator it would have been impracticable. Robert couldn't be left on his own for more than a few minutes. Because of his violent spasms, someone had to be present at all times. He needed drinks, meals, tablets, cigarettes, newspapers and lifts. He also needed company. My parents installed him in his old bedroom, among the trophies and memorabilia. Mum gave up work to look after him during the day. Now that Dad was no longer coaching, he was able to spend more time with him too. His weekends were largely given over to 'babysitting' him, as he sometimes embarrassingly put it. I visited them frequently and sat out on the deck with Robert while Dad gardened haphazardly below. I listened to their ceaseless conversation about cricket or football.

184

The alternative domestic arrangement was unpalatable. The proposed hostel for the disabled was still just an unacknowledged possibility. Until it opened, the only place for paraplegics and quadriplegics requiring accommodation was in nursing homes. When my parents went to Queensland for a short, needed holiday Robert went into a geriatric hospital. I couldn't look after him on my own, as it took two people to lift him and turn him at night. I visited him in the dismal ward which he shared with three silent septuagenarians. The thought of him living in such a place was unbearable, and he never went back. My parents intended to keep him with them forever.

Three months after Terry's departure, I too returned to Crosby Drive. The shared household in East Hawthorn had broken up after several altercations. My six-month initiation had been eventful but doomed. In the middle of the year I had belatedly completed my arts degree, a poet's degree if ever there was one. I wasn't sure what I wanted to do with my life, but I knew I didn't want to teach. I thought vaguely about going back to Europe at the end of the year. One of my Tuesday ethicists asked me to marry her—not just for altruistic reasons. I told A. that I was considering it, and he was shocked. Then in May, not long before Robert and Terry's parting, I made the mistake of falling comprehensively in love with A., my enigmatic gadfly. Propinquity and an unmatched mutual understanding finally broke down the old barriers. To my surprise, A. felt the same way. This passion was disastrous. A. had ghosts of his own and an acquired distrust of intimacy. After a short, euphoric affair, he crudely extricated himself, taking up with a woman. Never having been seriously infatuated before, never having known such killing rejection, I fell apart. It was the maddest time of my life. There had been too many drugs, too much experimentation. For several weeks I was in a deplorable condition, quite unhinged. My journal, often illegible, is full of the old self-hatred and a charged sense of worthlessness. I thought fondly of death, but then I remembered Robert and my parents. This all came to a head, all too memorably, at my twenty-first birthday party, which A. disconcertingly attended. My behaviour was extreme.

Happy majority!

So I moved into the bunker and began to piece myself back together. Robert had returned to the Austin for surgery on his painful right thumb. The night he came home, Dad was in an ebullient mood. I hadn't seen him looking so relaxed for years. Watching him, Mum said that he was happy because his two boys were home again.

I went to work in a factory on an assembly line, making air-conditioners. The tedium of the work was offset by the humour, life stories and sheer camaraderie of the other workers. I'm glad I spent time in a factory. Perhaps all university graduates and delusive romantics should be encouraged to do so. One day the foreman took me aside. I felt sure he was going to dismiss me for being cack-handed (or for my eight-hour daydreams about A.), but instead he offered me an apprenticeship as a welder. It was the proudest day of my life. I thanked him and explained that I was going back to Greece at the end of the year.

In due course the daydreams became real. A. returned,

having missed our marathon talks. We resumed our affair and I offered to take him to Greece. I remember an hilarious conversation with one of my more exotic confidants at the factory. Wayne, a New Zealander with an applied tan and ostentatious past, listened to my story as we ducked in and out of a wall unit with our power drills. When I told Wayne about my offer, which A. had surprisingly accepted, he was furious. He berated me for relenting and said I should go overseas alone to sort out my life. (Do young Australians still resort to Europe in that way: Europe as sanctuary or sanatorium?)

A. and I left in late November. By this stage Robert was utterly miserable. The new living arrangement hadn't been successful. It was too hard on everyone, himself included. Robert seemed dangerously depressed, and Mum and Dad bore the brunt of his moodiness. His infrequent meetings with Terry and Salli upset him deeply and he wasn't sure he wanted to see them in future. Yarra Me, as the hostel was named, had opened in early November. After a conversation with Mum and Dad and Dr Burke, Robert decided to put his name on the waiting list. A few days later the matron rang to say that he could move in whenever he liked. Robert, very depressed, elected to go next day. Mum, writing to me in Athens, thought he just wanted to get it over with. They packed up his few things and drove him to North Croydon. That, for all of them, was the most terrible day since the accident. The matron, who knew about Robert's moods, was understanding. Robert decided to share a room with two other men. The new hostel was large, well staffed and equipped, and designed to accommodate seventy disabled men and women. Referred to as residents, not patients, they were free to come and go as they pleased, but the matron suggested that Robert shouldn't spend that weekend at Crosby Drive. Home was elsewhere now, unavoidably.

Robert settled in reasonably well, but there were some teething problems with the staff, few of whom had nursed quadriplegics. The first time Robert went back to Crosby Drive, there were blisters around the sore on his bottom. Someone had tried to cure it with a hairdryer.

Robert started seeing Salli again, very happily. Dad took Robert to the cricket and sat with him when he was confined to bed. Thus began the long pattern of parental visits and encouragement. Dad told me in a letter that Robert was thrilled when he got away from Yarra Me. 'When he does come home he is quite excited—and we are too.' On Christmas Eve Robert was well enough to go to Adelaide for the Test against Pakistan, 'burnt bottom and all'. Dad drove throughout the night, with Robert stretched out on the back seat. They stayed at the same motel as the Pakistanis and partied with the Australians each night. During the Test Jeff Thomson injured his shoulder while fielding. His agent was reportedly in tears after visiting him in hospital. Thomson's career was in jeopardy. People said it was a tragedy. One night Dad and Robert dined with the Sachses. Dad described Janyne as an amazing person. When he got back to Melbourne he was exhausted, 'but it was worth it to see Robert enjoying himself'.

'Reuters' Rose, using my old Olivetti typewriter ('that bloody aaaa sticks every time'), told me that Dr Burke had published a letter in the *Age* imploring young people to be more careful on motorbikes. There had been a big increase in spinal care admissions at the Austin. That week, A. and I, now in Rome and fast unravelling, learned that a close friend of ours had been killed on his motorbike.

In Italy I often dreamed about Robert. Usually I was playing sport with him or reliving the accident and life in Ward Seven, always conscious of my parents' grief. In one dream we attempted to play tennis. Robert stumbled around the court on tin legs. Neither of us played well: I didn't record the score. In another, he was seriously burnt. I knew I had to get away. I invited Terry to go the movies with me, sensing my mother's disapproval.

Those weeks in Italy with A. were tempestuous. Wayne was right: it was never going to work. We both wanted different things. A. missed his louche life and all its temptations. Rightly, I suppose, he accused me of wanting a kind of marriage. He despised my gallery crawls and my paradoxical reverence in churches. Politically sterner than I was, and admirably anticlerical, he detested the papacy. Being in the Vatican turned his stomach; like an angry Adam he fled St Peter's. Quoting Nietzsche all the way, he upbraided me for swooning in front of Bellini's mooning Madonnas and passive Christs.

In Delphi we had met our witch, or so we liked to think. Judith, a radio journalist and possibly the smallest Canadian on earth, was travelling with a wealthy gentleman in a stetson who seemed to have adopted the courtship methods of Howard Hughes. He kept her locked up during the day and paid all the bills. Sex he deemed unhygienic. When Judith managed to escape from their hotel room she joined us for moody midnight strolls through the ancient site. We sat in the amphitheatre and watched A. sardonically mime some all too guessable tragedy on the stage. Later, Judith analysed us over endless glasses of whisky. Like many women she was fascinated by A., who was tall, manly and good-looking. She quickly recognised a fellow chameleon. She predicted that A. would circle and eventually rise in his own ambivalence. It was a good line and one I often thought about later. Turning to me, she said I had been hurt by someone and demanded to know why I hadn't been more assertive. Whoever it was had done a real job on me.

After Delphi the harmonious times were few but memorable. One day we visited the English Bookshop near the Piazza di Spagna for more Genet and de Beauvoir. A. asked me to indicate any book I desired. I walked through the bookshop in a saturnalian trance. As we left the shop I noticed that A. was moving rather awkwardly. Reaching the Spanish Steps, he stood and shook. I wrote about it in my poem 'Memorabilia' (always apologising to any booksellers in the audience before reading it in public):

> Great literature flew from you like doves.
> Humbled by such munificence
> I led you back to our hotel
> and now, when young colleagues
> wish to borrow my *Prime of Life*,
> I warn them, 'Mind you bring it back.
> It was stolen for me by a great friend.'

Finally, we parted in Venice. I moved to Padua and checked into a hotel. I felt compelled to write it all down in my journal, every insult and humiliation—a curious, self-coruscating act of reportage. Two days later, on leaving my room, I found the city palely transformed by two feet of snow. The worst blizzard in a generation had happened while I sat there auditing my woes.

I flew home at the end of summer. Next to me—I was in Economy, of course—was a massive, charming, high-strung woman. A purring Irishwoman, she introduced me to her new husband, an English television producer. Over the first of several whiskies, they showed me photographs of their recent wedding in Dublin. They were heading to Australia on their honeymoon. Each take-off or landing was traumatic for the Irishwoman, so we kept on talking. Politely she expressed interest in my poetry. She told me she was a journalist. She showed me a collection of her articles in the *Irish Times* and talked about her imminent first novel. I had never met a published author before, apart from Lou Richards. We swapped addresses. I wished her luck with her novel. Her name was Maeve Binchy.

Back home, Robert looked happier than he had for three years. He seemed to be adjusting to his new life at Yarra Me. He looked forward to each Saturday morning, when Dad collected him. In a way he was learning to hibernate during the week, anticipating the pleasures to come, knowing that for forty-eight hours he would live intensely, eat and drink freely, surrounded by people who loved him. He sat on our parents' deck improving his suntan. He asked about my travels, with one eye on the television. Summer, with its surfeit of sport, was a halcyon time.

On Sunday night, at the appointed hour, Dad or I drove him back to Yarra Me. Robert was becoming increasingly punctilious about such things and required us to be equally regimented. I was impressed by the facilities but at the same time deeply saddened by the place. The décor was clinical, but there were several large games rooms and common rooms where the more gregarious residents could congregate. Robert never wanted to join them, but asked us to put him to bed. We made him comfortable and left him after slightly awkward, protracted farewells.

Relaxed though he was at home, Robert's manner at Yarra Me was different, especially during those first few years. The hostel had rapidly filled. Those beds, too, were never empty long. It was an artificial and disparate population. As in any institution, strong antipathies and alliances quickly formed. Many residents were about Robert's age, still coming to terms with their disability, but some were middle-aged or older, sardonically inured to paralysis. Some had attentive families, some were abandoned. Some had independent means, most relied on the invalid pension, nearly all of which went to Yarra Me. Some wanted to be active and joined committees, others preferred to stay in bed and face the wall or the stultifying screen. Some acknowledged us when we pushed Robert down the corridor, others dully stared. Some were churlish with the inexperienced staff, others diplomatic, knowing that this was the best of all possible worlds. Some had a future, others hated the thought.

Robert remained aloof at first. He rarely mixed with other residents, preferring to read his newspaper or sit in the large native park surrounding the hostel. The sun became his companion. He was wary of new staff members. Once they had earned his trust, once he was confident they knew how to lift him properly and weren't going to poison him accidentally, his reserve dissipated. He was equally discriminating with other residents. As we pushed him along the corridor he would indicate with a raised eyebrow those he regarded as whingers or nutters. His sympathies were still black and white.

That year I discovered Carl Jung. Dutifully I began keeping a dream journal. Each morning I wrote one or two foolscap pages. I should have gone into analysis if only to justify my prolixity. I admired Jung's theory of didactic dreams. I still dreamed about Robert. In one of them, haunted by a demon-lover, I became the cripple, inexpertly wheeling myself through a soulless government office in search of a bargain bookshop. Then I was standing beside Robert's hospital bed when an old football idol arrived. The conversation was strained; I was self-conscious about being crippled. In another dream the whole family was together. Our kitchen was situated on an oval. My parents showed me a large oven in which Robert liked to sit. He said he enjoyed it more than anything. Fire began to infiltrate my dreams.

My mother, who has a fertile unconscious, told me that she had dreamed about a kitten with no back legs. She was desperate to feed it. I made the fairly obvious connection with Robert. She surprised me by saying that she had only dreamed about him once since the accident. In her dream Robert was sitting outside the MCG beneath a tree, after a football game. No one in the dispersing crowd went near him. They all shunned him.

Six months after moving to Yarra Me, Robert announced that he might go and live in Perth. He had just run into Terry and her new boyfriend at the Collingwood Social Club and was feeling low. Someone had told him about a new home for quadriplegics in Perth. It was said to be more progressive than Yarra Me. Other residents were thinking of moving there. The warmer climate also appealed to Robert. In retrospect it was a bold step for him to contemplate, given his reliance on my parents, especially my father.

Nothing came of it—I'm not sure why. Perhaps his failing health stopped him from going. A serious pressure sore formed on his ankle in October 1977, consigning him to bed. The knob of his ankle must have rubbed against the sheet one night. We had no idea the wound would become chronic. It's difficult to credit that a sore on his foot could isolate him for so long. But Robert's regenerative powers had begun to wane because of his immobility. His skin was becoming thin and discoloured. When we put him to bed at night his feet would be blue, frozen and swollen.

The pressure sore deepened and a new ulcer formed. Incredibly, it kept Robert in bed until August 1979. It was the most trying of his confinements, until his final illness. I used to wake up in the morning and think of him lying there. I tried to imagine what it must be like spending two years in bed, being turned every few hours, gulping down handfuls of pills, watching stupid quiz shows, wondering if the ulcer on your ankle was any better—betrayed by your body, by your own sluggish blood.

The effect on Robert's morale was catastrophic. During our visits he usually managed to remain stoic, but now and then he became sullen and incommunicative. Sometimes it was more than he could do to look at people. My father saw the worst of it. Because they were so close, because Dad's role was to rally him, Robert was frank with him and didn't conceal his despair. His dark moods and outbursts distressed my father. He felt helpless when Robert lashed out or refused to converse. But he always went back. Not all parents do. Dad was always thinking of new tactics, new diversions, new outings.

The relationship between Robert and my parents was becoming one of intense mutual dependency. They began to live through and for one another. So great was my parents' devotion that they too were greatly affected when Robert was miserable or debilitated. Activities that didn't involve Robert engendered a kind of guilt or unease. The only thing that mattered was Robert's equilibrium. When this was threatened, the effect was shattering. Mum, in particular, was devastated by new setbacks (another fortnight, another month, another year in bed), with deleterious consequences for her own health.

Latently I began to regret the burden my parents unconditionally bore. Watching them age, I worried about the toll it was having on them. Neither of them had had an easy life. They belonged to the generation that had grown up during fifteen years of Depression and world war. Just when they were reaching middle age and should have been able to relax, they had more worries and obligations than ever.

I knew there was nothing worse for parents than watching their child suffer. I also knew I would never feel such emotion, with its abjection and exaltation. They were going through a kind of mental torture of their own. Their compassion was instinctive and limitless. I never heard them complain about the cost. Somehow they had to keep Robert going. Their own health didn't matter now. If they could have swapped places with him they would have. And I couldn't help them.

Part of me—consciously, subconsciously—resented the demands Robert inevitably made on them. Part of me wanted it to end, I suppose. Sons fear for their parents as much as for their brothers. But I was sickened by my disloyalty.

Robert was allowed out from time to time, but he wasn't well enough to go to the football. Dad would bring him home for a few hours, just to get him away from Yarra Me. Usually he had to go straight to bed to rest his ankle. Salli, now six, visited him one afternoon. She had grown leggy and independent. I noticed that she was very tender with Robert. 'Daddy can't do that,' she would explain with an adult sigh, 'because he's in a wheelchair.' Her insight wasn't surprising given the series of muddles, tragedies and upheavals she had witnessed during her short life.

At the end of 1978 Robert was able to spend a couple of days at home. My journal records some of the tensions and pleasures of those occasions:

*When Robert is able to get up he is quite jovial;
there is so much cricket on the television I would be*

very surprised if he wasn't; but when his bedsores,
spots, marks and carbuncles ground him he becomes
miserable and everyone becomes very desperate.
This prompts in me uncontrollable sensations,
ranging from anger to sympathy to universal revul-
sion, as though I cannot bear outlaying emotion on
a situation so hopeless and pathetic. To see a grown
man bundled up in his father's arms, protesting all
the way, scowling at the void, knowing his condition
will never improve. But then...a flash of humour;
Robert is allowed up; Lillee bowls someone; sitting
in the backyard, reading a translation of Horace,
I hear Dad shouting 'Cyclone Peter is harassing
Darwin', and jokes are made. There is life in us yet.

Even after Robert's bedsore healed, enabling him to
return to his wheelchair, the situation remained uncertain
because of his delicate skin. (The wound itself would have
to be dressed for the next twenty years.) Six months later,
in early 1980, he was back in hospital:

Robert was taken to the Austin Hospital yesterday
with another bout of bedsores. It was only last
August that he was allowed up after two years in
bed. Mum thinks he may have a complete breakdown
if his general health doesn't improve, and I must
say when I visited him on Monday he was almost
catatonic with despair. But I can't help thinking that
he's incapable of breaking down further. Even that
is impossible. He can't run away from it—he can't

197

beat his brow. All he can do is sit there, lie there,
thinking, always thinking, becoming more and more
depressed. Thought is all that is available to him—
suffering petrified by virtual incorporeality. And it
is terrible.

And meanwhile the rest of us go on criticising each
other and bemoaning our lot because our job doesn't
pay enough or our lover forgets to telephone us.

Terrible not even to be able to destroy oneself.

Dr Burke told me recently that it was around this time
that a psychiatrist reported that psychotherapy would be
of no use to Robert. His depression was entirely due to
his disability and to the necessity for him to live in what
amounted to a nursing home. Medication—or rather, more
medication—would also be futile.

Medicine often begs a few questions.

'I remember that time too,' Dr Burke said, before
continuing in his understated way. 'Robert was really
quite depressed for a while. That's when I would have been
worried about his long-term expectations. A depressed
person—particularly with a severe physical disability—
can just about will himself to die. But that's when your
father stepped in—well, your family stepped in too, not
just your father, but your father particularly was just such
a wonderful influence for him.'

I asked Dr Burke if he was surprised by Robert's
longevity.

'Well, yes, in a way,' he replied, 'because he didn't enjoy
being a quadriplegic. Nobody does. But Robert perhaps less
so than most.'

7

YARRA ME

In the middle of 1980 there was a welcome, if unexpected, development. Robert became involved with another woman.

Jenny Anderson was twenty-one at the time, seven years younger than Robert. Jenny had known my family for several years. She lived next door with her parents. She was bright, talkative and gregarious. Not always happy at home, she was fond of Mum and Dad. She understood that the best way to cope with Dad's cheek was to tease him right back. She was good at it, better than most. She had also visited the bunker when Robert and Terry were living there. She adored Salli and regarded Terry as the kind of older sister she didn't have. Terry was fun and never short of a word. Terry, for her part, had visited Jenny's mother when she needed a break or when things were tense in the bunker.

Jenny hardly spoke to Robert at that time. She went to a girls' school and wasn't used to men. Nevertheless, she intuited that Robert appreciated her visits; they helped to break the ice. She must have remembered this a few years later when she got her licence and began visiting friends who lived near Yarra Me. She called on Robert and generally talked the leg off a chair. Sensing his appetite for news about other people's lives, she told him about the primary school where she was now teaching. One day Robert invited her to a party. When Jenny accepted he nearly fell out of his chair, she told me recently. 'He was really stunned,' she recalled. They had a good time, as Hemingway once wrote with admirable economy. 'I just thought, I like this guy, he's really good fun. And it sort of went from there.'

Robert and Jenny fell in love. This was not without repercussions in Crosby Drive, and beyond. Things were rarely uncomplicated in Robert's life, and this was no exception. My parents were overseas at the time. I had seen Robert several times while they were away. Oddly, we always got along much better when Mum and Dad were absent. I once wrote that our relationship was much saner at such times. We were more relaxed, and a greater warmth seemed possible.

Matters came to a head on my parents' return. Jenny's mother, aware of the situation, became agitated. I was present when the four parents discussed the 'predicament'. The fact that Jenny was an adult seemed to be overlooked. It became clear that parental fears could unnerve even those who had previously shown sympathy towards Robert. Someone said that a serious relationship between Robert and Jenny would be a tragedy and that Jenny had no idea what she was letting herself in for. Here I rather spoilt my

200

copybook by saying that Jenny must have known what it was all about. After all, she had seen enough of Robert and Terry when they were living next door.

This helped not at all.

It was left to Jenny's father, normally rather inscrutable, to remind people that there was no point in leaping to conclusions, that he had great faith in Jenny's intelligence and decency, and that he wouldn't allow anything to come between himself and his daughter. It was a simple and rather eloquent speech. Dad said much the same thing later as he drove me home. He told me that even when Robert was behaving outrageously in his teens he had tolerated his excesses because, as with me, he would never do anything to jeopardise their relationship. I listened to this in silence. Although I had always known it to be the case, his affirmation filled me with a warm and reassuring light.

Jenny and I reminisced about this domestic crisis when I called on her recently. We had arranged to meet at the primary school where she is now deputy principal. Situated in one of Melbourne's outer working-class suburbs, it was a long way from Paul Sheahan's bluestone principality on St Kilda Road. It took an eternity to get there, but, determined not to be late for school, I arrived as the morning bell was ringing. Jenny, with her busy gait and cheerful sense of chaos, led me down a festooned corridor and showed me into a small conference room. We hadn't seen each other for many years, apart from a brief conversation after Robert's funeral, which neither of us remembers well. She still looked wiry and energetic, but for the first time she reminded me of her mother.

An emergency had arisen at the school. Knowing that we didn't have long, we dispensed with pleasantries. Jenny spoke contemptuously about some people's reactions to the affair. 'I used to get so angry,' she told me. 'People would say, "How could you?" and I would be thinking, What's the difference? I think your boyfriend's ugly. Robert's good-looking. And he's funny.'

I asked Jenny if she was surprised by the source of such opposition. 'Oh, Peter, I lost so many friends. And yet it was the best thing that ever happened to me. Because they were the people who, when the chips were down, where would they have been? I am a very loyal person ...' She paused. 'As it turned out, I probably wasn't as loyal as I should have been—but I was very defensive.'

Jenny told me about one of her closest friends. 'When she had her twenty-first she said, "Jenny, here's an invitation for you, but I've left Robert off. I think my friends would be embarrassed by him." That was it. From then on I had nothing to do with her. I just thought, What a shallow person.'

Other people, though well meaning, were condescending. When Jenny danced with Robert at a party, a bloke went up to her and told her he really admired her for what she had done. 'I thought to myself, How wet!' Others were fabulous—'once they'd got over the shock of an unusual coupling'. Jenny remembers the Canobie brothers with great affection. Colleagues of Jenny's welcomed Robert into their circle and went to great lengths to ensure that he was able to get into restaurants and cinemas. The problem of access to venues or houses was more exasperating. 'It

202

drove us both mad and could be very restrictive,' said Jenny. She realised that some of her male friends liked the situation because of Robert's connections. 'Things came out of the blue. You saw the best side of people, and you saw the worst.'

After a while Robert and Jenny became good at avoiding those who weren't simpatico. 'Obstacles tended to be more physical than attitudinal because we gradually weeded out those who had difficulty coping with an atypical couple. We discovered some wonderful new friends in the process.'

Gradually even the doubters calmed down and accepted the relationship as a fait accompli. Jenny, though young, was every bit as single-minded as Robert. Nothing was going to separate them. Indeed, it seems to have been a serene relationship. Jenny can recall only two arguments: the first when Robert, rather drunk, woke up people in the house where Jenny was boarding (she had thought it prudent to move out of her parents' home); the second when Jenny danced with another man and left Robert stranded at a party. Both times Dad acted as mediator. As in so many other ways, there was little privacy for Robert, which troubled Jenny. Otherwise the relationship was surprisingly calm.

Jenny attributes this smooth passage to the fact that she didn't know Robert before the accident. 'I never viewed him as being really handicapped because I only knew him when he was like that. I never knew him when he was fully able. This was important in our relationship. There was no "He used to be this" or "I feel so sorry for him". I knew what I was getting. It was a fairly even, equal-based relationship

203

on the spiritual side—if you want to talk about it like that. Obviously it wasn't a really physical relationship— although, you know, you always find ways and get out of it what you need, I suppose, to a certain degree.'

During the week, Robert and Jenny spoke daily and saw each other as often as possible. They spent the entire weekend together. Jenny, a keen athlete herself, enjoyed watching cricket and football, which was fortunate. She took Robert to matches and got to know his friends. She was conscious of the flustered affection of some of his old team-mates, who didn't know what to say to Robert and whose only way of coping was to buy him another beer. As a consequence, he often got drunk at these functions. The combination of lager and Valium was potent.

By then my parents had acquired a minuscule Morris van. Dad had the roof raised so that Robert could sit in the rear compartment without having to be lifted from his wheelchair. We wheeled him up a ramp and bolted him into a steel frame. The Yellow Peril, as it became known, was good for our backs, hard on our aesthetics. A bulbous air-conditioning unit on the roof completed the space-age effect. Driving the Yellow Peril was bizarre. Pedestrians and motorists gaped as it went past. It became famous throughout Melbourne.

'Did you ever feel like an idiot driving that thing?' Jenny asked me. 'I used to wish it was painted unobtrusive white every time we pulled up at traffic lights and became the focus of everyone's attention.'

But the Yellow Peril had its uses. After school Jenny often went to Yarra Me in her own car and took Robert out for a drink or a meal. 'I always had to go into the public bar and ask a roomful of strange men if they would help me lift Robert out of the car. Without exception people were always great, but it used to freak me out having to do it. That was the main reason I kept moving back home— I was close to the yellow van.'

They often went to the drive-in, one form of entertainment that allowed them to stay in the car. 'God, we saw some garbage films during those years,' Jenny groaned. We laughed about Robert's appetite. 'We were forever stopping at Chinese restaurants to feed him up. He must have been Ringwood's biggest consumer of fried rice.'

Jenny's arrival eased the pressure on my parents, especially Dad. No longer did he have to keep Robert entertained or think up new ways to lift his spirits. It gave Dad a breather. I don't think he expected the relationship to last forever, but while it did it was hugely therapeutic. My parents were fond of Jenny, and she became part of the family. When she turned twenty-two, Dad jokingly presented her with his old Collingwood guernsey, which bore the same number. Jenny teased him by keeping it for years. The five of us spent most Sundays together, watching the football and attacking the newspaper quiz during half-time, with Robert as quizmaster. Jenny still remembers his amazing head for numbers: dates, telephone numbers, cricket records.

The transformation in Robert was profound. Early on, Jenny became aware that she was doing all the talking and that Robert had little to contribute when she asked about his days. All he seemed to do was sit in the sun listening to the races. She urged him to use the gymnasium. Within days he was lifting quite impressive weights with the aid of hoists. Robert hadn't begun to waste as many quadriplegics do. He was still upright and broad-shouldered. Although his stomach was expanding, he looked quite fit. People often remarked that if he had got up from his wheelchair and walked across the room they wouldn't have been surprised. In photographs he looks youthful, tanned and very happy.

Robert's exertions were good for him, as Jenny observed. 'He probably saw that he still had something to offer. For me he was fabulous. I tend to get upset about situations, and he could calm me down and sympathise. He was totally for me. To have someone totally for you is such an honour. The years Robert and I had together were really wonderful and a time we both benefited from.'

This explains Jenny's frustration with those who opposed the relationship. Although she appreciated that her mother wasn't unusual in wanting a different life for her daughter ('I think she thought I was wasting my life, as I suppose you would, knowing that it would be a hard life if I went that way'), she was annoyed by the disregard of Robert's loyalty and support. 'He was just the most wonderful person,' she told me, 'and so good for me with my volatile temperament.'

We talked about Robert's astuteness as a psychologist. 'He was actually a philosopher without knowing it,' Jenny proffered. 'He would have been shocked if you'd even suggested that. But he understood human nature better than most people, because he had lived through so many different reactions and learned the hard way.'

Robert never complained to Jenny about what had befallen him. The closest he came was when Moving Pictures released a song called 'What About Me?' 'He used to play it a lot when it came out,' Jenny recalled. 'And he really meant it. It *wasn't* fair.' But Robert accepted his fate. He never thought there would be a cure in his lifetime. 'He nursed no anger towards anyone or any thing. He just thought, well this is what happened—and what a bastard!'

Music solaced Robert. 'He loved those old bands like Genesis, the Supremes, the Animals. We spent many Sundays listening to their records in the lounge room—after the obligatory footy replay, debate and stats. We even went to a few concerts at Festival Hall to see the Kinks and Genesis. I think Robert fancied himself as a would-be drummer. He loved Phil Collins or anyone else who let rip on the skins.'

Jenny's arrival, combined with her warm personality and affinity with children, helped to normalise Robert's relationship with Salli. At first Robert didn't know what to say to his daughter, now about seven. Jenny, again, did most of the talking. The three of them would set off in the Yellow Peril for day-long outings. Salli, used to the protean nature of families and relationships, was quite relaxed with Jenny. The best time, as far as Jenny was concerned, was when the three of them went up to Nyah West. This enabled Salli to see Robert's large family responding to him warmly and unaffectedly. There was no tension between Terry and Jenny. Terry, now divorced from Robert and about to marry Darryl Butler, was pleased for him, if somewhat mystified.

At the beginning of 1982 we all went to Warrnambool to give Robert some respite from Yarra Me. Holidays were like military operations (pillows, medication, hoists, suitable bathrooms and facilities), but Elsie was the ablest of marshals. Madly looking forward to a week of tennis, I slashed my thumb while shaving on the first morning. 'Anything to get out of a lift,' the mockers chanted as I was led off wanly to Casualty. Warrnambool proved to be the windiest place on earth, but Dad persuaded Robert to go in the sea, knowing it would be good for his ankle. We drove the Yellow Peril down to the water's edge and carried Robert into the whipping surf on a tyre rubber, I holding my bandaged thumb out of the water like an aching buoy. Happy as a dolphin, Robert floated on his back, his plump stomach poking out of the water. Holidayers on the beach watched this ceremony in shaded astonishment.

Soon after we got back Robert turned thirty. Old friends and team-mates gathered on the deck. For Jenny, that was one of the best times. 'It was a great night for Robert. For a moment it seemed like it was back to old times. He was surrounded by all his old sporting mates, reliving past matches and joking as if nothing had changed. It was one of the happiest times I can remember.'

Trevor Laughlin, Robert's closest friend, made a speech and we all laughed about their youthful pranks. Trevor had played a few Tests for Australia during the Packer wars in the 1970s. As a journalist Robert had always promoted him. I wasn't there when Trevor's State selection was announced. Dad told me about it afterwards in a letter. Robert became upset and wept, something he rarely did. We all knew why.

Robert wasn't jealous. He was probably the least envious person I have ever known. He just wanted to be out there with Trevor. But he promptly sent Trevor a congratulatory telegram. 'I know Robert very well,' Dad wrote to me, 'but it's impossible to know what he is hiding inside.'

Trevor had also played county cricket in Lancashire, where he became friendly with Ian Botham. When the hero of Headingley came to Australia for an Ashes tour, Trevor and Robert spent a long boozy night with him. Botham taught them how to play indoor soccer. No Anglophiles, they both said he should have been an Aussie.

A few nights after the birthday party Dad reminisced about Robert's playing career. He talked about how good he might have been as a footballer (something Robert always denied), and even tried to inveigle me into his dynastic dream. Then Mum piped up with stories about the pair of us as little boys. It was of course St Valentine's Day.

In March 1982 Yarra Me began having financial problems. The hostel owed half a million dollars, of which Rupert Hamer's Liberal government, facing re-election, offered to pay less than one tenth. Yarra Me's survival was tenuous. The residents were warned that they might have to find other accommodation. Robert and my parents were naturally alarmed. It was one of those periodic crises that left them sleepless and apprehensive. We began to consider our options. A geriatric home was clearly untenable. I told my parents that I would move back to Crosby Drive if Robert went home.

Dad, a political novice, decided to use his media clout, Robert being reluctant to do so. A natural conservative, on the morning of the election he gave an interview to the *Sun* in which he deprecated the health minister's 'stupid' offer. Hamer lost the election, and the new Labor government, under John Cain, increased spending on health services, including Yarra Me. The residents' first emergency had passed, but not without casualties. Management dismissed fifteen nurses to reduce overheads. It was the first of many purges. The worst happened ten years later, when the entire nursing staff was sacked and replaced by agency nurses and aides, much cheaper but unable to build the same rapport. The residents were devastated by these departures. The nurses, as my mother said, were like family.

By early 1983 Robert and Jenny's relationship was in trouble, but we still saw her every weekend. Neither of them had much money (though Robert always insisted on paying when they went out), so they tended to spend most of their time at Crosby Drive. Jenny must have been frustrated by her sedentary life. We laughed blackly as we recalled those marathons in front of the television. 'That killed me a bit in the end,' she admitted. 'I'd go to the football and, while I liked it, it took up your whole Saturday. I stopped playing netball. I used to sit there and think, I used to be so active and now I'm just sitting, sitting.' Mostly, though, Jenny enjoyed her years with my family. She still speaks with awe about Mum and Dad. 'If ever anyone could wish for parents they would be the two. I mean, you hit the jackpot! I have never seen such a close relationship between a father and son—and between you and Elsie. It's just the most wonderful family unit.'

I was reminded of a comment I made once, several

years later, when Dad and I gave one of those silly father-and-son interviews. Asked what I thought of my parents, I said, 'I chose well'.

Until their difficulties began, Jenny had seriously contemplated a permanent relationship with Robert. When she bought a house she chose one that would accommodate someone in a wheelchair. I asked her if Robert wanted to marry her. 'Oh yeah,' she said, remembering. 'Look, I would have loved to marry Robert.' Happy though they had been, she hesitated because of the risk of another divorce. 'I couldn't have put him through a second marriage break-up. Obviously I know the break-up we had was really hard. It was for me. Sometimes I think I made that break completely because it wasn't like a divorce, it wasn't a nasty break-up. It was just—I couldn't do it any more.'

Jenny had fallen in love with someone else. She describes their meeting as a fluke. 'I wasn't looking for anyone else. It just happened—out of the blue. I had met someone else, who I did love.'

When I asked her how Robert took the news she told me, 'He had always said, "When it's time to go, you just tell me".' Now he sensed that something was amiss. 'Rob kept saying "What's wrong?" He knew something was up. In the end I just blubbered it out. And he just said, "Don't worry, it's okay".'

(I thought about his words to Mum when she found him alone in the bunker after Terry's departure—about everything being all right.)

Jenny remembers leaving Crosby Drive hurriedly, without speaking to my parents. When I arrived later they

211

told me what had happened. That night I wrote in my journal: 'Saddened tonight to learn that Robert & Jenny have parted, at least temporarily. She is still genuinely devoted to Robert, but wants to expand socially too. Robert was so wise & jolly & brave; I drove him to Yarra Me & just wanted to cry—but whom was I crying for?'

Robert and Jenny tried to remain friends, but whenever she contacted him it was as if the relationship hadn't changed. She knew that Robert was likely to go on misconstruing her calls. The situation felt helpless, even deceitful. 'I just thought that I had to stop it because it was killing me and he didn't know where he stood. He needed to try and have another relationship.' Ten years passed before they met again, accidentally, at a Christmas function. She found Robert unchanged. They talked as freely as ever.

When Robert died Jenny's husband offered to take her to the funeral, but she preferred to go alone. 'I felt that was cleansing, I suppose.' She ended up sitting with her mother—a turning point in their relationship. 'I have never sobbed as I sobbed at that funeral,' she volunteered. 'I lost control.' (Someone had told me that Jenny became distraught in the church.) She spoke about the feelings of guilt that arose during my eulogy. She thought I was referring to her when I alluded to friends who had gone missing after Robert's accident. ('Robert had a tremendous gift for friendship,' I said. 'But not all the associations of his youth survived the accident. Not everyone can cope with disability as profound as Robert's. Infirmity doesn't just afflict the victim: it also tests onlookers and reveals any limitations of compassion or imagination.') I assured her that this wasn't the case. The two moral truants I had in mind were in a different category altogether.

I didn't add that I was thinking of myself too.

Outside the church Jenny was upset, even affronted, by a couple of asides from other mourners. An old friend, with whom Jenny and Robert had spent many rollicking weekends, vaguely recalled that Jenny had 'liked' Robert. Then she went up to Terry. There was an awkward moment when Terry struggled to place Jenny.

'He was my life—for so long,' Jenny told me vehemently. 'I knew him inside out.'

She was reminded of something a friend said during her relationship with Robert. He told her that she was a saint. 'No I'm not,' she wanted to say to him. 'I'm just a woman who's fallen in love with a man who's had a terrible accident. A lot of people think that because you can't have a sexual—well, you can have a sexual relationship, to a degree, but they obviously thought I was just a carer or a nurse. I didn't mind. I knew what it was. And he knew what it was.'

The bell rang to signal morning recess. Jenny realised she was late for a meeting to discuss government funding. I wished her luck. Jenny escorted me along the decorative corridor, greeting midget students by their first names.

'He was so likeable,' she had told me towards the end of our interview. 'God, he was funny. Such a good person.'

She too had had her part, and it was a worthy one, in the doleful comedy, and she too had been changed— changed forever, it occurred to me.

213

Robert's relationship with Jenny altered him incalculably. It proved that, despite losing his mobility, his independence, his coltish pride, he could still help and protect and amuse someone. Loving, and being loved, had saved him. Without Jenny's intervention, I think it would have been a much edgier recovery.

Apart from one or two brief friendships, Robert never had another relationship (or none that we knew about). But nor did he succumb to the sort of depression that had afflicted him in the 1970s. Even when his health failed, as it often did, he remained stoic and good-humoured, and rarely talked about his condition. If you asked him how he was, he was evasive. There are fewer references to him in my later journals, but this one, from 1984, is typical: 'Robert too unwell to attend Dad's birthday but came home today, his (now) usual cheerful self'. He had accepted what had happened. He would never allow it, or any complication, to torment him in the old way. He would enjoy life as much as he could. He relished friendships, outings and family gatherings. He became an indispensable and hugely popular guest at parties. He had the best sense of humour, a quip for every occasion. He who had always been incurious about non-sporting matters suddenly became chirpily inquisitive. He always wanted to know my news. I was conscious of never having enough news, or of not being able to share my real news with him. I wish I had now. And all this time the bond between Robert and my parents was deepening. Always systemic, even in troubled times, it was now prodigious, unqualified and profoundly tender. I found it awesome to watch.

At the end of 1984 Collingwood was once again in a state of flux. Dad was vice-president, with the former newspaper owner Ranald Macdonald as president. At the end of the season John Cahill, the coach, interrupted a board meeting, dumped his resignation letter on the table and walked out without a word. (I do hope Dad eventually writes that book about his experiences in the Collingwood boardroom.) Overnight, Dad became coach of Collingwood for the second time, precisely forty years after arriving at Victoria Park. Although he wasn't the oldest coach in the League, we had qualms about his new burden. Didn't he have enough to worry about already? Mum, though aghast, put on a brave face. That night we all gathered at Crosby Drive and toasted him with champagne. The media coverage was huge, but this time there were no morning romps at the oval, no photo calls on the verandah, no exposed flies. 'It begins again,' I wrote in my journal.

Dad was partly motivated by a desire to reinvigorate Robert after Jenny's departure. Robert, with his tactical flair and matchless knowledge of players, proved to be an asset. He often sat with Dad in the coach's box—when he could reach it in his wheelchair. On Saturdays he stayed at the social club long after my parents left. Often he didn't get home until the middle of the night. Mum and Dad would stagger out of bed like sleepwalkers and begin the long process of putting him to bed. Annoyed that they were forced to do this, I often went out to Crosby Drive to help. Sometimes I rocked the boat by suggesting that they should have a weekend without nocturnal duties. Other times I wanted to go further, wanted to say to Robert that the

215

demands on them were unfair—but could not. I began to feel like a scold, a policeman, on the outer.

Since the early 1980s I had worked in a medical bookshop for a few days each week while trying to write a play. I was also dabbling in poetry again, without any success. The Monash University Medical Undergraduate Society was a cooperative bookshop associated with my old university's clinical school. Eventually, I got sick of explaining what the acronym MUMUS stood for and began telling new members that it was Aboriginal for medicine. They went away strangely moved. In 1984, on a whim and needing some money, I applied for the managership and was interviewed by the board, whose members included a young intern called Michael Wooldridge, the sullenest of my interrogators. Unexpectedly, I got the job. Even more bizarre was the enjoyment I derived from my new role. I may have been the most squeamish medical bookseller in history, but I learned a great deal about running a small business and serving a large membership. Within a year the run-down business recorded its first substantial profit. Soon after that Oxford University Press asked me to market its medical and science list. I felt privileged to be joining the publisher of the OED, in which I had esoterically lived for several years. On my arrival I was given the title of Medical Executive. I wondered if I would be expected to perform elective surgery after hours.

Around this time I became involved with a young man whom I shall call B. Since my mini-demise in Venice several years earlier, I had remained totally isolated. Then B. called one afternoon while I was writing. Like most of

216

my acquaintances, he was an artist, not a writer. Henry James, himself attracted to the breed, once said it takes courage to be a sculptor. I sometimes felt that it was even foolhardier trying to love one, which I went on doing long after worldlier types would have desisted. There is gloom in deep love as in deep waters, as Landor said. B., not unlike his forerunner in this respect, had his own demons. They made him alluring, impassive and unready for intimacy. He showed scant interest in my family or my upbringing. Being curious about his past, I probed him for clues, but he stayed mute about mine. One year we went to Canberra to visit his father. As we drove through Wangaratta I told B. about the night ten years earlier when my brother became a quadriplegic. 'Was that a difficult time for you?' he asked nonchalantly. This was typical of his attitude. Our relationship lasted for several years, but B. never once asked about Robert. Even now I am astonished by my acceptance of such indifference. Why didn't I get out of the car and hitchhike back to Melbourne? It is amazing what you bury when you crave gods. With some people I learned not to mention Robert, so as not to bore them or test their powers of sympathy or find out too much about them.

This avoidance, this silent negation, deepened my chronic despondency. Notwithstanding our moments of tenderness and communion, my involvement with B. cauterised me in a way, reviving my nihilism and confirming my pessimism about relationships. Would I always be attracted to cool and inexpressive men, ambiguous types who missed their women? I felt ossified, unworthy, invisible. At the age of thirty, despite the fact that things were starting to happen in my professional life, I was as prone to depression as I had been in my youth. Outwardly gregarious, I knew periods of intense dejection. It paralysed me. I would stare at the bedroom wall and ponder abysses. I should have done something about it—I had those dream journals, after all—but I never did. I was a boy, I was a Rose, I could cope. And of course there was Robert.

Other people were more empathetic and often asked about Robert. Even before I joined OUP in 1986, my circle had begun to change. At the age of thirty I published my first poem, a fervid, Eliotian piece about B. of course ('You are the infection and the squalor / The charnel-house of desire / The vicious simultaneous waltz'—quite a happy tune, really). Until then I had never mixed with writers. Soon I was meeting poets, editors, publishers and academics. One night Imre Saluszinsky came to dinner with some other people associated with the stylish *Scripsi*, which had published my first poem. Imre remembered my brother, as I noted in my journal: 'He wanted to know about Robert and said, without a trace of guile, that his tragedy had altered his own outlook, his faith'. Like Imre, other people spoke about the effect it had on them and their friends.

In 1990, B. went to live in Italy. It was the end of something, but also an opportunity. New friends in the literary world taught me a new kind of trust. Astutely, persistently, they wore down my reserve and introduced me to what Henry James called 'the religion of friendship'. Withdrawal wasn't tolerated in that circle. They recognised a lapsed hedonist and reminded him of the pleasures of openness, intimacy and excess. A decade of conviviality was launched. Old scourges began to recede. Before long, when I considered the captive of melancholia I had allowed myself to become, I no longer recognised him. He seemed like a miscreation. I had eclipsed him, with a little help from my friends.

A few months after B.'s departure I was to my considerable surprise offered the job of publisher at OUP. Nervously, I accepted and began calling on key authors. I was bemused by people's reactions when they found out, indirectly, about my sporting pedigree. I didn't expect, when introducing myself to influential professors, to be greeted with the question, 'Are you really Bobby Rose's son?' This hadn't happened in decades. Previously I had mixed with people to whom my family ties meant little or nothing, or who felt they couldn't betray any interest in football. The prurience of the professors took me back to the 1960s when people cocked their heads and asked me if I was going to play for Collingwood. I sensed a kind of incredulity behind their questions. Could this lean homosexual bookman really be a bona fide son of Victoria Park? Carlton, clearly, was agog.

One night I had a drink with one of our leading social commentators, whom I wanted to lure to OUP. He seemed rather more interested in extracting secrets of the locker room, and was piqued when I steered the conversation back to the book that we might produce together.

A striking example of this prurience occurred at Ormond College when I launched the first issue of *Scripsi* to be published by OUP. After the State governor was piped in by a single bagpiper (bizarre in itself), I was formally introduced by the Master, Alan Gregory, who would soon be embroiled in the so-called Ormond College affair, which prompted Helen Garner's book *The First Stone*. Gregory, an ebullient man, told the large and exclusively literary gathering that if they couldn't have Bobby Rose they would have to make do with his son, and that a Rose by any other name would smell as sweet. On and on it went. Stunned by his effusions, I spoke cautiously—a stern, unpresuming speech, Paul Carter remarked. Over the next ten years I would be required to speak at innumerable OUP launches, few colleagues being willing to brave the microphone, but my debut at Ormond College was certainly the weirdest of these occasions.

By this stage Dad was no longer coaching. Early in the 1986 season, after a succession of losses, he had resigned, happily making way for his deputy, Leigh Matthews. In the ensuing coup Ranald Macdonald had also resigned and Dad was pressured to assume the presidency. 'That's a job I don't fancy,' he is quoted as saying in the *Age*'s Quotes of the Day column, next to Ronald Reagan, Colonel Gaddafi, Margaret Thatcher and that other great leader, Frank Sinatra. Dad accepted the vice-presidency and held the post for another fourteen years.

One never sees one's parents through rose-coloured glasses, but even I was conscious of Dad's new, legendary status. By the 1990s his reputation, already strong as a result of his playing and coaching achievements, had grown because of his dignified attitude towards adversity and his unwavering devotion to Robert. He seemed to generate more newsprint than ever, though his scrapbooks lay idle now. One journalist gushed that he was 'a specimen who is half saint and half knight'. Still regarded as one of football's finest exponents, he was a unanimous choice as Collingwood's premier player when it came to select its 'team of the century'. There were many panegyrics, not all of them relating to sport.

Dad's popularity with young people was still potent. In the busy 1950s he had found time to coach the Collingwood boys' team to premierships. In Wangaratta, boys of my age and older bodgies had flocked to Dad's sports store for spirited teasing and banter. Dad called them all Tiger. Back in Melbourne, young neighbours were always knocking on the door wanting to shake his hand or to ask him to sign things. Children adored him because he was funny, uncondescending and genuinely interested. He signed their autograph books, asked about their families, then sent them back to their parents with a pat on the head. In this second, venerable stage of his life it wasn't unusual for Dad to be surrounded by shy admirers sixty years younger than himself. Somehow they always knew about his reputation. Earlier this year two old blokes watched one such besiegement and finally exclaimed, 'They *still* know who you are!' It can happen anywhere. Restaurants, beaches, theatre foyers, foreign cities bring out the little loyalists. One evening the three of us went to the opera. It happened to be *The Magic Flute*. At the Opera Australia party afterwards, the First Boy with the excellent treble, now in his Melbourne Grammar blazer, walked up to Dad and told him that his father always said it was a travesty that he had never won a Brownlow Medal. 'Cosmic,' said my mother.

In 1990 I published my first collection of poems, *The House of Vitriol*. My parents, while protesting that life at home hadn't been that bad (the title in fact alludes to parliament), were there when Gwen Harwood launched my book. The fact that Dad chose to leave midway through a final in which Collingwood was playing in order to attend the launch proved much more newsworthy than the book's release. Robert, it goes without saying, stayed at the football. Dad was incredulous when I told him about a couple of eminent poets who lurched up to me and tried to unsettle me by saying they had reviewed my book in ways that would give me no joy. All of us would become inured to the pusillanimity of the poets. My response to this pair of pissed scolds was to ignore their reviews.

Much though we all enjoyed the launch, nothing rivalled our elation two weeks later when Collingwood finally claimed the premiership that had thrice eluded Dad. There is a superb photograph of him wheeling Robert into the celebratory dinner. This dual portrait captures their excitement, dignity and rarest of rapports. We placed it beside Robert's coffin at his funeral.

Nothing dimmed Robert's new equanimity. Gone were the old introversion and taciturnity. Some weekends I marvelled at this garrulous, high-spirited brother of mine who had transcended his troubles, even as I sat there brooding over a hangover or publishing dilemma. After lunch he would accompany Dad and me to our tennis club and umpire our games, blithely tolerating our howls and overrulings. Elsie rarely went with us. She found our creaky competitiveness far too intense.

222

No one expected Robert to reach forty, but he did, in 1992. There was a surprise party with many guests and an arresting cake in the shape of a cricket bat. Several of us spoke, none so feelingly as Robert, who congratulated Darryl and Terry on the way they had brought up Salli, a tribute that must have required great humility and insight in a father. He described Dad as 'top of the tree'. I read from one of Peter Porter's poems: 'Nobody feels well after his fortieth birthday. But the convalescence is touched by glory'.

Salli, for once, was persuaded to speak. She expressed the hope that Robert would be there to toast her when she turned forty. Later I asked Robert if he was looking forward to another forty years. 'No way,' he laughed. Twenty? 'Maybe ten.'

In February 1995 I did a poetry reading at the St Kilda Town Hall with John Forbes and Dorothy Porter. This felt otiose, as if we didn't have a quorum. That morning I had read about the sudden death of the revered American poet James Merrill. I had come to Merrill ridiculously late, introduced to him by my friend Philip Hodgins, himself terminally ill and a wonderful poet. 'How death populates its text,' I wrote in a memorial poem about Merrill.

No sooner had I read about Merrill's death than Mum rang up to say that Robert's situation had worsened overnight. He had suddenly lost power in his wrists. This deprived him of the ability to feed himself, smoke a cigarette or steer his electric wheelchair—simple gifts, but liberating for someone as disabled as Robert. Degeneration of this kind often happens to long-time quadriplegics. Apparently surgeons had predicted it three years earlier, without informing Robert or my parents. Corrective surgery on the neck was possible, though Robert was sceptical. Other quadriplegics had undergone similar surgery with unfortunate results.

It was clear that Robert's health was failing. Whenever I saw him he seemed to have aged. His face was deeply lined and he had gone quite grey. He had been in a wheelchair for almost as long as he had been on his feet. He spent more and more time in bed with various ailments. He even came down with a heavy cold, his first in two decades, incredibly. This was dangerous because of his weak lungs. Each illness, each long stint in bed, demoralised my parents. They lived for Robert now. In a frank feature story written by Mike Sheahan, Mum was quoted as saying, 'You adjust. You don't think you will, but it doesn't come with an alternative.' The relationship between the three of them was now ineffably close, like a religion. Mum's role was pivotal, more and more rock-like. Subtly, she held it all together. No sacrifice was too great. Nothing was allowed to interfere with Robert's pleasure and relaxation when they had him to themselves. But it took its toll physically. At times of stress Mum developed a maddening rash over much of her body. It plagued her for years, resisting all treatment. The nerve deafness had worsened, and she was now very deaf. She had other chronic health problems. In 1996 she underwent major bowel surgery. The surgeon told her that her intestine, always prone to kink, was fifty per cent longer than most people's. Robert and I listened to this diagnosis without thinking much about it.

Parents of disabled children always look for reasons, answers, even when solutions are unavailable, panaceas hollow and exhausted. The temptation to blame themselves is strong, and terrible to watch. One evening Mum and I talked about Robert. He had just heard about a smaller hostel near Crosby Drive and had put his name on the waiting list. It was very convenient and would mean much less driving for Dad, who was now in his late sixties. Dad had driven tens of thousands of kilometres over the years, picking up Robert and taking him home, ferrying him to functions, taking him on holidays.

Mum and I discussed Robert's refusal to speculate about his condition or his increasingly bleak future. Mum blamed herself, not for the first time, for allowing Robert to become too attached to them, for not making him develop other relationships. Yet she went on to say, unaware of the contradiction, that she was looking forward to seeing more of him when he moved into the new hostel. They would be able to visit him and take him home for dinner during the week. I worried about this—the endless sacrifices and mutual reliance. When would it end? When would they have some peace?

Robert's strength continued to wane. When I saw him at the MCG in August 1996 he had lost what little movement he had in his arms. He was on antibiotics because of the cold and stayed inside behind the glass during the match. Finally, ominously, he had joined the toffs.

Football functions were elaborate by then. It was a long way from the chook pen. Like me, Mum enjoyed the football and the opportunity to catch up with old friends, but she detested the publicity. One day she told me about her mounting aversion to cameras, the hoopla, the dazzlement. She had gone to a lunch at the MCG knowing that their table would be surrounded by television cameras. John Howard and James Packer, falsely rumoured to be about to join the board, were among their guests. As they approached the MCG Mum had a strong urge to flee. She got through the lunch, of course, with her usual decorum. The next day she was photographed in the *Australian* sitting beside John Howard, who was gnashing his teeth rather ferally.

There was more exposure when Dad was named Father of the Year. If this seemed slightly belated ('Grandfather of the Year more likely,' I joked), it was highly deserved and enabled Dad to do more proselytising on behalf of the disabled, with an efficacy we only learned about later. Before the official dinner Dad and I worked on his speech. Dad talked about Robert's accident and how it had changed the family in every conceivable way. He dedicated the award to 'all the parents of disabled children who require our love and care and all the wonderful consolations that families have to offer'.

Dad and Robert were interviewed for one of those father-and-son articles. By now most of the sentiments were as familiar as 'Good Old Collingwood Forever', but Robert said a few things that made it special. He reminisced about playing cricket with Dad for the Waverley Fourths. (I wasn't alone!) 'Those days were terrific, being with each other. It was like later on when I kicked on to Shield cricket. I'd always look around at the crowd to see him and, sure enough, he'd be there.' He talked about Dad's abiding stamina. 'I think I am the reason my father wants to keep in good shape for as long as he can. He's never said that, but I am pretty sure that is why he keeps so fit.' He spoke about his dependence on others. 'When you rely on other people, you have to be careful not to tread too heavily. They can soon get sick of you.' But Dad was in a category all of his own. 'I try not to ask too much of Bob. I try to wait until he gets off his stool or takes a break from gardening or something before I ask for a drink or a cigarette. I watch and wait. And I know he is watching, too.'

In late 1996, twenty years after his despondent arrival, Robert left Yarra Me. There was no future there. The staff and services were always being depleted. One year they dispensed with the supper service. The residents, fed at five o'clock, were not even given a cup of tea in the evening—this during a period of general economic prosperity. This coincided with one of Mum's terrible dreams, in which the only place allotted to Robert was underneath a house while everyone else was warm inside. It reminded me of a subterranean dream of my own. I was living at Crosby Drive and Robert was downstairs in the bunker. One night Dad emerged from the bedroom to tell me that rain had flooded the flat and that Robert's electrocution was certain. I wanted to turn off the electricity to avert this, but Dad was reluctant, regarding his fate as inevitable.

Other accommodation was now favoured for quadriplegics. The ParaQuad Association, which funded Yarra Me, had informed the residents, of whom only twenty remained, that they would be moved into small houses in the community. Robert, more averse to change than ever, hated this prospect. No one could convince him that living in a non-institutional environment, with greater control over his life and resources, would be an improvement. He just wanted things to stay as they were.

The transfer to the hostel close to my parents' house was a debacle. When I saw Robert two days after he moved there he was very upset. He described the new place in nightmarish terms. The nursing aide who put him to bed did so unassisted and was inexpert with a hoist. Robert was sharing a room with a young man who had just become a quadriplegic. Foul-mouthed and abusive, he maintained his rage throughout the night. Robert, without earplugs and apprehensive, hadn't slept at all. In the morning there were three people to shower and dress thirty patients. Robert didn't get up until midday. I had never seen him so agitated. He was desperate to go back to Yarra Me. Dad, knowing how intolerant and unadventurous Robert could be, spoke to him sternly. Robert agreed to go back and try to be more positive. My parents, both exhausted, left for Queensland on a holiday.

When I spoke to Robert a few days later the situation was even worse. He said the place was full of fruitcakes. His voice was different—weak and despondent. He had never sounded frightened before. I went in and told my boss that there was an emergency and that I needed to see someone about it. As I did so I broke down, something I had never done before. I wondered if we were all cracking up. Not long before that, Dad had spoken at a football function at Waverley. Neil Sachse had paid a rare visit to Melbourne.

228

Dad got up to welcome Neil and his wife Janyne, but broke down completely.

When I spoke to the staff at Yarra Me they offered to take Robert back. He was vastly relieved and moved back the next day. He sounded stronger, more assertive. I was pleased that my parents were away and that he had been forced to act on his own, without turning to Dad for a solution. It was his choice, no one else's. By this stage, getting Robert to make up his mind was a major achievement.

Robert seemed increasingly frail. When we put him to bed one night I noticed the change in his physique. His upper torso was wasted, his legs spindly, but his stomach was enormous. I stayed behind to insert his favourite CDs. Phil and Carly and Eric and Diana always kept him company throughout the night, despite the arsenal of sleeping pills, which failed to knock him out.

Salli was now in her early twenties. As a teenager she had flirted with the idea of becoming a vet, for she was passionate about horses. She owned several and was a bold hurdler. Even after being kicked in the face and breaking her jaw she rode fearlessly. I could never watch her going over hurdles. Eventually she abandoned veterinary studies and started work at the Collingwood Football Club, in marketing. With her engaging, diligent manner, she was good at it. Long acquaintance with the politics of the place also helped.

Robert and Salli grew very close. Their bond and the marked similarities between them were surprising, given how little time they had spent together when she was young.

There is only one photograph of Robert holding Salli before the accident. Wearing one of his more flamboyant body shirts, he dangles her above his head.

Salli doesn't remember this, naturally. The paucity of her childhood memories is more surprising. When I called on her recently she told me that she doesn't have any early memories. 'I don't remember being a child at all,' she said. She barely remembers primary school or events before her teens. This shocked me. I recalled some of the things we had shared—first moons and rainbows and witticisms—and was sad to think it had all been effaced. Salli wondered if her amnesiac state was a reaction to the shock of her childhood. She seemed self-conscious about forgetting. 'It must be unusual. Everyone remembers bits of their childhood, but I don't.' She said she was looking forward to reading my book, especially the chapter on the accident. Until now she had blocked it out. Even when she met Ken Lynch at the club she didn't ask the old groundsman about the accident. 'I didn't want to know anything about it,' she admitted.

I had a sinking sense of my authorial responsibilities.

Salli often visited Yarra Me. She introduced Robert to all her friends. Strangely, they seemed more relaxed than Robert's contemporaries. He was always amused by their nocturnal adventures and relished stories about Salli's nightclub marathons. He loved giving her things. His trust fund, skilfully invested by Elsie, had begun to thrive, so he could afford to be generous. Robert never wanted birthday gifts from Salli. 'Just give me a new spinal cord,' he would say with a chuckle. But he never burdened her with complaints about what had happened to him.

230

One night, as we put him to bed, Robert talked about Salli. He said it was good to have got a daughter out of life—and a good daughter.

Robert's return to Yarra Me was short-lived. Work started on the designated house across Maroondah Highway. By early 1997 only thirteen residents remained at Yarra Me. Finally, in June 1997, Yarra Me closed. (In a sign of the times, it became a rehabilitation centre for drug addicts.) This had been coming for years, as Dr David Burke told me when we met at Ivanhoe Manor. The ParaQuad Association had been aware for almost a decade that the Americans now favoured more independent living. He said it took longer to crack up the nursing home model in Australia. He was blunt when I asked him to name its main limitation. 'Too many people shoved in together in an institution,' he replied. The new aim was, by placing the disabled in smaller, bespoke houses, to reintroduce them to normal activities, opportunities and responsibilities. 'You need alternatives,' Dr Burke told me. 'It's better to have people in homes with four or five people, giving them the same level of care but living in more of a home environment rather than a hospital. And it's important to have enough of these places so that you can move people around.'

Robert resisted the innovation until the end. When the other residents set off to buy furniture he refused to join them. They could buy what they liked; he would take his old furniture from Yarra Me. Interior décor wasn't high on Robert's list of priorities. We all shared his concerns, mainly because of doubts about the level of medical care he would

231

receive. When D-Day came, Robert moved out reluctantly.

He shared the house with three others, including his old friend Brian Martin, a former jockey. I went back there recently and sat with Brian in the sunny living room where Robert used to listen to music. Near the altar-like sound system was a carefully framed tribute to Robert, with familiar photographs and clippings. I knew Brian must have organised it.

Brian moved into Yarra Me shortly before Robert. He had become a quadriplegic in 1966, eight years before Robert and a few weeks before his twenty-first birthday. He was in a hurdle race at Flemington when his mount, Dark Gleam, jumped too early and landed on the hurdle, spearing Brian, as he put it. Brian was the first Australian jockey to become a quadriplegic in a fall. He had no idea what the word meant. Dr Burke admitted him to the Austin Hospital but didn't tell him that he would never walk again until one month later. They did things differently then. Brian was glad he wasn't told immediately. Even thirty-four years later, it was difficult enough. 'I can't say I've accepted it,' he told me. 'It's something that's happened to me, and I've just got on with my life and done the best I can.'

Brian's fracture was lower than Robert's, and he regained more movement. His family was devoted to him. Brian was one of the gentlest and most courteous men I've ever met. He still addressed my mother as Mrs Rose, though all the Roses regarded him as a member of the family. 'Knowing Robert has got me another family,' he told me, taking deep breaths between phrases. 'I feel quite proud. I'm a better person for knowing Robert.' He spoke slowly because of breathing problems. His health for some years had fluctuated.

Robert and Brian were inseparable for twenty years. They shared a smallish room at Yarra Me for the last eleven years. I asked Brian what Robert was like when he moved there in 1976. 'He came across as a bit of a loner,' he said. 'Then all of a sudden he came out of his shell and was a different person altogether.' I asked him if Yarra Me changed Robert's personality. 'It changed him a lot. You could see these changes each year—and I mean changes for the better.'

Brian and Robert became fast friends. 'We hit it off straightaway, probably because we were both sportsmen and had the same interests.' They both loved horse racing, and Brian also knew a bit about football. Each year Uncle Colin and his wife took them to the Kilmore Cup, a highlight on their calendar. One year they picked the trifecta and each won five cents. They laughed about their silken luck.

Robert trusted Brian absolutely. 'He confided in me a lot—quite personal things that he wouldn't have told anyone else,' Brian said. He knew how intensely Robert looked forward to his outings, how much living he packed into his weekends. When he got back to Yarra Me he told Brian everything.

I had often marvelled at their closeness, sharing a room, often confined to bed, for more than a decade. When I mentioned this Brian said, 'We went through some great times and we probably went through some hell too—illnesses and a lot of...' He broke off. 'It's not just the paralysis that knocks you around. It's the hundred and one other little things.'

233

Brian was well aware of Robert's hostility to the closure of Yarra Me. It was always difficult to ignore Robert's displeasure. But the new arrangement worked out well. Even Robert had to admit that it was an improvement. The house was spacious and well equipped. Each resident had his own room plus a choice of several living rooms. There was a large garden where Robert could smoke and sun himself. Two aides were always present, and the residents had access to, and often needed, medical staff. Robert, incredibly, became house-proud. The residents looked after the administration and took it in turns to do the shopping. The last time Robert had shopped was for LPs and pizzas, but once a month he too set off with one of the aides and bought the groceries. Occasionally he and Brian got into their mobile chairs and went out for a counter meal. I always cringed when I heard about these outings, for I knew they had to cross the busy eight-lane Maroondah Highway.

Brian told me about a recent tragedy that claimed one of their friends. This man had been a quadriplegic for thirty years, having fallen off a haystack near his church when he was fourteen. One day he had followed the same route that Robert and Brian took, only to become stuck on the railway track at a level crossing. He sat there for a couple of minutes, unable to free his wheel or even look around, his neck having been fused in an operation. When the train came round the bend there was nothing the driver could do. Three carriages went over him, Brian told me softly. We both sat there blinking at the cruelty of it all. There was nothing to say. I thought about all the sorrow, the diurnal indignities, the suspended supper services and other suave economies that poor man must have endured along the way. I wondered what went through his mind as he sat there, listening to hysterical voices of distant onlookers, the train pulling out of the station. Haystacks...fourteen...church function...express line...

I asked about Brian's family, then said goodbye. He accompanied me to the front door, which opened automatically, and sat there as I drove off, just as Robert used to do.

Sadly, three months after my visit, this memorably good man died suddenly of a cerebral haemorrhage.

In August 1998 the Rose clan and many of Dad's old team-mates and friends gathered to celebrate his seventieth birthday. Naturally the festivities took place at The Club, in the President's Room, where toffs smoked cigars and Bob Hawke once listened to the races on his pink tranny. Dad loves a speech, so Mum and I drew up a long list. She asked me to MC the event. When I sat down after welcoming the guests, Lou Richards said I should be working in television because of my elocution. I thought about the sixteen-year-old boy who had fretted about his high, suspicious voice and who had willed himself to 'enunciate less clearly'. I had failed.

Lou himself spoke, as did Keith McKenzie, representing the opposition. Keith, debonair as ever, was wearing the best suit seen at Victoria Park since Graham Kennedy's royal visit. Des Tuddenham, still in rude health, regaled us with stories about Collingwood's glory days in the 1960s. Afterwards Terry, often present at such family gatherings, told me that Robert had wanted to reminisce about their early years, as he frequently did when they got together. Lou came over and draped his arms around the three of us for a photographer. Everyone was in high spirits, especially Robert. His stomach, I later noticed, was bloated, like a stage girth.

Towards the end the stayers formed a school around a huge round table. Peter McKenna and Barry Price were there with their wives. So was the great Ray Gabelich, famous for his run in the 1964 grand final. Thorold Merrett, who had played with Dad, still looked young enough to execute a stab pass. Des Tuddenham wanted to sing, of course, so we heard 'Click Go the Shears' several times. Colin Rose told stories about the profane messages he used to deliver to the players, and about being chased off the field by an enraged opponent. Like Judy Garland, no one wanted to go home. Dad's elderly Aunt Ethel, down from Lake Boga and fitter than most of us, slowly rotated her thumbs and took it all in. When Robert's faithful cab driver arrived to take him home, he pulled up a chair and seemed disinclined to leave.

I watched these jovial survivors—some my age, others quite old. I was struck, as always, by their invincible camaraderie. Nothing had changed over the decades: the tales and tunes, the harmony and hyperbole. How sane they were, and affable. I thought about what an extraordinary boon it had been for them joining Collingwood in their teens, instantly forming dozens of friendships, and retaining them for the rest of their lives. I did so without envy, for I had never aspired to this fraternity, but when I pondered my own world—solitary, bookish, egoistic, self-reliant—it seemed impoverished by comparison. Although there was something profoundly innocent, even boyish, about these men as they poured late beers and slapped each other on the back, I felt sure they knew something about kinship and contentment that the poets didn't.

8

INTENSIVE CARE

Robert was promptly confined to bed because of another pressure sore which had almost prevented him from attending Dad's party. None of us would have been surprised had he rung up that morning and said he couldn't go. The gods' timing was always exquisite.

Ten days later Robert was unusually sleepy during the day. When Brian Martin went down to check on him Robert was always dozing. That night he ate only half his meal, which was unprecedented. When the aide mentioned this to Brian he became worried and asked her to keep an eye on Robert during the night.

Robert was restless and couldn't get comfortable. He asked to be turned onto his left side, though he normally slept on his right. Then he asked to be turned onto his back, which was even more unusual, for it was liable to trigger spasms. Finally he went back on his right side. The aide noticed that he wasn't draining. Perhaps his catheter was blocked. They summoned a nurse. Even after they changed his catheter Robert didn't pass any urine. By now he was distinctly ill, so they called for an ambulance. Brian, unwell himself, was already in bed. As they pushed Robert down the corridor past his room he said goodbye to him and told Robert he would be all right. Robert looked apprehensive as they took him away.

His condition deteriorated rapidly en route to the Maroondah Hospital. He became so ill the ambulance officers had to pull over and work on him for half an hour, trying to stabilise him. By the time they reached the hospital he appeared to be dying. When my parents arrived soon after midnight he was unconscious. His stomach was hugely distended. The attending doctor asked permission to put him on a respirator, as he was having trouble breathing. They consented. The doctor advised them to notify Salli. It was too early to specify the exact cause of the illness. Robert's paralysis and unconsciousness made it hard to diagnose. It could have been an infection, or a twisted bowel, or something else. Mum was surprised when the doctor said they had administered morphine. Robert couldn't feel pain there. 'He would feel *that* pain,' said the doctor.

Meanwhile, the doctor began contacting the major public hospitals, since Maroondah wasn't equipped for major surgery. After midnight, as many readers will know, isn't the best time to be searching for an emergency bed in Melbourne—or most Australian cities. The doctor spent hours on the telephone. Neither the Austin nor the Royal Melbourne, the optimal places for Robert, had a free bed.

Even now I am astonished that someone as vulnerable as Robert couldn't be accommodated without the usual struggle. Why should *anyone* in extremis have to suffer like that? Decent societies don't consign their unfortunates to the corridors of care.

Finally the Knox Private Hospital agreed to take Robert. My parents were told that surgeons were standing by to operate on him. They went home and waited. I joined them there in the morning and we set off for the hospital. We got lost walking through the modern, maze-like building. I felt slow and soporific amid the cheerful office activity. How could they all look so perky and positive? How could they glow like that?

The doctor in Intensive Care told us that the operation had revealed a twisted bowel. The surgeons had removed 42 centimetres of Robert's stomach. Mum asked if he had an abnormally long bowel, but was told that there was no mention of this in the report. We stood by Robert's bed, appalled by the battery of tubes and machines that were keeping him alive. Robert was still anaesthetised. Dad peered at the huge wound, but I didn't want to.

I drove to work and functioned numbly. Robert's illness coincided with one of my busiest times at OUP. Each year I published approximately thirty titles, mostly dictionaries, histories and reference works. That year's key title, *The Oxford Companion to Australian History*—an encyclopedic work with seven hundred pages and more than three hundred contributors—was about to go to print. This was to be followed—more bracingly for some of the eminences in Oxford proper—by a companion to Australian feminism. I was also busy away from OUP. A Sydney publishing house was about to issue my third collection of poems. I had also for some time wanted to write more prose. Since February I had been working on a novel, writing each night from eight o'clock until midnight. I was also writing reviews, serving on a few boards, giving occasional papers and talks, programming and participating in festivals, and judging the Miles Franklin Award. It never occurred to me that I was overreaching myself. My social life was equally packed. I had some extraordinary friends and a reputation as a party animal. After several relationships during the 1990s—heady but different, less consuming than the earlier ones—I was quite contentedly single again. Remembering my teenage belief that I would always be alone, I didn't expect to end up in a permanent relationship. So what else was I going to do with my spare time?

When I returned to the hospital later that afternoon Robert's condition had worsened. He was conscious, but feverishly so. His eyes darted about wildly. Grimacing, he tried to disgorge the thick respiratory tube in his mouth. When I stroked his sweaty brow he desisted, but only to stare at me pitiably, as if imploring me to put an end to this sophisticated torture. It was the most confronting sight since the days of the calipers, and all three of us were deeply shocked. I wondered if Robert's distress was caused by his changed medication. His frantic, agonised expression suggested that he was going through some kind of withdrawal. None of the medical staff had treated Robert before. Quadriplegics were rarities at Knox. They knew nothing of the stupendous quantities of drugs that

Robert had taken for a quarter of a century. When a nurse contacted my mother later that day to inquire about his medication she couldn't believe that he took 60 milligrams of Valium daily. The dosage for most quadriplegics is about a quarter of that. The nurse thought Mum must have been mistaken.

During the night—the first in this final, wretched, drawn-out chapter of Robert's life—he thrashed about, eventually dislodging the tube. They tied his arms to the side of the bed, so he bit through the tube. He had had enough of tubes. He was no better in the morning, still delirious, beyond recognising people. He was unchanged the following day, but, being a public patient, he still had to be transferred to a public hospital. Knox wouldn't keep him indefinitely. An ambulance transferred him to the Austin Hospital where he was moved to Intensive Care.

In all the years we had been visiting the Austin we had never set foot in this sanctum on the fifth floor of the penitentiary-like building on Burgundy Street. Intensive care units are frightening places, throbbing with emergencies. We got to know the nurses, who were uniformly superb. Because Robert was critically ill, the nurses never left him unattended for more than a few seconds. I was struck by the technical demands at this level of nursing. Robert was surrounded by intricate digital equipment. Just negotiating the squid of tubes draining, nourishing and monitoring his body was complicated. I noticed that the nurses spoke to Robert even though he was unconscious, explaining each procedure to him. When we arrived—only the immediate family was permitted to visit—they made us feel welcome, told Robert who was there, and insisted on our sitting right next to him, though we felt in the way.

Infection and pneumonia were the greatest dangers. Robert's condition wavered for a time. He eventually regained consciousness, but he was too ill, too full of tubes, to speak. As in 1974, the pattern of hospital visits began. I tried to alternate with my parents, so that Robert was rarely alone. I usually visited after work. Night after night I saw the same patients in the concrete forecourt leading to Intensive Care. They sat there pallid and robed, trailing their drips, sucking on last cigarettes for the day, surrounded by generations of staring, vaguely identifiable relations. Salli, very shocked, was a constant visitor. Tacitly, we all began to wonder if Robert would still be alive when she got married in December.

Three weeks after the operation Robert was still being fed intravenously. Life went on fitfully. Chris Wallace-Crabbe launched my new book, *Donatello in Wangaratta*—soon to be followed, he predicted, by *Don Bradman at Wagga Wagga*. My parents, though worried and exhausted, were there of course. For a few hours they could think about other things. I had at last, in the title poem, after a mountain of drafts, found a way of transmuting into poetry what I regarded as the most clarion event of my childhood: my discovery, when I was six, amid a roomful of robust footballers, of a reproduction of Donatello's David, a recognition that was accidental and epiphanic, furtive and transfiguring. Only one other poem had eluded me for so long: 'I Recognise My Brother in a Dream', which took seven years and thirty drafts.

When Robert was well enough to mouth words he asked about the launch. I was hopeless at lip-reading. Sometimes I tried to communicate via an alphabet board, but this soon tired Robert. Usually I sat there nattering away about anything under the sun, racking my brains for new subjects. Robert nodded his head before dozing off.

My parents were typically staunch. Every day they stood beside his bed for hours. Dad was worn out. Collingwood, under Tony Shaw, had had another inglorious year. In early September Dad resigned as vice-president, citing family reasons but also condemning the perennial rebels who had set out to destabilise the club. He told me about one remarkable act of treachery by a person who had sabotaged the board's plan to find a new coach. Some of these people would flourish in publishing. Dad's long career at Collingwood thus ended in discord and disappointment. Meanwhile, Eddie McGuire smoothly lobbied for the presidency, which Kevin Rose happily relinquished at the end of the season.

After three weeks in Intensive Care, Robert was moved to Ward Thirteen. We all sensed it would be a long convalescence. Major bowel surgery is debilitating for anyone: a full recovery for someone as infirm as Robert seemed doubtful. In the following weeks his stomach began to work, but unpredictably. He was forced to stay on a light diet: those gelatinous soups and custards we fed him.

Ward Thirteen was different from Intensive Care. Missing were the elaborate technology, the crisp urgency, the ubiquitous nurses. Supplementing the regulars, agency nurses did their best but were unfamiliar with the patients.

Above Robert's bed was a television the size of a postcard. It didn't work. The Austin lacked the money to fix televisions, the invalid's opium. Everywhere was evidence of skimping and neglect. The staff battled on with antiquated resources. Little appeared to have been done to the place since I was last there in the 1970s. The contrast with Knox—so shiny, so well staffed, so plush—was telling. This, you couldn't help thinking, was what society really thought of its most powerless members. This was how canny governments treated the unlucky ones. Robert's story, the quadriplegic's case, was by no means exceptional. Newspapers and talk-back programmes bristled with accounts of declining hospital standards and fatal mishaps and delays.

As Robert's condition stabilised he was moved around Ward Thirteen. No sooner had he got used to one spot, near a window or in a corner, than he would be relocated. He shared rooms with six or eight paraplegics and quadriplegics. Salli would go in after work and gave him his dinner. One evening Robert joked that he didn't want to go home because then he wouldn't see her every day. Mum told me that Salli had asked about the feasibility of Robert's living with her when he was well enough to leave hospital.

Recently I spoke to one of Robert's most attentive nurses during those months. Kate Breadmore, a pleasant, softly spoken young woman, commented on the strength of Robert's relationship with Salli, which seemed to deepen in the Austin. Kate noticed that Robert's face always lit up when he talked about Salli. Kate was also struck by the freshness and normalcy of Robert's relationship with his parents. 'They seemed to be very good friends,' she observed. He could talk to them if he wasn't feeling well; he didn't have to pretend.

Robert had many visitors. The two sporting identities who dropped him in 1974 stayed away of course, but no one expected to hear from them. Around this time a television producer contacted my mother. One of the heroes was about to be feted in a special tribute; his family wondered if Robert would like to appear on the programme. Mum put it to him without commenting. He knew how she felt; he had always defended the pair: now it was up to him. Robert listened in silence, then talked about other things. As they were leaving, he said he would prefer not to take part in the tribute.

Robert became popular with the nurses. 'He was always a dignified person, proud, and really independent despite his disabilities,' Kate Breadmore said. 'I know he was highly respected among the staff, despite his taunts and jokes about football.' She remembers his laughter, his irreverence, his concern for others, including the staff. 'He never really worried about himself,' she said. 'He was always very supportive of all the other people in the room.' She was amazed by his resilience. 'We saw him at some of his low times, but they never lasted long. He never seemed to let them get hold of him.'

Three months after the operation, Robert was still in bed. His bowels worked spasmodically, often when least expected. The old pressure sore, neglected during his other crises, kept him out of his wheelchair. This tested his patience more than anything. Boredom set in as the pressure sore resisted treatment. Sitting at my cluttered desk at OUP, coping with deadlines and challenges, I used to wonder how Robert endured those endless days in the bare ward. All this sun lover could see from his bed was the odd cloud and a riot of trees. Attending Salli's wedding seemed out of the question. But Dad was determined to get him there somehow. He said that he would take him there in an ambulance and push him up the aisle on his hospital bed if necessary.

Then, in November, they sat him in the wheelchair, knowing how much he wanted to give Salli away. Everyone in Heidelberg seemed to know about Robert's mission. As in 1974, he had to learn how to sit up all over again, in gradual stages: five minutes, ten minutes, then half an hour.

Salli and Mark Caruana were married in December 1998, on the hottest day of the year. One of Melbourne's noisome northerlies blew over the city. Flies pestered the wedding guests. The Roses found unwonted sanctuary in the Catholic basilica. Robert sat up the front. Newly beardless, he wore a shirt and tie for the occasion. He had aged dramatically. His face was worn and drained. Suddenly he looked like Dad's father. The heat in the church knocked him about; unlike the others, he couldn't fan himself. He seemed to be struggling for breath. But he relished every second of it and took everything in. Proudly he gave Salli away. He had made it. Afterwards, the elder Rose brothers stood around while photographs were taken. Robert appears in some of them, grinning broadly. There is a fine one of Salli, dressed spectacularly like a meringue, as she put it, leaning over his wheelchair.

Dad had planned to take him back to the Austin after the wedding, but Robert decided to attend the reception. During the formalities he spoke briefly and generously. Later there was dancing. Salli and her girlfriends pushed Robert onto the dance floor and swayed around his chair. By midnight he looked haggard, and ebullient. When Dad got him back to the Austin it was so late they were nearly locked out. It reminded them of other late homecomings, such as the time Dad tried to lift Robert out of the car on his own and Robert ended up rolling down the drive, laughing all the way.

I wasn't at the wedding. I had gone to Adelaide instead, to attend a long-awaited *Ring* cycle. Never had I been so torn between functions. I knew I should be there when Salli got married, but how could I miss the first complete Australian performance of Richard Wagner's masterpiece in a hundred years? I had fallen in love with Wagner's epic tetralogy. (I often thought about Dr Capes and my adolescent faux pas.) Two years earlier I had attended my first *Ring*, at the Berlin Staatsoper, with Barenboim in the pit. The effect was transcendent. Nietzsche summed up Wagner better than most: 'He knows of a chord which expresses those secret and weird midnight hours of the soul'.

Still, I felt like a cad when I declined. Wagnerites are imperfect creatures. Salli, though doubtless hurt, didn't say a word. In Adelaide I was joined by my great friend Sonja Chalmers. Salli's wedding coincided with *Götterdämmerung*, the final opera in the cycle. Sonja sensed that I was feeling awkward about not attending. That morning she said I should fly back to Melbourne. I decided to stay. It was a mighty finale. Afterwards we went to the post-*Ring* party in the Hyatt. As we joined the queue to congratulate the triumphant maestro, Jeffrey Tate, a mutual friend introduced us to a striking young man. We spoke for a minute or so, but he seemed preoccupied. He assumed that Sonja and I were an item, and he was also about to speak to the conductor. I circled the ballroom with Sonja, who works in public relations and was intent on distributing her business card to any stray Rhinemaiden or Nibelung. We nattered with Wotan. Donald McDonald got up and made one of his unctuous, shivery speeches. Crossing the room again, I noticed the stylish young man in the distance. During the long seconds that followed I gazed at him more intently than I had ever looked at anyone. Something had taken over, whether daring or Wagner or instinct perhaps. Startled at first, he held my gaze. By the time we drew close something, assuredly, had been exchanged. My life would never be the same. In one of his books, John Fowles talks about 'the strange dark labyrinths of life; the mystery of meetings'.

For the sake of alphabetical consistency, I shall call him C.

A few days after Salli's wedding and my surpassing Twilight of the Gods, Robert insisted on going home. The pressure sore hadn't healed, but he was able to spend Christmas Day at Crosby Drive. Everyone was in high spirits, including Robert. That evening I collected C. at the airport. He had flown in from Adelaide. It was our first reunion since the *Ring*, the first of many during the next fifteen months.

249

As we drove home around the Ring Road I played the third act of *Siegfried*—very loud.

On 29 December I returned to work. This was always a quiet time at OUP, ideal for catching up with the midden of manuscripts that was my office. I was editing one of our major publications for 1999, a biography of Les Murray, written by Peter Alexander. I had commissioned it back in 1991, one of the first books I signed up. Even then several people had remarked that it was a brave (meaning, foolhardy) thing to do.

Early that morning Dad rang to say that Robert was ill again. He had become unwell overnight. Despite vomiting up some kind of filthy black muck, he had refused to go back to the Austin. Only when he began to dehydrate did he relent. Brian Martin and the other residents were fearful as Robert was taken away. Incredibly, the cruellest phase of Robert's life had just begun.

My parents went straight to the Austin and spoke to Robert in the emergency ward. He was quite lucid this time. 'They want to cut me,' he told Mum. She saw some of the black filth he had vomited, and was horrified. Some of it had got into his lungs overnight, and he already had pneumonia. He was operated on that afternoon. The surgeons found that his bowel had again become twisted. When my parents saw him they were told that the operation had been successful and Robert was expected to be off the respirator in the morning. Robert woke up during their visit. They went home feeling reasonably sanguine. I went to the Austin later in the evening, meeting a wan Salli in the forecourt. Robert was unconscious.

By the following morning his condition had sharply deteriorated. He was now listed as critically ill. The doctors performed a tracheotomy. The whole family convened for a meeting with a professor who talked sympathetically about the gravity of Robert's plight. He knew that Robert didn't want to go on, believing that it was too much for Mum and Dad. Mum would have none of this. 'That can't be the reason, not for us,' she said. The professor outlined one possible course of action: a controlled trial involving some new accelerated protein. This was still being tested under the auspices of the Washington drug agency. Because it was a clinical trial, half the guinea pigs were being given placebos, not the drug. No one would ever know which one Robert got. Beeped about another crisis, the professor left us to consider our options. Dad reminded us that Robert had no desire to spend the rest of his life in bed. Terry asked Mum and Dad how much more of this they could take. Mum and I, in the absence of any express advice from Robert (who had, after all, agreed to the bowel surgery the previous day), felt we had no alternative. We signed the papers, and the test began.

The following day I flew to Adelaide for a holiday. Robert was still unconscious and likely to remain so, I was told. I was struck by the paradox that my brother and my parents were going through hell during what was proving to be the most euphoric time of my life. I had found happiness as my brother was dying. (Salli walked the day Robert stopped.) The contrasting emotions couldn't have been more stark, and engendered the old sense of guilt.

251

On my return a fortnight later I went straight to the Austin. Robert was no better. He lay on his back with the same paraphernalia in his veins and orifices. We tried to communicate. He couldn't speak of course, because of the tracheotomy. At first I thought he was mouthing, 'I don't want you here, I don't want you here'. Then I realised he was saying, 'I can't hear you'. Something, possibly the drugs, had deafened him. He dropped his head frustratedly and shut his eyes.

Everything was going wrong. One of the doctors let slip that Robert's temporary hearing loss wasn't his only concern. He said what a pity it was that they couldn't take him outside: the sun would be good for his golden staph. No one had mentioned this before. Golden staph, the curse of modern hospitals, was in his stomach wound, one of his lungs, and the pressure sore on his rear. It all made sense to Mum. She had wondered why Robert's cubicle was labelled 'Isolation', the only one so designated. She had also noticed that the nurses assiduously put on gowns, masks and plastic gloves before treating Robert. And yet no one had alerted Mum and Dad. Meanwhile, they had stroked and sponged Robert a hundred times, unprotected. Every day Mum took home and laundered his soiled lambswool rug. How different it had been the last time Robert contracted golden staph, back at Yarra Me. On that occasion, looking after him was a highly sterile procedure: we were all required to don masks and protective clothing.

Robert's temperature continued to fluctuate. His long wound was badly infected and wouldn't heal. Then it began to open. They had to leave it like that, hoping it would eventually close. The pneumonia worsened. Even now I find it impossible to convey how ill Robert was. I kept looking at him and wondering how he was still alive.

One day Mum was standing by Robert's bed with the professor who had recommended the protein trial. He said it was such a pity that Robert had such a long bowel. No one had mentioned that either.

Three weeks after the operation, I sat with Robert and fed him ice blocks. Because his stomach wasn't working, he still couldn't eat. He wasn't sleeping at all. They couldn't knock him out. Yet he smiled at me almost roguishly as he took each soothing ice block and moved it around in his mouth.

There was a further crisis on 17 January. He told Dad that he didn't want to go on. Then he broke down. He repeated this to an orderly and a nurse. Both were upset. Salli was due in that night: we feared that Robert would say the same thing to her. The man had had enough.

There was a conference with his doctors the following day. They recommended more surgery. Robert declined. Again he said it would be too hard on Mum and Dad. They had suffered enough. Having none of this, Mum and Dad told him they were willing to look after him for as long as necessary. They said the whole family believed that a full recovery was possible and that he should fight on. So Robert had the operation. The doctors inserted a peg in his stomach, which had filled with gas. Brian Martin was alarmed when he heard about this. He knew someone who had been pegged: he never ate normally again. Brian went in to see Robert that afternoon. They were allowing more visitors now, knowing how low Robert's morale was. He was quite calm when I saw him. My parents seemed more relaxed. In some ways the ordeal of confidence had been cathartic. Everyone knew where they stood now. There were no limits. There had never been any limits, but Robert needed to hear it again.

Knowing how critical things were, I cancelled some readings in Britain and the United States. I told Peter Porter that I wouldn't be able to MC his seventieth birthday celebration at Australia House in London.

When I saw Robert two days after the operation he was still groggy. His condition hadn't changed, except that one of the lobes in his right lung had collapsed. A physiotherapist tried to straighten his arms, which had become bent from lack of exercise. This involved placing each arm in an inflatable brace. I helped her as she secured the crooked limbs. Once so muscular, they felt bony and breakable. His wrists were slender and white.

The following day Robert became so agitated they had to sedate him. Whatever they gave him worked like a vault of Valium. He slept for a week. Next visit, a nurse told me they were planning to do an EEG to determine why he was sleeping all the time. It was probably related to his medication, but they wanted to rule out seizures, presumably epileptic ones. A few days later Dad was shocked by Robert's condition. Conscious but unresponsive, he stared at the ceiling all day. Dad seemed desperate. What were they going to do to help Robert? Why hadn't they performed the EEG?

Finally, almost unbelievably, Robert's condition improved a little. In early February, five weeks after becoming ill, he was well enough to leave Intensive Care. He went back to Ward Thirteen where he shared a small room with a young Fijian who had recently become a quadriplegic during a social game of soccer. The Fijian's wife visited him each day with their irrepressible two-year-old son, who romped around the ward and rapidly got bored. He wanted to be outside playing soccer with his father. His mother sat there for hours threading rings through plastic labels. They had a new house to pay off.

C. and I visited Robert on 6 February, his forty-seventh birthday. It was the only time they met. I had never introduced Robert to any of my partners before. Robert was in excellent form. He still had the capacity to lift on special occasions. He spoke softly to us, despite being partially respirated. He asked me what was new, then told us that he was due to have two operations on his tail the following week. I gave him a CD for his birthday. My choice of music may not have been appropriate. It was the blues, sung by his favourites. Above his bed were stray photographs from Salli's wedding and a warm fax from Dennis Lillee. Robert began to fade. As we left I asked him if we were the last of his visitors. 'I hope so,' he said, smiling.

A few days later they finally removed the tracheotomy, so he was able to eat once again, though only mushy food. I went down to the kiosk and surreptitiously fed him a meat pie. He told me how good it was to speak. He seemed vague, unusually forgetful. Neither of us acknowledged that it was the twenty-fifth anniversary of his accident.

Brian Martin, intensely worried about his old friend, visited him each week. Mum was there one day as he was leaving. Brian turned to Robert at the door and said, 'I love you, mate'. 'I love you, too,' said Robert.

The pattern during the next few weeks was erratic. Robert's mood varied. One day he was depressed, the next quite chirpy, in the old way. 'I'm sick of this,' he told me one night, but that was all he said. He changed the subject and asked me what I had been up to. Usually this involved predictable slog at OUP or frenetic interstate rendezvous, so I mentioned other things. He always liked hearing about my late nights.

In the middle of March, C. was in Melbourne when his father suddenly died in his sleep. I had met him several times and liked him. Ridiculously, the morning after the funeral, I flew back to Melbourne for a management meeting. Around this time one of my bosses described me, tentatively, aware of its pejorative connotations, as a good company man. I shuddered. Sometimes I feared I would never escape the whirligig of publishing, the turgid meetings, the moral compromises, the bottomless bottom line, the exposing nature of the business. During the past ten years I had turned myself into a kind of public animal by publishing my own and other people's books. When I looked at that creation—giving talks, programming festivals, making friends, making enemies, airing poems of some intimacy—I became increasingly sceptical. I missed the anonymity and absorption of my twenties. I wanted to write again. I wanted, simply, to *be*.

Back in Ward Thirteen, Robert was moved from room to room as his condition stabilised. One day in March I found him in a new room with four strangers, all of them fierily tattooed. Robert was most unhappy about the shift. He was nowhere near a window; televisions throbbed all night; he couldn't sleep. All he wanted was to go home, but he knew that was weeks, even months away. No sooner did the pressure sore begin to close than it would erupt again, requiring further surgery (more than thirty stitches on one occasion). It was doubtful that Robert's bowels would ever work properly again. We wondered why a colostomy hadn't been recommended after the second twisted bowel. When I joked that he'd just have to stay well when he got out of the Austin, Robert said there was no way he would ever go back. He meant it. He would sign a form if necessary, refusing further surgery. Indeed, one of the doctors in Intensive Care had already told my mother that there would be no point in Robert's coming back there if his bowels became twisted again.

Kate Breadmore was still nursing Robert. Despite his prolonged ordeal she found him as self-contained as ever. She was surprised by how normal he seemed, given what had happened to him. He wasn't self-involved, as she put it when we spoke recently. I told Kate, more bluntly, that I still marvelled that Robert remained sane that year. 'Absolutely,' she agreed with alacrity. 'I didn't want to say it, but that's exactly what I meant. To be able to still have the relationships he had with all of you...not to crack.' She hesitated. She then talked about his composure, his single-mindedness. 'He directed his own care. He kept quite independent. He never gave that up. He never surrendered to any of his illnesses. He'd keep us on our toes for sure. But that was fantastic, because it meant that he had respect for himself and for us.' She remembers his concern for the staff and for other patients in the ward. Robert was now in a smaller room. He grew close to Dale Tripcony, a paraplegic who was in the Austin for some treatment. There was much banter across the room between Dale and Robert. The football season had begun. They had that in common, and an irreverent sense of humour.

By early May all of us privately feared that Robert would never leave his bed again. When I asked him how his wounds were faring he told me coolly that he had no idea. He didn't want to think about it. He said the boredom was killing him. Our parents went away for a few days, their first break in months. For Mum these rare respites were always problematic: she felt she should be by Robert's side. They rang every morning and were told that Robert's condition was unchanged. I went in on 5 May and found him depressed and suffering from a bladder infection. By Friday, 7 May, this had cleared and he was in a better humour. The doctors had told him they hoped to sit him up in his wheelchair on Monday. He hadn't been up in almost six months. I gave Robert his dinner, then we went through the menu for the next two days. Life in the ward was so torpid we actually looked forward to this ritual. I dutifully read out the choices and ticked the familiar staples: orange juice, stewed fruit and custard, anything with beef. Salads he eschewed like a card-carrying carnivore. As always, he wanted to check the menu before I put it away. He never trusted my handwriting—my cacography, to give it its proper name.

As always, we talked about Salli. I asked him what he

was giving her for her birthday the following Wednesday. We also went through the television guide. There was a football game on that night. I wanted to stay and watch it with him, but C. was over from Adelaide and a friend of ours was due for dinner. Before I left, Robert wanted to tell me a joke. His jokes were marginally better than mine, which is not saying much. It was one of those 'Knock, knock, who's there?' jokes. I didn't get it, of course. I never did. As he told me the answer he shot me amused, sidelong glances. We chuckled at the folly of it. I studied Robert's cheerful, careworn profile. Then, a little awkwardly, I said goodbye and withdrew. That night I wrote in my journal, 'At one point he told me a silly old joke and watched me laugh, and it broke my heart. No one deserves to suffer as he does.'

I still wish I could remember that joke.

On the Saturday, 8 May, my parents got back from the country and went straight to the Austin. Dad asked if he could see the pressure sore while they dressed it. Mum said he was ashen when he rejoined her. The sore was in a dreadful state. It must have opened overnight. One of the nurses was shocked too. Dad said it would be at least a year before Robert could sit on it. They didn't tell Robert, knowing that he couldn't bear much more.

The next day there was a family gathering at Salli's house. C. and I put in a brief appearance. Mum was depressed. They had seen Robert en route. He was sweating profusely, always a bad sign. He was still unaware of the true state of his pressure sore.

259

On the way home we passed the Austin's ominous grey tower. I suddenly wanted to go in and see Robert. I thought about him lying there while the rest of us were out and about enjoying ourselves. The unfairness of it, the undeservedness—his torment, my dispensation—haunted me. But C. had to catch an early flight back to Adelaide, so I didn't mention it.

That night I had a disquieting dream. Robert and I were attending a rather tense party. Also present was a friend of mine with whom I had fallen out rather spectacularly the day before. When she beckoned Robert, I warned him not to trust her, but he went to her nonetheless. I hadn't dreamt of him walking in years.

The call came the following morning soon after I got to work. Dad told me that Robert had become ill overnight and had some sort of infection. My boss, just back from Oxford, came into my office, obviously wanting to discuss something. I told him about Robert's deterioration and left immediately. I drove to the Austin expecting to find Robert dead. He was alive, but in a pathetic state. He was still in his room, opposite Dale Tripcony. He had been in good spirits the previous night. When Kate Breadmore went off duty she thought he looked particularly well. Robert and Dale were watching another football game on television. Midway through the game Robert said he was feeling unwell. Within a short time he became seriously ill. By Monday morning he was delirious. 'Oh, fart,' he kept saying. 'Oh, fart.' We had never heard that one before. He had been raving all night, which must have been terrible for Dale, who had grown fond of him. We tried to comfort Robert but nothing worked. His

260

arms flailed about, as if he was in pain. Now and then he stared at us derangedly. I looked at the untouched breakfast tray with the scribbled menu.

The family conferred with one of the doctors. Terry was there, with Salli and Mark. We reminded the doctor that Robert had been explicit about not wanting more major surgery. He knew this already. The hospital would respect Robert's wishes. But, while he appreciated Robert's feelings, he said that if it was something relatively simple they should treat it because Robert had been such a fighter. He sought our permission to perform an MRI to determine whether the problem was minor. Dad, very agitated, was adamant that this shouldn't happen. Mum and I both felt that if there was a chance that the problem could be ameliorated simply, with drugs, we should authorise the MRI.

There was an absurd moment as we waited for this to happen. A brusque surgeon marched into the room and told Mum that as soon as Robert had had the scan he would be taken straight into surgery. 'No, he won't,' said Mum, repeating Robert's instructions. 'Then why on earth is he having the scan?' barked the surgeon. 'And how long has he been like this anyway?' he snapped at my mother, as if she was responsible. Mum was often astonished by the lack of communication within the hospital. She never saw the surgeon again.

We sat in the forecourt for hours while the tests were conducted. Finally the original doctor informed us that Robert had septic poisoning and an acute renal infection. His bowels, this time, were not the problem. They were treating the infection with antibiotics and also administering

261

morphine. Robert wouldn't be moved to Intensive Care. The doctor was candid about Robert's chances. He wasn't optimistic about curing the infection in Ward Thirteen. Mum asked him how the infection could have started so quickly. 'As simply as cleaning his teeth in here,' he said.

I went back to work in the afternoon. My boss called me downstairs for a chat. Yet another restructure was imminent. This time I was offered overall responsibility for academic publishing in Australia and New Zealand, and a place on the senior management team. I listened blurrily. I said yes to everything. I didn't want to think about it. My brother was dying.

Robert was moved into a private room at the other end of the ward, a recent creation intended for patients with terminal illnesses. When Kate Breadmore came back on duty that Monday afternoon Robert was still delirious. There was one moment of lucidity when Kate asked him how he was. 'I'm ready,' he told her. Gradually he relaxed. 'Maybe he wasn't accepting of it to start with,' Kate told me, 'but then he started to calm down.' One of the spinal technicians asked him what day it was. 'Wednesday,' he kept saying. But it was still Monday. Kate asked me if there was anything special about Wednesday. I told her it was Salli's birthday.

Salli saw him that evening. He was still saying, 'Oh, fart…oh, fart.' It was a pretty good assessment of the situation.

Tuesday dawned murkily. Morning light on such a day, the day of a likely death, is uninviting. Action, like daylight, seems futile, each movement an anomaly.

For Mum, Tuesday started even earlier. Sleep, reviving sleep, was impossible. Insomnia was her reality, almost a responsibility. A mother's watch, as I would discover, is infinite. At 4 a.m., sitting in the living room so as not to wake Dad, she rang the hospital, unable to wait any longer. She didn't recognise the perky voice that answered the phone in Ward Thirteen. She asked how Robert was. 'Oh, he's well,' said the nurse. Mum assured her that he couldn't be, that he was seriously ill. 'Oh well, he's well now,' the woman insisted. Mum thanked her and hung up. She didn't bother waking Dad and telling him. Let him sleep for a while. She knew it wasn't true. It was another mistake. They were multiplying. The gods were sporting with them now. She sat there amid the shadows, watching the silhouettes in the garden. Parrots began their wake-up calls. The large house creaked around her, with its empty bedrooms. There wasn't even a dog to keep her company.

Ten minutes later, one of the familiar nurses rang to ask Mum if she had just called the hospital. The nurse who had spoken to Mum—an agency nurse, as it happens—had briefed her after becoming alarmed by the caller's incredulous response. Unfamiliar with the ward, she had thought Mum was asking about a different patient—someone who was well. The second nurse apologised to Mum. Quite unsurprised, Mum told her not to worry about it. She woke Dad and began to dress. Soon afterwards they set off for the hospital.

I had heard of a similar error four years earlier. This was shortly before Philip Hodgins's death. Philip's leukaemia had advanced to the stage where a final 'blast' was both expected and untreatable. He went into hospital for blood tests. His haematologist rang him upon getting the results. He told Philip that there had been a mistake—it was only a minor blast. Philip had another twelve months to live, which, in Hodgins years, considering that he had already lived ten years longer than expected, could mean anything. Philip and his wife, Janet Shaw, both euphoric, began making plans for the future. They rang his aged parents. Then someone called to say that an assistant had put a figure in the wrong column and that it was the fatal blast after all. Philip told me this quite nonchalantly. The grotesque was inevitable by then.

On Tuesday morning I went into work to discuss the new arrangements. OUP wanted me to go to New Zealand to meet my new authors. I had done some odd things in my life—running a medical bookshop, writing poetry—but this seemed especially bizarre. Later in the morning I went to the ABC to help record a tribute to Peter Porter, who was in Australia for the antipodean leg of his birthday celebrations. I had written the preamble, which the producer asked me to record. I had also chosen the poetry, a somewhat morbid selection containing some of Peter's finest poems, several of them about his unhappy first marriage. Peter was to record three of them. The actor Robert Menzies, with whom I had gone to school, would perform the rest, which was a coup.

Robert read the Porter poems with requisite gravity and sonorous nuances, then Peter took over. Soon he had everyone in the studio laughing. Although he had recorded a thousand talks for the BBC, he pretended to be inexpert behind a microphone, with his trademark self-deprecation.

Eloquently he recorded a couple of poems about death ('the anaesthetic from which no one returns,' to quote him). Peter is also the most death-haunted person I know. Years ago he told me that he wakes up every night thinking about death. Clive James, another admirer of his, once wrote: 'in [Porter's] imaginative universe…everything is about to die about noon next Wednesday'. Peter's existential terror surprised me. Mortality, as yet, didn't torment me. The death of others, yes, but not my own.

We asked Peter to read 'Basta Sangue', a late poem about a nineteenth-century genre painting which depicts a ewe standing over her dead lamb, surrounded by crows. The sentimental painting always reduces Peter to embarrassed tears.

A melody
Can gong the executioner's axe awake,
A painting take away our appetite
For lunch, and mother-love still walk all night
To lull a baby quiet.

After the session was over, our producer took us to the staff canteen. Familiar faces, familiar *voices*, queued for sandwiches and lattes. Then word reached me that I should ring OUP urgently. I could almost hear the air being sucked out of the canteen. Dad wanted me to go to the Austin without delay. When I arrived, at about 1 p.m., I was directed to the small room at the end of Ward Thirteen. I spoke briefly to Kate Breadmore, who was just going off duty.

Robert was lying on his back with his battle-scarred arms and torso exposed. Mercifully, there was no respirator. The invasive rigmarole was over. They weren't giving him antibiotics, just morphine. Although his breathing was laboured, he hadn't looked so calm in weeks. He was through to another state. There were no outbursts, no furious mantras. Perhaps he was comatose. But his eyes were open. Mum tried unsuccessfully to close them. All of us sensed—hoped—that he was distantly conscious of our presence. We felt as though he was still listening to us. Onlookers are just as needy as the dying.

On seeing him like that, knowing what this strange calm denoted, we all broke down. I spoke to him and kissed his brow. It was warm and sweaty, but alive. I withdrew to a corner of the room and tried to compose myself. Terry told me not to be embarrassed. 'He's your older brother,' she said, almost defiantly. 'Cry as hard as you want.'

My parents were there of course. Salli and Mark held each other's hands, saying little. Uncle Kevin came in to say goodbye, stern-jawed, poker-backed, fond of his nephew to the last. So we were all there, the originals.

Everyone was grateful for that private room, which had been funded by an entrepreneurial medico and his supporters. He had recognised the need for an isolated space where patients could die in peace. Previously, vigils like ours would have been played out openly in the ward. Mum had taken in a portable CD player so that Robert could listen to his music. Carole King sang moodily, but I missed Cream.

A Chinese doctor came in and stood by the bed. He

commiserated with my parents. 'I'm sorry,' he said simply. 'I liked your boy.' Another doctor had told them at midday that Robert's death was imminent, which was when I was summoned, but he was still alive at 3 p.m. Two nurses came in and disconnected some tubes and machinery. Nothing was keeping him alive now. They couldn't even detect a pulse. Yet somehow he went on inhaling spasmodically, almost lunging for breath. He was struggling to die. He must have had a very strong heart.

I went outside and rang a few people. Believing that Brian Martin should know, I rang him—at 4 o'clock, he reminded me when I spoke to him recently. I heard Robert's precision in that remark. I sat in the forecourt and snuck a cigarette with Terry, just like the old days. Salli joined us, very despondent. I told her that she had added ten years to Robert's life.

Three hours later, another doctor came in and stood at the foot of Robert's bed. I hadn't seen this one before. I thought about all the people in Robert's life whom I hadn't known—all the carers and admirers. Without approaching the patient or so much as brandishing a stethoscope, the doctor announced that Robert was taking his last breaths. Mum and I looked at each other across the bed. He didn't know our Robert.

At 9 p.m. Robert's breathing was unchanged. He seemed likely to survive the night. My parents and I went down the hill for a plate of something. We sat mutely in the bistro where, back in 1974, I had felt uncomfortable at one of those fundraisers for Robert. I drank several espressos to prepare for the tide of instant to come.

267

When we got back the nurses produced blankets and cushions. As fear and shock gave way to something else— languorous acceptance, I suppose, a kind of relief that Robert's horrors were almost over—we began reminiscing about his eventful life. Mum, with her peerless memory, related incidents from his childhood that made us laugh. I had never watched anyone die before. After the agonies and absurdities of the past nine months, there was something very sane and basic about what we were gropingly doing, this conversation around the dying, this fond guard as the body wound down and stopped. Now and then we moistened Robert's mouth and spoke to him. I shall never forget my mother's tenderness.

Only Dad seemed uncomfortable. He paced around the room and couldn't settle. He wanted to talk about the arrangements for the funeral, which disconcerted me a little. What if Robert was conscious at some level? What if he could hear? Dad persevered. He drew up lists of people to be contacted when it was over. He asked me if I would speak at the funeral. He who had been magnificent for a quarter of a century was edgy and desolate and anxious for it to end. His work was done. He didn't have a role now. It was all, finally, up to Robert. It was his labour, his burden, his self-overcoming. Dad couldn't help him. We watched and learned. Dad could not.

Midnight passed without comment. Finally, someone realised that it was Salli's birthday. Robert had lasted until Wednesday, as predicted. Nurses kept dropping in. One was in tears as she encouraged Robert. She said he was a very gentle man. As Kate Breadmore said, Robert was well loved in Ward Thirteen.

I asked one nurse how long this was likely to go on. She admitted that people had been known to last in this state for twenty-four hours, or even longer. We began to contemplate the possibility that Robert might live until the weekend. Not for the first time, I wondered if he was indestructible. At 4 a.m. Dad went home for some needed sleep. He had become very restless, almost angry at everything that had happened. He had a right to be. While Salli and Mark dozed, Mum and I stood on either side of Robert. I couldn't persuade her to rest. Now and then she murmured to Robert and stroked his brow. She pulled down the sheet to sponge his chest. It was spotty, battered, white-haired and traced with a networks of scars. Mum said it was intolerable to outlive your own child. She said she envied women in foreign countries who could stand up and express their grief without inhibition, wailing openly. But she was quite composed, even relieved that it was almost over for her firstborn.

We timed Robert's breaths—about three or four each minute. At one point he stopped breathing. Nothing happened. Mum and I waited, holding each other, then gestured to Salli. We all stood around the bed. Then Robert took another twisted breath, and for a time his breathing improved. At 6 a.m. we persuaded the young ones to go home and get some sleep. I stepped out with them, intending to go back to St Kilda, but suddenly realised I couldn't leave Mum on her own. So we stood around the bed, very calm now, all anxiety past. An hour later, there being no change, I persuaded Mum to go home and rest. We withdrew quietly, whispering to Robert.

I drove home along the Eastern Freeway, astonished by the volume of early-morning traffic, surgent and aggressive. I didn't belong in it. The telephone rang soon after I got home. Robert had died a few minutes after 8 a.m. Before leaving the Austin I had sensed that he was reluctant to die in the presence of his family. I just hoped he hadn't expired alone. Kate Breadmore, when I spoke to her, told me that this wasn't the case. Kate had gone back on duty soon after Mum and I left the ward. As she walked into Robert's room the night nurse was saying goodbye to him. 'It's okay, Rob, you can let yourself go now,' she told him. Kate freshened him up and turned him. 'He looked very comfortable at the end,' she told me. She was happy for him. 'It was like a winding down. He seemed to relax into it, in a way—it's hard to explain.'

Kate stood by him as he died.

Everyone wanted the funeral to happen as soon as possible. I was impressed by the funeral director's tact and efficiency. We asked our cousin Tom Rose if he would conduct the service. Tom, a cricket-playing contemporary of Robert's at Haileybury, had recently been ordained as a minister, trading a banker's suit for white vestments. He reported that the preferred church was available on Friday. The two of us had a relaxed theological discussion about how much could be claimed in the service.

Dad spoke to several journalists, including one obituarist. 'I have seen a lot of champions,' Dad told him, 'but none of them held a candle to Robert.' Salli, asked for a comment, was proud and emphatic: 'His entire life should be an inspiration to people'. A little sheepishly, Dad warned us that a television crew was coming to interview him and to film Robert's memorabilia. Mum and I withdrew to another room while a journalist fossicked for footage of Robert among my parents' video collection.

When Mum phoned through the death notice to one newspaper, the woman who took it down told her how touched she and her husband always were when they saw Dad pushing Robert's wheelchair at the MCG. It was the first of a thousand tributes. In coming days we became aware how many people had been moved by Robert's ordeal and inspired by his life. They had been watching him, strangers as well as friends. They may not have all known him personally—and those that did may not have been able to express their emotion while he was alive—but they had heeded his message and they had honoured him. For Robert had come to represent something tragic but uplifting, something that was possibly needed—an old-fashioned way of outfacing misfortune. This man who had suffered so silently and stoically, who had known great sorrow and pain without complaining or disintegrating or losing his character, was indeed well loved. As an old family friend stated in one of the hundreds of letters that began arriving, 'He had a wonderful charisma'.

The premier, Jeff Kennett, went on radio that morning and talked about Robert. He spoke about the effect Robert's resilience, and the publicity Dad got when he was named Father of the Year, had had on his government's attitude towards the disabled. When the health minister sought additional funding—tens of millions of dollars—the premier was much more sympathetic. In a letter to me, written while I was preparing this book, Kennett talked about the bond between Dad and Robert.

> It was during the countless times I saw your Father behind Robert's wheelchair, ensuring that Robert could see or attend a particular function, that I observed a special relationship, a singular calm, a great dignity. There was never any fanfare... just a Father in love with his son, and that love reciprocated. There was an aura around them, and Robert's condition, and the wheelchair, seemed to be incidental...They set a high standard, a great example for others. I regret Robert's passing, but he and your Father left me with a picture I will never forget.

By Wednesday evening all the arrangements had been finalised. Much of the Mallee was on the march, and several people were flying in from interstate, including Trevor Laughlin, whom Dad had asked to deliver the second eulogy. I was about to set off when the telephone rang. It was the funeral director, very upset. There was one more indignity to endure.

Apparently there had been a bureaucratic hiccup at the Austin. The doctor who had completed the paperwork had indicated that Robert's death was the result of his original accident, not his recent illness. Forget pneumonia, septicaemia, renal failure, golden staph and two twisted bowels. Consequently, in accordance with State legislation, the coroner had become involved. He had declined to release the body to the funeral director, an autopsy was now likely, and the funeral couldn't go ahead on Friday.

This was more than anyone could bear. As the folly of it sank in, everyone became highly upset. I feared that the shock would prove catastrophic for my parents. The funeral director gave me the name of someone at the coroner's office whom I could ring. I called him. Never had I been so outraged, so vehement. I pointed out the effect this cock-up was having on my parents. Cruelly, I asked him if he knew what it was like to watch a child suffer for a quarter of a century. I warned him that unless the situation was rectified immediately they were likely to have more Rose corpses in the morgue. Mum, watching me pace around the kitchen ranting at the man and exercising all the worn-out rhetoric at my disposal, felt sure I was having a stroke. Finally, the official, who had not of course caused this calamity, explained how it had come about and confirmed that he was hamstrung. He wanted to help, but first a couple of steps had to be followed. I listened.

Just then, Uncle Kevin arrived. Before he could even sit down or condole with his brother I told him he had to drive us around for a couple of hours because none of us was in any condition to get behind the wheel. First we had to go to a police station and make a formal statement about Robert's death. Dad and Kevin and I went to a local one. A young constable, forewarned about our visit, led us to a cubicle. He took down our names as if we were minor criminals. Surprisingly, Dad's and Kevin's meant nothing to him. This reminded me of a choice story about Joseph

273

Gutnick, Melbourne football club's plutocratic president. The year before, while hosting an official lunch before a Melbourne–Collingwood game, he had welcomed all the dignitaries. When he read out the names of Collingwood's president and vice-president he stopped, clearly nonplussed. How curious—first Kevin Rose, then Bob Rose. What a coincidence for the club, having two officials with the same surname.

The constable asked us what was wrong with Robert. I enlightened him. And how should he spell quadriplegia? I could help him with that too. I had mastered it by now. The young man was a clumsy typist, so it took a while. He asked us if Robert had ever been ill before his death. I began listing his afflictions, but eventually summarised. The constable didn't look at us, clearly discomfited by this procedure, which he rightly resented. Finally we completed the statement, which the constable said he would promptly dispatch to the coroner's office.

That was our next destination. We set off down another teeming freeway. I had cause to remember that Kevin was famous for his wayward driving. We began to meander across the freeway. I thought to myself, We're all going to be killed. But we made it to the city and located the State coroner's office, just behind the ABC. Only yesterday I had been there recording threnodies and listening to Peter Porter's bons mots. How long ago it seemed.

The man to whom I had spoken met us in the foyer. We shook hands rather awkwardly. He, too, regretted the whole affair, for which he was not to blame. My uncle was diplomatic and thanked him for seeing us. The coroner led us down a corridor and showed us into a small room. Behind glass, in an adjoining cubicle, Robert lay with a sheet over his body. His mouth was open, his eyes finally closed. The people at the funeral parlour hadn't got to him yet. His hair was greasy, which he always hated. I thought about the hundreds of times I had shampooed it. I wondered who would wash him now.

Dad's legs nearly crumpled when he saw the body. He let out a cry and turned away. He hadn't realised that the purpose of our visit was to identify Robert. Either I hadn't made it clear after my telephone conversation with the coroner, or Dad, similarly befuddled, had misheard. He was just expecting to sign a few papers.

I stood looking at Robert's body. I wished he didn't have to spend the night in this fortress, surrounded by other cadavers. I thought about everything that had happened to him during the past nine months and wished it had been different. I had intended saying goodbye to him in more decorous circumstances before the funeral, but this would have to do. I remembered the wounds beneath the sheet. *Ecce homo.* What had they done to him?

Finally, with a pang of something that would never fully dissipate—incompletion, incomprehension, rich regret—I recognised my brother.

I Recognise My Brother in a Dream

Run to ground in a desecrated cemetery
by the Murray River, I am told a power failure
has occurred in the town's electricity plant,
throwing the entire region into darkness,
an existential night in which the ubiquitous
love-maddened cicadas and the Jewel Hotel's
sun-wizened inhabitants fall silent for a moment
before droning intoxicatedly on. Immediately
I set off for the library where I work,
to help offload books and reassure chiefs,
the computer no doubt having gone down,
thrown into a sort of crimson chaos. As I go,
rushing down broad avenues of sullen ochre,
avoiding the prams that flash across my path,
my feet send up hurricanes of dust and I glimpse
neurotic women clambering into fetid attics
laden with tawdry hatboxes. Frightened,
I tell myself I am not afraid and resolve
to creep quietly on. On the pavement
oily, parasitical insects insinuate themselves
in sandy rivulets like scorched flesh,
so that, near the town hall, all gothic emanation
and tarnished gargoyle, I find myself longing
for the unspeakable rites of a carrion crow.
Arrived in the main street I weep.
The library, imposingly situated between
the blood bank and the football oval,
is ablaze, everything in it presumably lost:

276

library staff, manic borrowers, the erudite.
Undismayed, teams of earnest young firemen
compete to douse what yet might prove
superior to flame, unleashing swollen hoses
and flicking them about like nightclub singers
with their microphone cords, so officiously
I no longer misgive. Further along
stands a two-storey block of flats,
ugly, stuccoed, rented, utilitarian,
designed only to withstand the erosion
of a certain stoic architectural standard.
Upstairs three boys are leaning out of
a window festooned with purple ribbons,
jeering at something which I cannot make out.
The youngest is shorter and blonder than
I recall, his face vivid and suntanned
and smiling like that of an angel.
With uncanny attention to detail
and though I am many years his senior,
he describes the furnace for me:
how its flames torment the woodwork,
lifting great sheets of bubbling yellow paint,
and hordes of camera-laden spectators
cringe behind their cordoned safety.
Only then, as in a paradisic dream,
do I recognise my young guide as my brother.

9

THE BANNER

Robert's body was released the following morning. The death certificate followed some weeks later. The cause of death was given as sepsis, retroperitoneal infarction and quadriplegia. Quite!

I went to work that Thursday and tried to catch up. A miasma of emails confronted me. I thought about our sales conference, due to start on Monday, at which I would have to present my major titles for the year. Much remained to be done in Auckland after the recent changes. I now had twice as many authors to commission, edit, hector and pacify.

That night, the eve of the funeral, we launched Peter Porter's *Collected Poems*. This was slightly ticklish because of OUP UK's recent abandonment of its poetry list, a cavalier decision that had incensed every militant poet and headline writer in both countries. Peter had always been published by OUP UK, not by us (I produced anthologies, including one edited by him, but not slim volumes), but this distinction wasn't widely appreciated and we found ourselves thoroughly implicated in the parent company's clumsy schema.

The launch took place at Readings in Carlton. I was supposed to introduce our launcher, but a colleague stood in for me. I went along numbly, wanting to congratulate Peter. I stood near the exit. Most of the guests knew about Robert's death by this stage. The men, by and large, responded differently from the women—or rather, didn't know how to respond. Most of them stayed well away. The women seemed to know what to do inconspicuously and without effusion. Morag Fraser steered me to one side and stood beside me during the speeches, keeping an eye on me. I was grateful for her company and tact.

I left soon after the speeches and returned to St Kilda. C. flew in from Adelaide later that night. After he went to bed I sat up and worked on the eulogy. I had never written one before. In the morning—I have no idea why—I went into work to discuss the editorial consolidation of New Zealand and related changes in the office. So there I was, swapping stratagems, drafting emollient letters and press releases, a few hours before my brother's funeral.

The mood at Crosby Drive when C. and I arrived was sombre. I read the death notices and that morning's crop of letters. I found Mum in her bedroom and sat with her on the bed. She looked elegant and bereft. Staring at her hands, she spoke softly, a new note of desolation in her voice. She wanted to talk about her own regrets, or some of them. She felt guilty because she hadn't acted on her latent anxiety about Robert's swollen stomach. I told her that she and Dad had done everything they could, that they had been magnificent. Hanging there between us was the knowledge that Robert's final year had been appalling—and so futile. After twenty-four years of anguish he had been subjected to untold misery in the place he dreaded most. What good had it done? Why hadn't he been spared? In what way had he benefited from that pegged convalescence? Robert's final suffering made the parting rank, like a perpetual wound.

Consolation—the theme of my eulogy, such as it was— would have to be grafted, magnified, earned.

The funeral director didn't want us at the church until the advertised start. Mum concurred; she didn't want to have to speak to anyone until it was over. She also dreaded the prospect of television cameras in the church, but was told that they would be placed in the choir, not up the front. For Dad—always the first person to arrive at a function—our half-hour delay was anathema. He wanted to go straight to the church, greet the mourners and be with his family. We kept inventing reasons to postpone our departure. Finally, the chauffeurs led us to the cars. We set off, only to drive around the block—wonderfully slowly. I didn't even look at Dad.

Seven hundred people had descended on the church. It was full, as were two nearby halls. They had set up speakers for those standing outside. Many of Robert's old team-mates were there, as well as current League footballers and cricketers, and survivors from the 1940s and 1950s, who had come along to commiserate with Dad. Lou Richards wisecracked with a group of old cronies. The Collingwood board was present, led by its new president, Eddie McGuire. The board had invited everyone back to the club for a wake. Ron Barassi, who like me had tried to interest Robert in chess, arrived late, walking into the church with his amazing, loose-limbed gait. Asked on television a few weeks later if he ever cried in public, Ron said he wept that day.

Half the mourners signed memorial books. Some of the autographs are illegible, scrawled with emotion. Later, flicking through them, I recognised the name of one of Robert's abandoners—the star of the television tribute.

On arrival we were led through a rear door into the church. We walked past the coffin. On top of it were Robert's Collingwood guernsey and his Victorian cap. C. and I sat with my parents and Salli and Mark. We were the family now. It felt small, vulnerable. I thought how difficult it must have been for C., attending another funeral so soon after his father's and meeting so many of my friends and relations on such a day. But I was very glad he was there.

The congregation was bizarrely quiet and expectant. It was like walking into an ominously subdued classroom. Although I tried not to look at the gathering, I was aware of a few familiar presences—Sonja and Michael Shmith; Morag beaming encouragement at me from behind a pillar; Brian Martin to our left, with three other gentlemen in wheelchairs; a few friends from OUP.

As I sat down I felt sure I wouldn't be able to get up again and move to the lectern. My legs seemed to have dissolved. Then Tom Rose, his regulation Haileybury haircut now tinged with grey, began to speak. He too was nervous and stumbled over his opening remarks. I looked at a coterie of

281

champions in the right transept. Lou Richards was ashen. Neil Balme, another legendary strongman, was visibly upset. Behind me, in the nave, was a formidable sadness. I sensed the pull of people's sorrow—their deprivation, their commitment, their needfulness. I realised that we were all in the same boat and that it wouldn't be ignominious to stammer or stall in such company.

Tom, in his cousinly, deliberate address, was eloquent. 'We come believing that all human life is valuable,' he declared. He extolled Robert's qualities. 'The gifts Rambles offered us will never be lost.' He spoke of my parents' devotion. 'This too is a story of exceptional commitment that stirs and will continue to stir the heart.' Then he touched on qualms that swarm around any death, but especially one like Robert's. 'Part of our grief may be regret for things left done or undone, words said or never said. Forgive us those times and ways we failed Robert and help us to forgive him for any hurt we feel he has caused us. Help us to forgive ourselves for any harm we may have caused him.'

Sonja, a stalwart friend, took exception to this, she later told me. But I didn't.

Terry read from St John. Then it was my turn. I was determined to express my revulsion at the suffering inflicted on Robert. I described it as grotesquely cruel, like a stupid, vicious swipe from the gods. I wanted the high ceilings and elongated crosses to resound with some kind of refusal, however feeble. I spoke about Robert's sporting career. Many in the church, I knew, were unfamiliar with his record. I drew on crucial incidents and images, some of which will be familiar to readers of this book. I cited the photograph of Robert kicking a football at the age of two, which had appeared in one newspaper that morning. I recalled the queer sound he made in his throat while dispatching imaginary balls to boundaries of the future. I reminisced about the day he took on D.K. Lillee at the MCG. Then I turned to my consolations: Robert's closeness to Salli and my parents and his genius for friendship. Perhaps inevitably, encapsulating and doing justice to Robert's relationship with Mum and Dad was the hardest part:

> Bob and Elsie's devotion to Robert was unqualified from day one and remained passionate and limitless, and always so intelligent and considerate of his physical and emotional needs. Robert returned that love in full. The love and mutual respect swirling around that little hospital room on Tuesday night, even as Robert slipped further and further away from us, cannot be captured in words. For this son, it has been an extraordinary education to observe this tacit and everlasting pact. Putting aside blood ties for a moment, I am left with a sense of awe and good fortune at having known these three people.

My final consolation was Robert's own unique fortitude, his resilience, his incredible self-possession:

> Virtually everyone was moved by Robert's determination and by the uncomplaining calm with which he faced his many handicaps. It is impossible to exaggerate the difficulties that quadriplegics have

to face day after day, year after year. What drew people to Robert was an awareness that here was someone who had suffered more acutely for a quarter of a century than most of us can begin to imagine. Pity never came into it. People wanted to know Robert because it was a privilege to do so. Here was someone who had looked into the abyss and had pulled back, never entertaining feelings of self-pity or futility or bitterness or desolation. They must have welled up, you would think, in private, in the dark—but if they did we never heard about them. Robert never once complained about his fate in my hearing. It was almost as if it wasn't worth talking about...Robert was, quite simply, the bravest man I've ever known. In a self-regarding and complaining age—the Age of Bleating, one sometimes thinks, when a bad night at the casino brings out the stress counsellors—Robert's courage was awesome, and exhilarating, and profoundly worth commemorating.

Naturally, I ended with a poem. Introducing Auden's villanelle 'If I Could Tell You', I said: 'As some of you know, in addition to my own sporting achievements I'm a poet'. The silence that followed was awkward and showed no sign of abating. 'That was a joke,' I felt obliged to add. Irony is wasted on a funeral.

Outside, a gale was blowing, battering the church, thudding on the roof. Several people mentioned this later, apropos one of Auden's lapidary lines: 'The winds must come from somewhere when they blow'.

Trevor Laughlin spoke next. His tribute was tender, hymn-like, Whitmanesque, each detail preceded by the phrase 'And I remember'. Trevor reminisced about country capers, soccer lessons with Ian Botham, the night the Volkswagen's battery caught fire—'all the things we used to do when we were twenty and thought we were bulletproof'.

I never thought I was bulletproof.

After the committal the funeral director rounded up his pallbearers: Peter McKenna, Colin and Kevin Rose, Robert's son-in-law, 'Butch' Canobie and myself. Afterwards, as we stood by the hearse, 'Butch' became upset. The national broadcaster chose to use this footage on the evening news service along with my Age of Bleating. I turned and watched the hearse leaving for the crematorium. Robert still had company. The police had offered to provide a motorcycle escort to Springvale.

As it pulled away, my brain began to shut down. I became incredibly vague when people spoke to me. My memory was addled. Familiar names eluded me. I was grateful to those people who stated their names as they extended their hands, sensing my plight. One or two people from the distant past teased me by asking me to identify them. An old girlfriend of Robert's whom I hadn't seen in years asked me who she was. I couldn't help her. I began to introduce Michael Shmith to Jan Bassett and Andrew Demetriou. 'It's all right, Peter,' said Michael, reminding me that we had all had dinner together at my place the previous Saturday. Jan, an historian, had been one of my authors since the beginning. Immaculate as ever, she was pale and quiet. Terminally ill herself, she had only five more months to live. I knew how grim that funeral must have been for her.

Several people commented on how much Robert had accomplished during his short life. Nathan Buckley told me that he hadn't appreciated that before. He was only a baby at the time of Robert's accident. Yet I never thought of Robert as middle-aged.

I spoke to Kate Breadmore, who was in uniform. Many of Robert's other carers were present. Kate told me that all the Austin nurses would have attended but for the patients. Those sixty-two beds were never empty long.

Fittingly, when we reached Victoria Park, a football match was under way. This was Friday afternoon, so of course they were playing football. It was a reserves game, quite a lively affair. Saturday contests were rarities nowadays. Three months later, the seniors would play their last game at Victoria Park. Much hoopla surrounded this occasion. Dad and Lou were driven around the oval at half-time with other veterans.

We ascended to the President's Room, zone of the toffs. Mercifully there were no speeches. Gin revived my spirits but did nothing for my scattered wits. Someone congratulated me on my 'urology'. I introduced C. to my aunts before crossing the room to speak to Brian Martin. He told me that Robert had been like a brother to him. A man came up to me and said he was one of those who had 'gone missing'. I'd never heard of him before. He said he was a journalist. I found it interesting that he needed to confess. I sat with C. and my friends, blissfully smoking. Never before had I been so sure of the blessing and constancy of friends.

Somewhere a photographer was studying my father—waiting for the moment. The portrait that appeared in the *Age* the following day was subtle and beautifully composed. Dad, unaware of the camera, moves through the nebulous company, glass in hand, slightly quizzical, looking for someone. He had pushed Robert around that room a thousand times. In the accompanying article the journalist lingers on the periphery, speaking to Brian Martin and some of the nurses. 'These were the people who had spent more time with Robert than anyone, and their praise was uniform. Such a nice person they said. Always interested in everyone's families.'

They even reproduced the auto-da-fé from my poem about recognising Robert. Conveniently, they printed this as straight prose, eliminating line breaks. They described it as my 'prayer and farewell'. I didn't care.

As we were leaving the President's Room, the wife of one of Robert's old team-mates stopped me on the stairs.

'I got your joke,' she told me.

'Which joke?'

'The one about you being a poet.'

None of us was ready to resume our lives, to confront the void. We decided to have dinner at a bistro in Richmond. Sonja and Michael and I had been there before, but we felt that sufficient time had elapsed for us to return. On that occasion we had cleared the restaurant with our show tunes and cigar fumes. This time we were ten. When we arrived the manager recognised Dad and shook his hand. I often wonder how he felt at midnight, for we were a boisterous group. Robert was endlessly toasted, a certain theme song lustily sung. Much wine was drunk as the anecdotes flowed. I loved hearing them for the umpteenth time. For once, I needed to hear them. Our patient waitress remarked that we looked as though we were having fun. 'What are you celebrating?'

Janet Shaw was there with my confrère and drinking partner Craig Sherborne. Someone let slip that Janet had twice been the Australian Birdcall Champion. Elsie wanted to hear her party trick: a horse whinnying. 'Only if you sing for us,' said Janet. Mum declined, and prevailed. 'You're not really going to do it, are you?' I cautioned Janet. 'If Elsie wants me to ...' she replied. Her two-fingered equine whistle silenced the restaurant. It would have stopped the traffic in Manhattan.

Robert would have loved it.

The morning after the funeral I was like a zombie. At midday C. and I went to Crosby Drive to retrieve my car. My parents had gone to the MCG for a Collingwood match. Although exhausted, they felt they should be there to see the team banner, a billowy tribute to Robert. We drove into town intending to find somewhere to have lunch. On the way I played some music. Suddenly I wanted to be there when the players ran through the banner. I asked C. if he would mind taking me to the MCG. I only wanted to stay for a minute.

Huge dark clouds hung over Jolimont. We arrived long after the crowd. The fans were all inside, and the match about to start. We ran through the boggy car park as hail began to fall. Between thunderbolts I heard the crowd greet the opposing side and abuse the umpires. I waited for the louder cheer that would signal Collingwood's arrival. There was maybe a minute to go.

I had no idea which entrance to use. Normally I had a pass, but not today. We dashed from gate to gate. Someone directed us to the paying gate. We queued with a few stragglers, thoroughly saturated. Just as we reached the cashier I heard the unmistakable roar. We turned around and trudged back to the car.

I remembered Mum's old dream in which Robert was stranded outside the ground under a tree. I searched for that tree.

Text Classics

textclassics.com.au